Baltimore Review

2015

Poems, stories, and creative nonfiction from the Summer 2014, Fall 2014, Winter 2015, and Spring 2015 online issues
baltimorereview.org

Founding and Senior Editor
Barbara Westwood Diehl

Editorial Staff

Elise Burke
Rick Connor
Taylor Daynes
Cody Ernst
Olumadebo Fatunde
Amanda Fiore
Jonathan Green
Julia Heney
Mallory Jones
Ann Eichler Kolakowski

Lisa Lance
Holly Morse-Ellington
Bobbi Nicotera
Lalita Noronha
Michael Salcman
Seth Sawyers
Joanne Cavanaugh Simpson
Dean Bartoli Smith
Holly Sneeringer
Lynn Stansbury
Jennifer Holden Ward

Webmaster: Matt Diehl

Cover art: Painting by Magan Ruthke. "Tense Like Wires" was painted as part of the Baltimore Ekphrasis Project, a collaboration between LED Baltimore and The Light Ekphrastic, which paired sixty-six Baltimore-area writers and artists to create new work inspired by the work of their partners. Final written works were presented as excerpts on top of art on the LED Baltimore Art Billboard in spring 2015, and in full in a special online issue of The Light Ekphrastic.

Baltimore Ekphrasis Project: http://thelightekphrastic.com/ledproject/

ISSN 1092-5716

Editor's Note

We are pleased to present the poems, stories, and creative nonfiction of contributors to the following online issues: Summer 2014, Fall 2014, Winter 2015, and Spring 2015.

We encourage you to visit our website to listen to contributors read and comment on their work. Stop by our blog, too.

About *The Baltimore Review*: The journal was founded by Barbara Westwood Diehl in 1996 as a publication of the Baltimore Writers' Alliance, publishing poems and short stories. The journal later became an independent nonprofit organization in 2004. Susan Muaddi Darraj led the journal from 2003 to 2010, expanding contributions to include creative nonfiction and interviews. In 2011, Barbara Westwood Diehl resumed leadership of the journal and now serves as Senior Editor.

In 1996, we began with a mission to showcase the best writing from the Baltimore area and beyond. Our mission remains just that. In our online format, we can now bring that fine writing to a wider audience, and more frequently. We can also explore new ways to bring you the world of writing, writers, and the writing life.

To our contributors, our editors, the Baltimore literary community, and the network of writers throughout the world—thank you for your vision.

Visit us on Facebook.

Contact us at editor@baltimorereview.org

Contents

Fall 2014 Issue

Poems

Stories

Creative Nonfiction

Winter 2015 Issue

Poems

Stories

Creative Nonfiction

Contest

Spring 2015 Issue

Poems

Stories

Creative Nonfiction

Contributors

Summer 2014

Jurisprudence

—————————

Evan Beaty

Those with the greatest love
of law are the war criminals' attorneys.
From the gallery, we admire their clean distinctions
and the rain falling outside speckled
with dust kicked up at Bagram.

In the Oval Office, a woman counsels
patience, warning, "You'll wonder why
you slapped the hornet." From the gallery,
we deem her far-seeing. At evening I push
toward the subway past walls tagged *V for Victory*
and nothing else.

How to Make a Thing to Believe In

Michael Trocchia

Start with a landscape. Dress the field with sun and dew. Put a wily man in it. Put him between the horizon and the river rushing by in the foreground. Have his back to you. Okay. Now take away the landscape. Spin him around. Fill the space around the man with the interior of a subway car. Slap a flat cap on his head. Have the man riding along, his chin jutting out. Have other passengers riding along. Now take out the man and put him aside for now. Pick any passenger with a mustache. And follow his commute. Follow him out of the train, up the grimy stairs, and onto the street. Have it so he smells the smells of damned streets. Have it so you follow him into a café. See him go to a table; see him see the other customers. See him sit down with, yes, the man with the flat cap. Remove the cap. Let them crouch together. Let them speak to each other discreetly, one with a thin smile on his face, the other with his eyes glancing down. Have them say something you cannot understand. Put a cough in the room. Okay. Now take away the table. Remove the walls of the café. Have the two men gesture in the blankness that remains. Have their gestures make shadows on nothing at all. Tear through the shadow of one man and find the photograph of his father's house. Open the door of the house and there find two other men, resembling each other, carrying on in the living room. Draw the two men into a conversation had between old cousins come together for a holiday. Turn the sound up so the rest of the family can be heard arguing and jesting and shouting from the kitchen, but keep these two men where they are; keep them sitting alone and discussing important matters, matters like wages, like disease, matters like helplessness and hindsight and other people's futures. Have them digress. Be sure there is an old coffee table there, chipped at one corner and with faint stains here and there. Be sure there is a couch along the wall, a bunched up blanket on one end. Be sure that one man is sitting on the other end, and the other man beside him in a chair that would recline if he'd like it to. Now listen to the cousins talk of a loved one. Listen to their concerns. Follow the head of one man as it shakes and then, moments later, shakes again. Read all kinds of things in their eyes, in the way they hold their hands, in the rise and fall of their voices. Read worry and hold it. Hold the worry there for a moment, like a lampshade. Now go into the kitchen and put the rest of the family members all around you. Have the family talking all at once. Notice the window is cracked open. Feel the cold air coming in. Feel it coming in and feel also a hint of heat from the stove and the smells of the family and their half-eaten food. Have it mingle with their breath, with the spit of their words, and holiday drinks. Make sure a street can be seen clearly from the window. Bring together the noise of their talk and the noiselessness of the street. Find yourself being drawn to the quiet of the street. On that street place a runaway cat. Move the cat up the street toward the horizon. Don't worry about the family in the kitchen. Don't worry about the two cousins in the living room. Stay with the cat. Follow the cat into each circle of night, into an unlit alley near the city center. Lose the cat in this somewhere. Make the darkness unbearable. Make the darkness into an object in front of you. Hold a match up to the object. Have it look back at you.

The Stylite Prays for Visions

Marjorie Stelmach

My sandals are deeply stained
with blood from the steep slopes and peaks
of my penitential stones, and still, not once
in my years of observance have I been granted
a vision.
　　　Worse, in my repeating dreams,
birds flock to feast on my sins, crying: *spite,
scrupulosity, pride pride pride.* In defeat, in defiance,
I take my stance atop this pillar, spread my arms
to the heavens. Stay.

Thus begin the decades of my lessening,
seasons of abiding Heaven's scorch and storm,
unwinding in my wake a pilgrimage as long
as the turning of earth.
　　　Below, my brothers, too, revolve
with the cities and graves of the plains, enduring
the circling demands of sowing and harvest,
canticle and psalm.
　　　Each evening, one of my order hoists bread
and goat's milk to my platform. At dawn, another
hauls down the emptied bowl. I see I am a burden
and pray to grow smaller.

In time, it becomes the way of things: a man
on a platform in the sky. No one gapes, no one cranes
in awe: unremarked, I wane in their eyes toward
sainthood.

When, day after day, my meals are lowered
from the platform untouched, they understand:
I have learned to live on air.

Now, with my flesh broken back
to its elements, my damaged soles returned to earth
after all these years, I rise into the grain, and again
into the loaves.
Because they have shared for generations
in the bounty of my bread, the birds assume
a formal demeanor winging off with my eyes.
Who can say what holy visions they see
as they go?

Thrift

_____

Marjorie Stelmach

You'd hear it edging a conversation—a lengthened vowel
   or the slight vibration of a consonant. Then the briefest

of pauses, the veer, and the squaring of a jaw. Even the idlest talk
   seemed mined with the broken bits of something someone

wished they'd said years back when it might have mattered.
   So little margin for error. What with the merciless winters,

the mines closing down, the pinch of hard times, you learned
   to parcel your words, scrimp, take precautions. Economies

everywhere: firewood leaning on tumble-down sheds, side-yards
   littered with salvaged machine parts, faded shirts and graying tees

strung on the wash lines. Food stamps in checkout lanes.
   Boarded-up stores. _For Sale_ signs that have stood for years.

Everything here says go, nothing allows the going.

Just watching, you learn it—how strength can decay over time
   to a sour endurance that fuels its own furtherance.

The way a place may seem, at first, severe but not unfair:
   you are equal to it. Then comes a winter so brutal you burn

the last of the woodpile and turn to the furniture. You never
   speak of it. Next season, you make such ample provision

the surplus stays stacked in abundance through a score of springs.
    Faced with such bounty in such a world, what else can you do?

You stay.

Iris Wants to Learn to Float

Carolyn Williams-Noren

Her hair knows already, freed
to its red vegetable self. Gravity dampened,
I hold her as I could her first year—
in two palms. *Tell me how.*

She's willing to lean back, stare through yards of humid
space. Willing to become still. I say *pretend
the water is your bed*, but that's not right.

Outside tall windows, the 21 bus courses by,
lit up. A walking woman's grey hijaab billows
and snaps. Two boys in down jackets, hands
in pockets. Branches bend, unbend.

The surface a fine chain around my shoulders.
What are the words?

We are the saint's saliva in a reliquary vial. I can believe
we are held here, carried along.

Think of music. Relax your legs.

     What does relax mean?

Like a cooked noodle. Her body lightens,

heavies back. I tap her up, slow upside-down bounce
against the beginning of air.

Briefly, pigeons clutter past, flash
of silver bellies as they turn.

Each lift longer.

And how to say
be. And how to say
float. How to say every
body floats differently. Feel
where you must hold yourself.

Evening, End of Summer

Carolyn Williams-Noren

The closed canning kettle
cools on the stove.
Steam collects itself inside the lid
among enamel stars.

One drop grows heavy
and falls. No sound in the house
lasts longer than its rippled ring
through water and aluminum.

On the counter, jars of sliced peaches
lose their heat, suck down the centers
of their wet lids. We wait
for each little metal breath.

Hospice

Suzanne Simmons

"Who is coming for him?" the nurse asked,
and in my confusion I thought the gulls were
angels rising and falling through the fog.
Or, they could have been fighter planes from
an old movie reel. Flyboy, I swear the moon
stopped climbing, sat like a whole note between
the power lines. One. Two. Three. Four. I counted
seconds between your breaths. The strength of your
heartbeat still shook the bed. Later, pulling
into the driveway, my headlights caught possum
slipping behind the shed, his long pink tail
curling into shadow. Then the moon rose.

Blue

_____

James Norcliffe

I should have had my suspicions
when I accidentally discovered that
she worked at the National Poisons Centre.
Perhaps, too, I should have been warned

by the scent of almonds, the scent
emanating, I presumed, from her clouds
of golden hair which, like Porphyria's, fell
about her lovely shoulders
in such sweet chords and shrouds.

Above all I should have recognised her eyes,
so blue, so deep and blue, like fluted phials.
But I did not. How could I be so disposed
when her lips were half opened
and her eyes half closed?

American Metal

Craig Buchner

My American Metal (Blog Entry): *December 13*
I never read much before, but here it kills time. *Band of Brothers. Catch-22. The Thin Red Line.* Most everybody watches movies. I can't take the violence on TV, but I'm excited to fire at something other than paper targets. Maybe everybody is, but no one's saying much. Guess I'm looking for insight into somebody else's experience. Just being away from home, I guess, is like every other deployment. So I lie in wait, and I read until the shooting starts.

My American Metal (Blog Entry): *December 28*
In our Combat Lifesaver course, I had to start a line on a guy named Dover, but he did me first. He was all shaky and massacred my arm, a lot of holes and blood. He probably thought I'd take revenge and stab him a hundred times, but I liked him okay so I got his vein the first try. We learned how to treat gunshot wounds: check the airway, breathing, circulation, disability; then apply pressure to the wound and use pressure points to control the bleeding. The instructor stood at the front of the room. He said, "There's an eighty-goddamn-five-percent chance you will need to apply what you've learned here in the next 6 months." Most everybody laughed, but he was dead serious.

My American Metal (Blog Entry): *January 2*
It's a land of extremes. Streets piled with trash, and you see an old man like your grandfather yakking away on a cell phone while he's steering a cart being pulled by a donkey then moving out of the way for a Lexus SUV with gold rims. You could drive by mud huts and then see a palace that looks like it came off the Vegas strip.

My American Metal (Blog Entry): *January 10*
The bars are in houses, like old time speakeasies. They're set behind this 20-foot wall that goes on forever, protected by a perimeter of security

guards. I met a girl named Lee Marie in the bathroom, and we made out next to some dudes pissing.

My American Metal **(Blog Entry):** *February 12*
At the range we shot every kind of specialty weapon we could carry without having a tank or an aircraft. We found this little tin shack about 100 yards away, big enough to hit with most handhelds. I fired all kinds of things: AK47, M16A2, MK47, minigun, LAW, Carl Gustav, PKM, .50 Cal, 240B, SCAR heavy, Barrett sniper rifle, M4 shorty/conventional, M203, 9mm pistols, a 6-shooter semi-auto grenade launcher. Before we left we had to clean up the area, which meant we blew a giant hole in the ground with some explosives, threw in all the garbage and shells, etc., and blew it all up with C4. On the ride back there were the same locals watching us cruise by, some kids waving, some staring like we were from Mars.

My American Metal **(Blog Entry):** *February 26*
Rumor was Rainwater and Dover got caught by the MPs. On the roof of our barracks. The official report said they were engaged in a "voluntary wrestling exercise." You can't talk about that shit.

My American Metal **(Blog Entry):** *March 13*
Finally. Got Lee Marie alone. But in bed you can hear Apache helicopters passing overhead. No matter how hard your dick is you never forget there's a war going on.

My American Metal **(Blog Entry):** *April 21*
Opium is cheaper than water. You see it on the streets: men, women, grandmas, everybody. I asked Sabir, the interpreter, why. He said the Taliban kill their families every day. "What would you do?" he asked me.

My American Metal **(Blog Entry):** *May 10*
A dozen light explosions at 0400. Harassment fire. Maybe RPGs. None hit inside the fence. Sometimes I think we're untouchable.

My American Metal **(Blog Entry):** *May 30*
In mess hall, Rainwater started up about Thailand again. He said a man-killing bull elephant killed every single mercenary group that's tried to

bring it down. "I'll be a fucking legend down there," he said. "I'll kill the son-of-bitch." We were all getting itchy.

My American Metal **(Blog Entry):** *June 15*
Woke to an explosion. Scared the holy shit out of me. Dover said it was some kind of weapon sent our way but not to worry. He said if I was still scared, I could sleep with him and pretend he was Lee Marie. But Rainwater walked in. I thought he'd rip us in half, but he went for something in his lockbox and left.

My American Metal **(Blog Entry):** *June 23*
Another mission outside the wire. Rode in an open hummer with a 240B pointing out the backend. I was like an action hero. We cruised through a tiny village and the kids chased us, smiling, waving. Half of them didn't have teeth. But they all had beautiful eyes.

"Sand nigger, sand nigger, sand nigger," Rainwater yelled, pointing at them, his hand like a pistol. "Bang, bang, bang."

Then he holstered his invisible sidearm and threw them a handful of breath mints.

We got to the range and fired off all the big guns, making sure everything was sighted, operating properly. We took Sabir. It was endless blue skies. Reminded me of the Palouse. I told Sabir it would've been great if we had some hard cider, but he had no idea. He just asked about New York City, and if I watched David Lettermen every night.

My American Metal **(Blog Entry):** *July 2*
We weren't trained for what happened. Somebody "found" opium and a Koran in Rainwater's lockbox. I figured Rainwater didn't believe in anything.

My American Metal **(Blog Entry):** *July 27*
Our first trip off base since the shooting. The convoy drove high into the mountains. There was nothing but rocks and the single paved road cutting through the creases of the world. All the locals squatted along the road and the kids ran toward us waving like lunatics. We drove to a big

open area into what used to be a Russian military camp. The building looked 50 years old. Abandoned, falling apart. There were radio towers and watchtowers. We stopped the trucks, looked around. We couldn't see another living thing for 10 miles. Looked like something out of an old movie set at the edge of the world. Everybody knew we were nowhere.

My American Metal (**Blog Entry**): *August 2*

The camp psychiatrist said there was no understanding people like Rainwater, that we can only understand ourselves. I told her I couldn't sleep, that I was having dreams of people without eyes. She said I should write about what happened, and I told her I didn't know how to start. She said it's easier in steps, like a cooking recipe. I told her that was a fucked up thing to say except I didn't say fucked up. She said it helps to think about it differently to move past it.

My American Metal (**Blog Entry**): *August 3*

~~Total Time: 30 minutes~~

- ~~4 Privates~~

- ~~1 Specialist~~

- ~~3 Corporals~~

- ~~2 Staff Sergeants~~

- ~~2 Second Lieutenants~~

- ~~1 Captain~~

- ~~1 Translator~~

- ~~Sand~~

- ~~1 Professional Size Volleyball~~

- ~~1 Volleyball Net~~

~~1. Set daytime temperature to 120 degrees. Place Privates, Sergeants, Lieutenants, and Captain in a 60' by 30' sand court. Play volleyball until sweating.~~

2. ~~Simmer Specialist with pinch of psychosis, jealousy, or opiate. Set~~
~~aside.~~
3. ~~Add Translator. Simmer 25 minutes with non-stop New York City talk.~~
~~Remove Translator. Set aside.~~
4. ~~Add Specialist with loaded handgun. Whisk Specialist, Translator, and~~
~~players in a large court. Keep whipping into frenzy for two minutes as~~
~~others react with their firearms until the Specialist is no longer alive.~~

My American Metal **(Blog Entry):** *October 18*
We got the names and emails of our replacements. It wasn't soon
enough.

My American Metal **(Blog Entry):** *December 25*
We spent our last night at the bar toasting cable television, in-door
plumbing, and real hamburgers. A few soldiers mentioned the names of
the ghosts we left. Somebody said, "Goddamn Rainwater," and
everybody fell dead quiet.

I could almost stand by the end of the night. I think I asked Lee
Marie to marry me. She said she thought so if I quit trying to drown
myself.

"There ain't enough water in the desert," I joked.

She said if anyone could drown himself in a glass of whiskey it
would be me.

My American Metal **(Blog Entry):** *June 5*
I remember it was 120 degrees. The sand whipped like flecks of red-hot
metal off a grinding wheel. We had a few hours so we raked a volleyball
court. Dover played in high school. Captain Vega too. Nobody wanted
Sabir, the interpreter, on their team. He was good at his translating. Had
no idea when it came to sports. He paced the sidelines, smoking
cigarettes, talking, talking, talking. Mostly about New York City. Just
named things: Sarah Jessica Parker, Empire State Building, Bob Dylan.

"You know Bob Dylan?" Sabir asked.

I said, "Bob Dylan's a robot."

He laughed, and asked, "It's like Disney Land?"

"New York?" I said, but I'd never been. "Yeah. Exactly."

I remember this part real good because it was like he started dancing, spinning on his heels. But when he faced me he wasn't grinning. It happened too fast. The gunshot, the blood. Shot in the neck. Still talking, talking, talking.

"Coney Island. Ellis Island," Sabir said. "Miley Cyrus."

He fell, and I fell with him. Grabbed his neck, pushing his wound hard, like I could snap his spinal cord. "Shut the fuck up!"

He said, "I love New York," until he couldn't speak.

Dover and Vega sprinted for the jeep. More gunshots. More yelling. It was Rainwater, pistol drawn, firing like a lunatic. But it didn't make any sense in my head.

Dover, ten feet from the jeep, dropped, a punch of blood on his chest. His head bobbed like he had fallen asleep, his legs giving.

I remember this about Specialist Rainwater:

- He was a middle child.

- Said he had a girlfriend in Knoxville.

- Was afraid of swimming in the ocean.

- Owned a hunting dog, Buck.

- That he didn't hunt.

- He was on medication for anxiety.

- And he was also in love with Private Brian Dover.

And I remember never saying goodbye to him.

Aralik

Joshua Idaszak

It never crossed my mind that Ahmet would jump from that minaret. I didn't think he had it in him. Over the year I'd spent with him I'd only seen what could be called intent in his eyes briefly, just once, toward the end of my time in eastern Turkey. He was a man of absence. If you grew comfortable with this fact he became your friend. I had no choice. I knew no one else in that town.

I met Ahmet in Iğdır. I had moved there from Gaziantep after a Foreign Service Officer found me a teaching position at Iğdır University. He was tall, and thin, a graduate student from Aralık, a village a few hours southeast of town. He wore white dress shirts that were always pressed and primly tucked into his slacks, billowing shirts that gave only the faintest hint of a body beneath. He was writing his thesis on some aspect of the province's soil. He seemed more of an idea than a man.

Iğdır University was two years old and existed, more or less, on the fifth and sixth floors of an abandoned shopping complex in the center of town. The days were dusty and the sun hung as if on a rusty wire, moving across the sky at an interminable pace. Dust blanketed everything. The buildings were layered with it, as were the streets. I tasted it in the food. It made its way into the water, the air, even my mind, which makes me wonder if I am misremembering certain people, or places, or occurrences. When it rained the unpaved streets and empty lots turned to mud.

The rector of the university was a plump man who had spent four years studying in Texas. He had a dark mustache and thick eyebrows that rose and fell with the intonation of his hoarse voice. He seemed eager and incompetent. The day I arrived, after tea in his office, he passed me off to Ahmet, who took me to my university lodging, a decrepit öğretmenevi on the edge of town, a block away from the north-south highway that cut Iğdır in half and led to places like Tuzluca and Kars and Doğubeyazıt. From my window I could see the highway leading off into the distance, running

19

parallel to the plateau that formed Ararat, which also ran north and south, as though everything in that part of the world ran north and south and there was no other choice, no other direction. At night the headlights of trucks beaded the dark road, their engines roaring as they zoomed in and out of town. Clusters of lights marking distant villages dotted the hills. I'd stand by the window, looking out at the desert and the highway and the wavering lights, fingering the American flag pin my father had given me the day I left Washington, almost two years before.

In the mornings Ahmet would come for me at the öğretmenevi. We walked everywhere. We would wander the streets and alleys, stopping at different teahouses, and eventually for börek or simit. Our conversations always started the same way. In each teahouse Ahmet would explain the specific process each owner used to make tea, and how it differed from the others, and how it was better or worse. Then he would talk about the Black Sea coast, how the closer you got to it the fresher the tea became. That would lead him to describe the hamsi from Trabzon and the mantı from Sinop. Then he would talk about his thesis and how when he was finished he wanted to move back to Poland, where the girl he had met during his Erasmus year lived. His tone always grew serious when he brought her up. He would speak about the emails she sent him, and sometimes even bring a copy, ask me to read it and tell him what I thought. I would tell him that I wasn't good with women, but he would insist, slide the pages across the splintery table of whichever teahouse we were in. Her responses were vague and overly polite. It was immediately clear she was trying to distance herself from him. Each email surprised me—the many ways she had to say nothing, promise nothing. I tried to sound both uncertain and positive. We never made much progress.

After the fourth or fifth stop we would head across town to the rektörlük, where I taught the university's agriculture professors. There was a fence around the building, and a security gate at its only entrance. Students stood around in clusters on the courtyard's patchy grass. There was a gazebo and a pile of bricks and that was it.

At night I had trouble falling asleep. I would lie awake in the early morning hours terrified of the stillness before the call to prayer. Its warble seemed forever imminent. I would close my eyes and wait in dread for its first notes, unable to relax until it had passed. After it came I would fall asleep until my neighbor switched on the morning news, or whatever it was he watched at full volume, and the sound would thump through the walls. A little later Ahmet would come for me and we would start our routine. Whatever the cause, I couldn't sleep. I had nightmares. My eyes started retreating into my skull.

One day Ahmet asked me what was wrong.

"I'm having trouble sleeping," I said. "I miss home," I added, after a moment.

"You miss home," he said. His tone was flat, devoid of everything but the words themselves. I couldn't tell if he was questioning me, mocking me, or even determining if and how he could help me. An impossible determination to make, yet somehow I felt it held the key to everything that followed.

"Would you like to come to Aralık?" he asked. "To see my home?"

I didn't. It was far, most likely, and I was exhausted and wanted nothing more than to sit in my room and imagine my impending return home. What my first meal would be, who I would visit.

"Sure," I said.

We left that afternoon, in Ahmet's rusted Iranian sedan. Halfway to Aralık the left front tire went flat. Ahmet and I got out to replace it. While we were changing it a man in a gray suit biked past us. I wondered where he was going. There didn't seem to be a house around for miles. Eventually we fixed the wheel and continued on our way. When we were almost there it started to rain, a shower that smeared the layer of dust on the windshield, creating a grainy paste that was impossible to see through or clear with the wipers. Ahmet cranked his window down and stuck his head out and drove like that the rest of the way.

In the village there were cows in the street, and deep puddles in the potholes. At scattered tables in front of storefronts, and on rickety staircases leading to second floor rooms and sometimes to nowhere at all, men hunched on low stools around low tables, holding tea cups, handling prayer beads, watching the sporadic cars that came and went down the main street.

We pulled up to Ahmet's home, a low cinderblock structure with a rusted metal roof. Ahmet told me we were even farther east than Iğdır. Right up against Armenia. He pointed down one end of the street, into the middle distance, past a stream and a clump of trees too sparse and scraggly to be a wood, and said it was just over there. That if there was time we would head through the trees and look at the line that separated the countries.

"Is it safe?" I asked.

He thought for a moment, nodded.

His mother was cooking when we walked in. She smiled at me and shook my hand slowly. I wondered if this was for me or if it was how she normally greeted guests. The floor was covered with rugs, and from where I stood in the front room I could see into the kitchen. She said something to Ahmet and he nodded.

"We will eat in thirty minutes," he said.

He spoke to his mother, turned, and went out the door, motioning for me to follow. We walked through the yard, past a strutting rooster and out the front gate. Some children were playing soccer in the street. They paused to let us pass, watching us in silence. We crossed the main avenue and continued down into a ditch and over a crude bridge of stones across the stagnant water of the stream, which upon closer examination was really more of a canal, or maybe a drainage ditch. We wandered through the copse of trees and then up a hillock where ahead of us stood a rotting guard shack and some spindly posts linked by rusted razor wire. I had never seen a military front before and it looked just as barren as I had always imagined one would. There was a sign with a cartoonish picture of a uniformed soldier warning, in Turkish, not to approach any further. I asked Ahmet if there were landmines and he shook his head.

"It's not that kind of border," he said. "Besides, this is not yet it."

In the distance we could see a guard tower and something glinting in the late afternoon sunlight that I imagined to be a tank, but was probably just a truck, or maybe a jeep. We stood for a moment in silence, looking off toward the east, toward the Armenian side. The land looked no different. A sluggish river winding through the cracked earth, a few low trees here and there, some bushes. Then Ahmet spoke.

"There," he said. "Do you see that?" He was pointing off past the guard tower. I squinted and tried to follow the imaginary line that connected his finger to whatever it was he was signaling at, but it was hard to see, even though the sun was behind us.

"What is it?" I asked.

"There," Ahmet said, still pointing.

And then I saw it, but only for the scattered cars parked beside it sparkling in the light. A church. Rounded domes, brown shingles, a burnt-red façade. I imagined all of this, of course. It was too far away to see any detail. Really, it could have been anything. But Ahmet told me it was a church. One of the most famous in Armenia, or oldest, or most important. We stood staring for a while. Then Ahmet said that dinner was probably ready, and we turned and retraced our path back toward the village.

We ate in near silence on the floor of the front room. Ahmet's mother appeared only to bring more tavuk sote and lavaş or to clear away dishes. By the time we had eaten and had tea it was late. Ahmet rose and said it was probably best that we return. I thanked Ahmet's mother and said goodbye. We walked outside and Ahmet abruptly stopped. He told me to wait, and disappeared inside. The village was silent, except for a dog barking in the distance. There was a full moon, or a near full moon. In its light Ararat was easy to find. A heavy presence on the horizon, reaching up past a house at the opposite end of the street from the path we had taken that afternoon. An enormous mound, all muscle and rock. There were no stars in the sky, a symptom of the smog that plagued all of the villages and towns in the east. Finally Ahmet reemerged. He apologized, and we walked to his car.

Neither of us spoke for a while. Then, about half an hour after we left his village, Ahmet started talking about his mother, and Iğdır, and the girl from Poland he had met, or was friends with, or had slept with.

"Between the border and the mountain there isn't anywhere to go," he said.

I nodded.

"Of course this isn't true," he said. "There are roads. An airport in Erzurum."

"Yes," I said. In that moment I was thinking of that airport, how soon I could make it there, where I could go.

"I would leave," he said, as though guessing my thoughts. "But there is my mother."

He didn't need to tell me she was sick. I already knew. It was the smell of the house, as thickly settled as Iğdır's dust. Ahmet removed a tape from his breast pocket and put it in the cassette player and turned up the volume. Through the scratchy speakers I heard a woman's voice over a sparse beat.

"That's her," he said.

I didn't understand.

"Ania. The girl from Poland."

"Ah," I said.

"She sings," he said. "Sometimes she travels to sing. She nearly came to Istanbul last year. I told her if she did I would come see her."

"That's nice," I said, staring out the window at the landscape blurring past. The horizon seemed to be glowing, almost imperceptibly, as if some object at the smudged meeting of land and sky were giving off a precious and delicate energy.

"When I was with her in Krakow we were inseparable," Ahmet said. "We spent whole nights walking around the city. She told me everything about her life. Then the sun would come up and we would wander into one of the city's cheap cafeterias. I think they were called milk bars. We would drink coffee and eat little pastries. She even took me to her hometown. I taught her brothers how to make gözleme."

I tried to picture Ahmet and this girl, imagine his feeling toward her, his feeling toward his home, what it would be like to grow up here, grow old. I wondered if I could do it. One of the girls who taught English at the university was pretty. I imagined settling down with her, working at the university, maybe even starting my own school. I squeezed the flag pin in my pocket, felt the prick of its pointed edges on my fingertips.

The song ended and Ahmet removed the tape from the player and returned it to his breast pocket. The highway began to curve. Soon we would be approaching the outskirts of Iğdır. We passed a shuttered fruit stand, the charred remains of a house.

"Do you have a minute?" Ahmet asked. "I want to show you something."

I shrugged, and immediately realized I should have been more affirmative. "Yes," I said, a little too forcefully.

He pulled off the highway and onto a dirt track. We rumbled for a few minutes, bouncing up and down on the car's worn suspension as we rolled over the pockmarked route. We crested a slight rise and Ahmet pulled to a stop. He turned off the car and got out. I followed. The moonlight seemed weaker here, as though the plateau had taken it and scattered it, dispersed it in ever-decreasing amounts until its effect was negligible. It was almost impossible to see more than a step ahead. I felt as though we were being watched, then felt immediately embarrassed for thinking this. Ahmet led the way with a sureness that made me certain he had done this many times.

We walked beside a row of bare trees and then I glimpsed what I presumed to be our destination, its angular shape almost indistinguishable from the pitch black night surrounding it, shadow upon shadow. The outline of its lone minaret pierced the emptiness.

The mosque's walls were unpainted cinderblock. It was clear that the building had been abandoned while still under construction. Many of the mosques in town were like this: suspended in some indeterminate state. Still, the structure had a charge to it.

We entered through the gap where the door should have been. The floor was packed dirt. A pile of smashed wooden crates in one corner, a mound of trash in another, ashes and charred wood scattered in a loose, hurried pattern. It looked hastily abandoned. I wanted to ask Ahmet why we were here, but my voice felt stuck, as though it had dried in my throat. I tried to cough and something hoarse and not quite human came out.

"Come," Ahmet said, and led me through the vacant space. I could not see the doorway or the crude cement steps spiraling upward into the emptiness until we were upon them. The minaret. Ahmet started up its staircase.

"Come," he said again, as though chanting. The steps were uneven. I had to feel my way against the wall as I climbed. At any moment I thought the wall I was pressing against would give out, and I would fall toward the earth in an avalanche of cinderblock and mortar.

We emerged from a small doorway onto a crude crow's nest of cement and wood planking about forty feet above the ground.

"This is a very special place," Ahmet said. He spoke staring straight ahead, as though addressing someone out in the darkness, or maybe someone in his mind. He raised his hand slowly, as if cupping something, then extended his finger and pointed off at the horizon, alive with the distant, wavering lights of Armenia's capital.

We stood for a moment in silence. Then Ahmet spoke.

"When my mother can live without my help I'll return for Ania," he said.

I knew Ahmet would never leave, that his mother would die soon, and that Ania would exist, for the rest of his life, in the sad scratch of a cassette and the distant glow of a city across a closed border. At the time, I thought he couldn't see this, and that's what gave him such power. His oblivion, willful or otherwise, at the sad details of his life, looking out across the border at the lights of a city a world away. A city only he could see.

"You are leaving soon?" he asked, turning to me.

I nodded.

"When?" he asked.

"When the semester ends."

"You miss home," he said.

I nodded.

"I would also leave," he said.

I searched for something to say.

"I know," Ahmet said. He smiled.

"Here," I said, reaching into my pocket for the pin. "Take this."

It was a pathetic gesture. I knew it as soon as I spoke, but it was too late to stop.

Ahmet took the pin, turned it in his fingers. He nodded, whether in acknowledgement of the gift, or in resignation that after all he'd shared with me this trinket was what I chose to give him. What he said next I've been turning in my head ever since.

"Sometimes, up here, I feel as though that is not Yerevan, that this is not Turkey. That if I jump I will not fall," he said. "That I will just..." and he trailed off, made a motion suggesting he would just float away, or maybe that he couldn't find the right words in English, or even that the right words didn't exist.

"Maybe I will leave soon, too," he said, after a long silence. He pinned the flag to his shirt. We turned and descended the spiraling stairs.

The Weeping Widow

Meng Jin

The first time I saw the weeping widow was on Qingming Day, a few weeks before my mother left for America. Every family was out visiting their dead. Summer's weeds had crept over the graves and autumn's leaves littered the stone plots; now the snow was melting, and the sun licked away the frost by noon. My grandmother, uncles, Ahyi and I climbed up the mountain to my grandfather's grave with brooms and baskets full of incense and offerings. Firecrackers cackled across the mountains in rounds of fading applause. Their red scraps covered the newly swept ground like thousands of exploded flowers.

A cry broke out over the din of the families at their graves, singular and sharp. I looked up. Above us, a woman was standing alone. The grave at her feet was so overgrown with weeds that the stone was hardly visible. The woman wore a white mourning dress with long billowing sleeves that had been stained gray and brown with dirt. She knelt before the grave. Wisps of gray hair hung over her face. The woman began to grab fistfuls of dried weeds with her bare hands, pulling them from the earth. As she ripped up the thorny stalks, she cried out, her voice cutting through the laughing echoes of firecrackers. She stopped when the plot was bare. The headstone rose up before her, lonely and gray. The woman dropped to her knees on the ground. Her hands, torn and bloodied, fell at her sides. Drops of red dotted the piles of yellowed weeds she had thrown to the ground.

I looked at Ahyi and then back at the woman. No one seemed to notice her. Ahyi had gone on scrubbing grandfather's gravestone and putting out bowls of food. When she saw me watching the woman she stopped and turned my head away. My hands and my eyes stung. The sun was setting, and the incense we lit had burned low, bending over in drops of white ash. I raced down the mountain and led the way home.

~

The door to grandmother's house was open. The high floral whistle of a woman's voice rang out from inside. "Where's my xiang xia daughter?" I

27

ran past the gate and stopped in the doorway. A pretty woman was sitting on the wooden bench, rifling through her traveling bag. She looked up. It was my mother.

"Come on inside," my mother said. "No need to be shy around your Ma-ma."

She pulled a white dress from her bag and held it up by its shoulders, snapping it in the air to smooth out the wrinkles.

"Look at what Ma-ma brought for you."

I hadn't known that my mother was coming. I didn't know much about her—only that she was a scientist in Shanghai, which was two long bus rides and a longer train ride from here. It was a trip that I had taken once, so long ago that all I remembered of it was Ahyi telling me not to stick my hands or head out of the windows, or a man with an axe would chop them off.

I walked towards my mother, carefully putting one foot in front of the other. My heart pounded in my ears. My mother was wearing a long sleeved black dress with a white floral print, and high-heeled shoes that would have sunk into the muddy mountain paths. Her lips were painted like candies.

She was even more beautiful than I remembered. The dress she brought me was made from a material I had never seen before. It looked like something out of a movie. I reached out to touch it.

"Aiya!" My mother grabbed my wrist and brought it to her face. The dress was gone, stowed back in the bag. "How did my daughter get so dirty? Come, let's give you a bath first."

"Hao le," Ahyi said as she walked in. "She can have a bath after dinner."

Grandmother and my uncles followed, calling greetings to my mother as they pulled off their boots and gloves.

Ahyi set her baskets by the door and walked to the kitchen, where I could hear her picking through the woodpile.

Grandmother said to me, "Have you greeted your mother yet?"

"Ma-ma hao," I said, looking at the ground. I ran into the kitchen to find Ahyi.

~

The kitchen was the warmest room. In the corner was a cement stove where burning wood heated two iron woks and boiled water in the copper

28

container between them. Behind the stove, my uncles had stacked up piles of wood. Vegetables and meat covered in wet cloth lined the wall. Ahyi and grandmother spent entire days there, wrapping dumplings or making tofu, warming their fingers over bowls of hot coal. When people from the village passed by looking for my grandmother, they knew to look there first.

Ahyi had started the fire and was fanning the oven. I pulled up a stool beside her.

"Do you remember the woman on the mountain?" I said. "The woman who was crying."

She fed a fresh stick of wood to the flame.

"Who is she?"

"Some people call her the weeping widow," she said.

Ahyi was often reluctant to talk about things. She would shake her head and ask why it was I wanted to know everything. But I knew that if I kept quiet she would go on.

"People say some strange things about her," she said. "They say she lost her husband many years ago. They say that grief drove her so mad she forgot she had a son, who was only two years old. Well, I don't know what to believe. But the facts are she once had a husband and a son, and now she doesn't."

"Does she live here?" I said. "I've never seen her before."

"Don't go bothering her, you hear?" Ahyi sighed and closed the metal flap of the oven. She turned to look at me, her elbows resting on her knees.

"She's had a hard life."

She opened the oven flap again, and with a shovel scooped out hot coals into a metal bowl. I thought of the weeping widow in her white dress, her bloody hands hanging at her sides. The sun had gone down and the air was frigid. I put my hands over the bowl of coals. Ahyi poured oil into the wok.

"Now go, bring that bowl to your ma. She's got to be freezing in that dress of hers."

~

Whenever my mother visited, the streets rustled with whispers. "Rumor mongers," Ahyi said, "Counting up her cash." Ahyi then disappeared. I'd find her in the kitchen scrubbing the woks or sorting out vegetables, but when I poked my head in she would run out to do something else. I followed my mother into the streets alone. My mother's hands were smooth and white. They gripped mine tightly.

According to Ahyi, my mother had gotten pregnant with me too soon. She was just beginning her doctorate, and my father was leaving on a fellowship to America. My mother didn't trust her clumsy country mother, my grandmother, to take care of me. Ahyi, my mother's older sister, hadn't finished high school and didn't have anything else to do but work in the fields. My mother had said it would be a good chance for her to come to Shanghai and meet a rich man to marry. "Like she was doing me a favor!" Ahyi laughed. "Who will want to marry me when they see a child in my arms?"

Ahyi, my mother, and I lived in a one-room apartment in Shanghai until Ahyi couldn't stand it anymore. Suffocated by the narrow, stinking streets, she packed up my diapers and told my mother that she was going back to Wantu. My mother hadn't wanted me to go, but with her dissertation to finish, she had no choice.

My mother never stayed in Wantu for long. During her three or four day visits, she made the rounds to all of our relatives, stuffing red envelopes of cash in their hands and explaining how to take the Western medicines she'd brought from Shanghai. I sat silently beside her as she gossiped, nibbling on yam chips or some other treat, looking up and smiling when I heard my name. During one of the visits I heard my mother say that Ahyi had a simple face. I thought it was a compliment. Ahyi's face was big and round like a plate, her cheeks always red as if they had just been pinched. Her skin was smooth and there were no wrinkles or shadows on it to hide secrets. "Men prefer a simple wife," my mother said.

On the walk back to grandmother's house, my mother and I passed the weeping widow. The widow stared at us, her head tilted and her eyes curious, and my mother pulled me into her side. "I remember that woman," she said when we turned the corner. "She's a madwoman who killed her own child. The grown-ups used to tell us that if we stayed out after dark, she would mistake us for her child and snatch us away. I thought she must have died by now." My mother quickened her pace. "You stay away from her," she said.

~

My mother was the first person from Wantu to go to America. In the months after her Qingming visit she was talked about so often that even her absence was inescapable. Whenever someone saw me, they would ask after her—"Is your ma in Mei Guo yet?" I nodded obediently, my head tucked down. "Tell your ma to bring you back something nice from America!" they said, by which they meant, tell her to bring them back something nice. They would beckon me inside their homes and stuff my hands with treats, and I would feel embarrassed to be so loved.

The first time I returned home with my pockets full of candy, Ahyi grabbed my elbow and marched me right out the door and back to the house I'd come from. She smiled and shook her head as she emptied my pockets onto the table, apologizing for me—bu dong shi, this child, she said, she understands nothing. She assured our neighbors that we had enough sweets in our own home. Save these for your children, she said, and besides, this one's got bad teeth. Ahyi was a master of evading favors. Before they could try to push the treats on me again, we were out the door and Ahyi was shouting a last thanks and good night over her shoulder. On the walk home, she said to me, "Be careful, shi-san-dian!" Shi-san-dian was Ahyi's nickname for me, her affectionate way of calling me "little idiot". "If you accept gifts from everyone, next time your mother comes back she'll have to empty her pockets thanking the entire town."

~

I was in the market with Ahyi when I saw the weeping widow again. She walked with her head tilted towards the sky and her eyes far away, humming as she veered from vendor to vendor. I watched her as Ahyi bought vegetables for dinner. Every once in a while, she let out a mournful cry that sounded like a bird flying straight at your heart. She seemed to be wailing at nobody.

Ahyi had once told me that living in the same place where our ancestors were buried protected us. I imagined the spirits of my grandfather, my great grandparents, and my great great grandparents rising to walk beside us, while their bodies kept the earth full and thick so it wouldn't collapse below us. I was not frightened by the weeping widow, walking as if among ghosts. I thought she was just living what was true.

On the walk home from the market we saw the widow again, up the road ahead of us. A group of boys were huddled nearby. The children all

31

knew about her, I'd discovered when I recounted what I'd seen on Qingming. Everyone had already been warned by parents to stay away. She was our woman in the dark, our ghost in the flesh, the one who would eat you if you if you stayed out too late.

The boys were laughing excitedly and throwing pebbles at the widow. One by one, they ran towards her, tossed a stone and darted back to rejoin the group. A small stone struck the side of the widow's foot, and a high whoop erupted from the boys. I squeezed Ahyi's hand and pulled. She was already snatching her hand from mine. She stormed over to the boys, swinging her bag of vegetables at them. "Chu! Chu!" she hissed. "Idiots! What did she ever do to you?" Ahyi carried a stout authority. The boys scampered, and I thought I saw the weeping widow turn back to look at us, her mouth curled in an almost-smile.

We walked home that evening, Ahyi trailing the widow at a distance, and I trailing behind Ahyi, counting the strikes of her heels. It was almost dinnertime. The smell of burning wood snaked from blackened chimneys. As we passed the houses of our neighbors, heads emerged from doors, shouting Ahyi's name. They asked us if we'd eaten and called us to join them, cradling bowls of rice and waving us in with their chopsticks. Ahyi shook her head. On a typical night, she would have thrown her head back and said, "Another time, Ah-gong, my mother's still expecting us at home!" But that night she walked on briskly without responding, only occasionally waving her hand to say no. She seemed distracted, as if she wanted to be alone. I walked faster to catch up with her. "Look at you," a woman said as we passed her door, poking her chopsticks in my direction. "Following behind your ahyi like a little tail. Come on! Your ahyi doesn't want to come, but you can!" I smiled weakly at her and grabbed Ahyi's hand.

Ahyi had told me that in the balance of giving and taking, I should always give more than I take. If I did this, good fortune would come to me. After the incident with the candy, I'd learned to refuse everything and anything as a rule of how to be a good person.

~

The summer after my mother left for America, the village roads swelled with rain then cracked dry under the pulsing sun. Everywhere, there were strange flowers to pick and berries to taste, blades of long grass to purse between lips in makeshift whistles, bamboo branches to brandish

32

like swords. My mother had sent her first letter. She enclosed in it a picture of herself taken by my father. In the picture she stood alone before a small white house, wearing a broad rimmed hat and suit dress with stately shoulder pads. Her face was still and unsmiling.

I had never seen my mother like that: frozen. During her visits she was a flurry of hands and bags, sitting down on one chair just to get up half a minute later to sit or stand somewhere else. It seemed that the person in the picture was not my mother, but rather a memory of her.

I knew that so long as she was not here in Wantu, it made no difference whether she was in Shanghai or in America. But the photo was glossy and hard, and it cemented in my mind the knowledge that my mother was far away. Looking at it, I felt I had lost her for good.

I shook away the empty feeling and ran outside. It was late afternoon and the sun's last rays peeked over the shoulder of the mountain. I ran up the road until my clothes were streaked with sweat and dirt. I splashed into the creek to cool my feet against the smooth, wet rocks. The sun dipped. The smoke of burning woodchips rose from the village. It was almost dinnertime. I started to wander back, turning down small roads without thinking where I was going, looking at the stones beneath my feet.

That was when I heard the song. There were no words to the song, just an unearthly melody that echoed in the hollow of my stomach. I was on a narrow path, and the singing was coming from inside one of the old houses on either side. I stopped in the middle of the path, listening. The singing grew louder. The figure of a woman appeared in the doorway of the house in front of me. It took me a moment to realize that it was the weeping widow.

She stopped singing and smiled at me.

"My child," she said. "Why, you're all alone."

I had never seen the weeping widow from so close. I hardly recognized her with her hair tied back in a bun. Her skin was lined but soft, her eyes crinkled and small, and her mouth wide. She was wearing black cloth pants and a brown shirt with a qipao collar, the same work clothes that my own grandmother often wore. She stood above me on the stone porch of her house. Peeling red papers from the New Year striped the dark wood panels on either side of her door. I wondered who lived in the houses next to hers.

"Have you eaten yet? Come on inside." the widow said. She waved her hand and turned into the dark mouth of her door, calling out over her shoulder. "I'm just making dinner."

Perhaps the heat had made me bold. I was suddenly very hungry. I climbed the stone stairs and stepped over the threshold into her home.

It was dark inside. The widow nodded towards a table at the center of the room and disappeared into the kitchen in the back. I sat and waited for her to return.

The table was made from heavy red wood, similar to the one used for meals in my grandmother's house. It was tall and my neck barely craned over it from the low stool where I sat. Along the sides, an intricate pattern of leaves and flowers was carved into the wood. At the corners, the floral pattern burst into heads of phoenixes and dragons. I traced the woodwork, collecting a thin film of dust on my finger. I wondered if grandmother's table had these same patterns. The carvings twisted and turned, deep red in the dim light. I thought they were the most lovely things I had ever seen.

The widow was singing again. From the kitchen, I could hear the sounds of cooking. The gurgle of running water, the hiss of oil on hot iron, the cackle of wood chips burning. Beneath it all was the steady thud of a chopping knife meeting its wooden block. Whatever was cooking smelled heavenly, smoky and sweet and savory at once.

The faucet turned off. The singing stopped. I listened for the scrape of a metal spatula scooping against the wok. I could not hear it behind the gentle thud of the knife, which chopped on at a steady pace. Unaccompanied, the knife sounded slower and duller than Ahyi's frenetic chopping. It shuddered through the walls like a great heartbeat of wood.

I looked toward the kitchen for the widow to appear. The doorway remained empty. I looked around the room, my eyes adjusting to the light.

Besides the table there was no other furniture. The windows were covered with yellowing tissue. The walls were papered with newspaper clippings, and the same photo of a young man had been pasted on every spare inch. The man's eyes looked alive. They watched me from each corner. Red candles lined the walls and melted into pools of wax on the floor. Between the candles, bowls of offerings had been set out. In the flickering flames, the rice in the bowls seemed to squirm. When I looked closer I saw that they were larva, and that flies swarmed around the bowls' cracked and soiled edges. At the table, I counted three place settings.

The widow appeared at the door of the living room. She was cradling a large, empty bowl and smiling serenely. I wondered what would happen to Ahyi if I disappeared. I pushed my chair back and fell out of it. My mother would never forgive her.

I stood up quickly and took a step back. The widow dropped her bowl. I ran for the door. I could hear the widow crying and running after me. Her voice sounded in a wail so sincere that for a moment I almost stopped. Then I remembered her face on Qingming, her wild gray hair and bulging eyes, and I ran, faster than I had ever run before, out the door and down the darkening path. My heart pounded stiff against my ears. It wasn't until I reached the end of the path, where it forked onto the main road, that I dared to look back.

She had stopped. She stood in the frame of her door, looking at me strangely. Her look was almost tender, and yet it did not seem like she saw me at all. It was as if she was struggling to see past an immense wall, squinting and rubbing her eyes, and with a swelling pain I thought I understood—she did not see me as I was but as a picture of myself, stilled and frozen and beyond her grasp. The look on her face was the same one my mother would have seen on mine, if her photograph had been able to see.

I did not dwell on our loneliness. I turned around, and I ran all the way back to grandmother's house where Ahyi was waiting, my lungs gulping so much air I thought they would burst.

Habte

Vincent Poturica

So gentle, soft-spoken, mild, say the eyes of the other soccer parents when they turn to wave to Habte, Paul's father, sitting alone three rows behind them on the concrete bleachers at Redondo Beach Elementary School. Aloof, a little strange, their eyes say, but what immigrant isn't a little lost? Habte nods to their eyes. He prefers to sit alone, to share his burrito with the blue pelican hopping on one leg beside him, the pelican he calls Lucy, for the woman from the TV show who kept him company during those long nights working as a security guard when he came to the U.S. for graduate school. Habte pats Lucy's head. He watches his son Paul: a flashing green jersey circling the ball. He claps when Paul makes a good pass. He thinks about the wood floors in his condo five blocks away that he's refinishing himself to save money. His research salary isn't enough to hire a professional, but Habte doesn't mind the work. He likes to run his palms over the wood's clean shave. He likes the dim outline of his face reflected from the polish: a rough mirror like the sea. Habte has always liked the sea. First the Red Sea that was quieter than the proud Pacific, so quiet that when he let his feet dangle in the water, he felt compelled to whistle. He was a boy then in Eritrea, in the village of Tiyo where fishermen spoke in whispers not to wake the water.

But then the war came and Ethiopia became a bad word, a word that meant evil, and everything was evil: children strung upside down from trees, black flies tunneling eggs into their swollen lips. The trucks crowded with older boys waving candy wrapped in bright plastic: sweet rewards for conscription. Two years later Habte hid his gun in a shrub along with his boots; it was harder to track a barefoot deserter. He wandered to Asmara, the capital city. He slept on benches, dreaming of bread and cool water sweetened with honey. Nothing to do but beg, or huff a rag soaked in petrol to make his stomach quiet. He scolded himself for not killing himself. He threw dice into the air and watched them fall: a three and a six, three plus six equals nine, nine is an odd number, odd meant Habte wouldn't kill himself that day. I'm so unlucky, he would say without bitterness to the other hungry boys, thinking of his mother's fingers that smelled like rice, fingers he would have eaten had she been there stroking his hair. His mother and the beauty mark on her chin that Habte liked to press for luck. And luck finally came—it always does—when another boy stabbed Habte, seeing him as a demon with his hungry eyes, stabbed him with a rat bone he'd sharpened and left Habte bleeding on his back, watching the stars grow until everything was shining: the gravel stones, the muddy puddle, his fingernails, his knuckles. Habte felt very light. He closed his eyes and saw a small grass house and his grandfather, tall with one leg missing, leaning on an elephant tusk. His grandfather pressed Habte's hand and said, My little lamb, I would love to give you something, but what would help? He pointed to a giant hole beside the house circled with crosses. It has no bottom, his grandfather said, taking a dried bird's wing from the brim of his straw hat, throwing it into the hole. They wish they had wings, his grandfather said. You hear them? Habte nodded. He heard so many voices. Habte listened to these voices—some sang, others were screaming—until some of the boys were shaking him. He felt a cockroach scuttle over his toes. He opened his eyes and saw a goat chewing weeds and kicking its feet like a spoiled child. Habte laughed as the boys carried him to the clinic where the doctor assumed his laughter was a symptom: he'd lost a lot of blood. The boys told Habte he wouldn't stop saying Not to worry, not to worry, while the doctor stitched his wounds shut. Habte healed. Still too thin but a little stronger with new scars raised above his eye and across his chest like ribbons, Habte slicked his hair back with rainwater the boys collected in a bucket. He combed his hair as neatly as he could with his fingers. He still had no money, but he wanted to go to school, to the University. He wanted suddenly to learn. Why? Who knows the origins of inspiration: one day the heart beats faster. Habte stumbled into a lecture hall, giddy with hunger. A molecule grew slowly into a fish on the dusty wall: no money for a projector screen or even a blackboard, only chalk in the professor's hand. But a shadow lifted in Habte's mind. A small sun rose inside him. The girl with thin arms sitting in the front asked him his name after the lecture ended. He told her. She smiled and told him her name was Haben and asked if he wanted to share lunch: stale bread and sour cheese. Habte swallowed his spit—he did this often to pretend he was eating—and nodded. He shut his eyes to hide his tears. Come, she said. Habte followed Haben to a shaky ladder they climbed to reach a tiny room: a thin mattress, clothes folded neatly in a corner, a picture of Madonna torn from a magazine and pasted to the wall, a red bow in her hair, aluminum foil smoothed beside the pop star to make a mirror. They ate, and Habte listened to the frogs talking in the puddles under the window. Haben found him a job at her cousin's printing shop where Habte's fingers became sticky with new paper and glaze. He took classes at night and saved all the money he didn't need to keep himself alive. He woke early in the mornings, bathed in a river still lit by the moon. He studied and struggled until slowly, very slowly—Habte doesn't know how—he is at this green soccer field, waving goodbye to Lucy the pelican now that his burrito is finished. He watches Paul run up the bleachers in his small bare feet, his cleats and shin guards in his hands. Paul is smiling. *We won, Dad, we won.*

Standing in Hawaii

Douglas Cole

I arrived in LA a little early. I didn't have to meet the group at the airport until four that afternoon, so I took a cab down to the beach. It was the first time I ever took a cab. It was the first time I really had any money. I had saved most of it, working at the hospital in San Francisco. I also took out a loan. I would have sold a relative to do this year abroad, to get out of Berkeley. Nothing was happening there, at least not for me.

The beautiful people of the beach. I just told the driver to get me to the beach, so he took me to Manhattan Beach. A bit skank, but hot and crowded with young tan beautiful bodies. I had a sandwich and a few beers in a little café and watched it all, the cars cruising, young hip rich kids, vampires, star seekers, working stiffs and students like me, homeless ragged wanderers, narrow-eyed junkies, you name it. And I loved it all. I was in love with it all, ready for the big adventure, loaded with hope and confidence and the feeling that nothing much mattered. I had come out of a beautiful lysergic death-maze, wept my past away on the shores of Stinson beach, crawled out of the shattered egg of what was, and I had no fear. Take everything I have. I'll walk right through walls.

Back at the airport, I sat a while in the bar and had a few more beers. I was underage, but a little number pasted onto my license upped my age a bit. No one cared except the cop at Tilden Park who took my old license away when he caught John Clark and me coming down the hill with a couple of Kirins and a fresh buzz, nothing else on us, thank god—but officer Freeman rummaged around in the bushes and found a few old dusty beer bottles to add to our mix, picked the little number off my license with a thumbnail, and slapped his cuffs on us for public drunkenness and underage drinking. There was no way I was going to cancel this trip to make the court date.

A pretty young girl drifted by in a light purple pleated skirt, and she twirled and her skirt flared out around her and she smiled and I waved and said, "Hey! Come on over." All smiles and light and good energy. She waved and twirled and flirted and floated on into another dream.

The beautiful hum of the airport, all that travel energy, all that tension. Even the weary been-here-a-thousand-times guys in their wrinkled suits were beautiful gargoyles perched in the bars of this cathedral. Bless you all on your journeys. Bless you all in the tinted light of those enormous floor-to-ceiling windows of expansive visions with religious expectations and halleluiahs to distance and desire. I kept expecting to see the ghost of Frank Sinatra materialize, saying 'Where's my jet?' 'Come fly with me' in the eyes of every woman I see.

Ablaze, I drifted over my own reflection in the polished floor to the little conference room where we were all supposed to meet, and I wasn't the first or the last as I slipped into that white cold room with its plastic chairs and oatmeal walls and long bland conference table, and then wham! She hit me. Long brown hair with ringlets, skinny in her blue jeans and red t-shirt and light little sweater with horses rearing up on the front, and her eyes, her eyes, her blue eyes bright annihilated me where I stood. And I stared, struck, paralyzed and, wow, awake as she glanced over at me and saw me and lowered her head a bit and looked again and smiled and looked away and looked back and smiled as though saying, what?

Magic. Kismet. Wonder. Desire. And the director, I suppose you might call him, came and said, "Hello everyone! Let's go ahead and get started."

And so we sat and went around the table introducing ourselves, "Hello, my name is . . . from . . . and I'm studying . . ." Yes, Gary from Oregon, nice hair; Linda from Arizona; long-fingered Suzie; Little stylish buzz-cut Brian with a lisp, and she stood and said, "Hi, I'm Mary. I attend Cal Poly. I'm studying British Literature." I never took my eyes off of her. When my turn came, I stood up, looked directly at her because she was at that moment the only one I wanted to tell anything to, and I said,

"Hello, my name is . . ."

Blur out. Focus in. Silence and slow time. Hubbub—lock. And she and I met for the first time.

We scattered to different seats on the plane. Take off and cruise. Not long in, I rose and sauntered down the aisle. There was already a small line-up at the bathroom, but I didn't really need to use it. I just knew that she was not sitting in front of me, so I headed back, scanned slowly as I walked, hand over hand on the headrests, and hello, there she was in an aisle seat. I knelt down and put a hand on the arm-rest. "Hello, Mary."

"Hello."

"What are the chances of us being on the very same plane?"

"Pretty good!" She laughed and gave me God's own precious smile. And we chatted a bit, casual, easy, known you forever . . . and we did.

~

Later in the flight, when most people had zoned out, sleeping under those thin blue blankets, heads crinked on those tiny fuzz mat pillows, I drifted back again and found her there by the emergency exit stretching her legs, and I stopped and leaned in towards the window and looked out at the twilight sky.

"Was England your first choice?" she asked.

"My first choice?"

"As opposed to your alternate choices?"

"I didn't have an alternate choice," I said.

"You had to. The application had you list two alternate countries."

"I left them blank."

She shook her head, and all I wanted to do was gaze at her, but by now that would be rude, so I looked out the window.

"What a beautiful color the sky is," I said. "I wonder if the altitude changes anything. You know?" I looked at her, and then I said, "Why? What was your alternate choice?"

"Spain."

"Spain?"

"Actually, that was my first choice. England was my second."

"How lucky for us. Saved us time."

"Right," she said, narrowing her eyes.

"So what would you have done if you hadn't been accepted to England?" she asked.

"Well," I said. I waited a moment. She was so open, so sincere, and yet there was this sexy, energetic pulse in her. "I never thought about that. I guess I figured I would get it."

"Really?"

"Really."

And the plane swept on over the clouds in a bright white arc as the sky went from Maxfield Parish blue to obsidian black and the stars emerged and swirled around us and the ocean below became nothing but abyss and darkness and everything far away rushing in a stream as Mary and I slipped into the bathroom stall and kissed and quick stripped the clothes from each other while all around us the passengers floated in their little bubble dreams sleeping and coughing and sighing and stirring in that long glorious flight.

~

I was standing out on the deck, smoking a cigarette and drinking a glass of scotch. Standing in Hawaii. That's what I had taken to calling the deck, Hawaii, because of the sunlight and the view west over the water. Perfection. That's what I thought. Perfection. Mary, the kids, the house, the job—the life. I don't think I thought it then, but if I could choose a phrase to sum up what I was feeling at that moment, sun going down over the Olympics, drink in hand, Chet Baker playing on the radio, it would have to be—this is the life! Maybe I was too complacent. Maybe I was smug or confident in a way that drew a bull's eye on my world. The gods look for that kind of thing. I'll never make that mistake again.

At first she started buying new clothes, sexy clothes, tight and low-cut. She said, "I just want to feel sexy." All right. Then she drifted a bit. You can see that sort of thing in the eyes.

I asked, "Is something wrong?"

"No," she said. But that wasn't true.

"Come on," I said.

"What can I say? I just…" She struggled for the way to say it, to put words to a thing big and vague and strange.

"What is it?" I asked. "I can tell there's something up. You seem so far away."

"Nothing. Just…" And she searched. I waited. Our bed never felt so huge. I looked around at the clothes on the floor, papers and pens and feathers and make-up and cups and money and bills and receipts and…all kinds of crap on the dressers. The place was a mess.

"You know," she said, "I guess I'm just wondering what the next thing is."

"The next thing?"

"You know, after achieving all this—" And she waved a hand up and around. "You know. You get the career you want, the life you want. You achieve your goals, and then what?"

I get it now. I got it then. She always had ambition. Drive. I never knew anyone who worked harder. She was awarded a Faculty Excellence Prize before she even got tenure. Her students loved her. Her colleagues respected and admired her. She was beautiful and smart and charming . Things really went her way, came without a whole lot of effort, though she worked hard. She made everything look easy, though. But I knew. You come from a poor background like she did, folks working hard but not making much money. Struggling, wanting more. She was the first to make it to college. Her aunt had helped her get a spot as a Senate page back in DC when she was sixteen. Senators attended her birthday party. Rich kids with privileges and power all around her. I get it. You get a taste of something like that, you get a feel for your own knack to work a world like that, and it gets inside you. Not that we were struggling, but we were basically middle class. I mean, Hawaii, sure, but without the colonnades.

Her hand was still in the air. Her ring glittered in the lamplight. Downed with light brown hair, I kept thinking. Funny, I thought, how two people can stand in the same corner of paradise and see two different things. I guess we both drew a bull's eye on our lives in our own way.

~

Then it was money. A little here, a little there. Then a big chunk just gone, and I said, "Hey, what happened here?"

She shrugged, looking at the bank statement. "I just paid off some credit cards."

It didn't add up, though. Money gone. Late afternoons. How many committee meetings can you go to?

I couldn't quite put my finger on it, so I started to investigate—the bills, her day-planner. I was going nuts. And I asked her flat out: "Are you seeing someone?"

She looked at me like I was the village idiot. But she was smiling a bit, too.

"Come on. When am I going to have time to see anyone?"

But I knew there were men interested in her. At one of her work parties, I saw a guy come up and put his hands on her shoulders and rub her and smile. I asked her about that and she said, "Oh, Brent? He's like that with everyone. Even if I were single I wouldn't date him. He's a mess!"

Then one time we had a party, and she was dressed in a mini skirt and bustier and fishnet stockings. She invited friends and some people from work, mostly men, and even her hair dresser. I said, "What's up?"

"What?"

"The outfit?"

"I just want to feel sexy."

During the evening, I didn't see her. At one point I went looking for her and found her out on the deck sitting next to a friend of ours, John, and smoking a cigarette. He had tried to kiss her at a party a couple of years ago, she told me, and in one of those conversations couples often have in which you ask, who of our friends are you most attracted to, she had said, John.

I went over and said, "Hey, what's up?"

John just about jumped over the railing. The energy was visible.

Then, a couple of weeks later, I was supposed to go to jury duty, but they let me go early. And when I got back to the house, John was there. He said he had come by to drop off some Christmas gifts. All the way from Edmonds. I guess he did have a bag of gifts with him, though he was out of work at the time. Still, Christmas was weeks away. At best, he was on a hunting mission.

And so I asked again, "Is something up?"

"You're crazy," she said.

I went to a therapist. I must be crazy, I thought. It wasn't a waste of time, though. I raked myself over the coals. Went over my whole history. Examined patterns. Interrogated myself. My therapist wasn't sure what to make of it all, either. She gave me exercises to control obsessive thought and told me about experiments she had read about in which people walk around holding the end of a pencil in their teeth, and by doing this they were forced to smile. They actually felt better. "Does it have to be a pencil?" I asked.

So I muddled along in a strange kind of limbo. I even convinced Mary to try couples counseling, but she was reluctant, saying it was my problem not hers.

The kids? How did they fare? I kept my anxiety hidden. But the house was full of tension. And I watched them fade into the television, into their rooms. I was usually the one to pick them up after school. We did art, watercolors, or took walks or played soccer in the backyard before she came home. And I usually did the bedtime routine, too, getting them into the bath, reading to them. She was always a hard worker, and work came home with her, sometimes accompanied by the smell of fresh perfume on her clothes. She graded papers or worked on her textbook, so in a way they never missed her. She was physically there, most nights, when there wasn't a department gathering or a reading or some other event with friends. She had even taken to going out dancing with some girlfriends, cruising the bars. Her schedule could fill up faster than a plugged sink.

In couples counseling we mostly went over what was wrong with me. My trust issues. Abandonment issues. The counselor suggested we go out more. Mary didn't want to. The babysitter would cost too much money. Whatever I might plan would cost too much money. But I pushed for it, even though it was a hassle to find a babysitter. Mary of course never found us a babysitter. That became my job, and I approached it like some strange cosmic search. I asked any girl between the ages of fifteen and twenty if she could babysit. It didn't matter where I met her. I asked girls in grocery store aisles. I asked girls at bus stops. I asked girls in bookstores. I was always very courteous, but I felt like some kind of predator. And I found babysitters that way, decent girls who came over and watched our kids and responsibly watched our house. Some even did a little cleaning. I had a knack for finding "good girls," at least to babysit our kids. And so Mary and I did go out. But the gulf was always there.

I knew something was up. I got to be like Sherlock Holmes in my powers of observation and deduction. She had bought two mail-order Versace belts and hid them in the closet. One was a woman's belt, the other a man's. But she sure didn't give the man's belt to me. Then they were gone. When I asked her about it, she said "I bought it for my sister."

"A man's belt?"

"She likes the style."

That was only one among many lies. Then I remembered that she had said her hairdresser was 'really into' Versace. That's when I found out, by checking the records at the bank, that she had made out a big check to him. I confronted her about the money. "I gave it to him as a loan, an investment to open his own salon."

"I didn't know he had his own salon."

"He deducts the amount of my cuts and colors from the investment, so it's not like I gave it to him."

She was going for a cut and color every other week. At least, that was what she had written in her day-planner.

"Are you having an affair with him?" I asked.

"I wouldn't touch him with a ten-foot pole."

I drove over there one afternoon when she had an appointment. I just showed up unannounced. It was the first time I had ever been in the place. He had it decked out with purple curtains and zebra-skin chairs. When I went in, no one was there. Then I heard them. They were in the back, a little alcove off the main part of his salon. I didn't go back. I waited. And when they came out, I said, "So, you have been fucking him!" They were both stunned. She smiled in a weird way. He slipped around the side of us and went out the front door.

"No." she said. "Just a little fooling around. Nothing serious."

We screamed it out for a while. Then I went out. I didn't say anything to him. He just stood there, looking scared and guilty. Then I drove off.

That was the end of it. I can think of worse things than being right. We muddled through, as they say, for a while. I mean, you have to give it a try, right? Everyone deserves a second chance and all. And there were the kids to consider.

But that deck. Every time I went out on that deck to smoke a cigarette, I kept thinking about that moment. And I stood there under the eaves as the winter came, clouds flowing in like an armada of woe. But I kept my thoughts to myself. I knew better. That's the only way to survive.

~

Everyone was out. She was out with the boys. No, wait. She was in California with the boys. That's right, because she had told me to move out right before Christmas. My first Christmas alone. The place was more a mess, though, with clothes all over and dog crap on the floor. I rummaged around a bit. Nothing of mine was really there. The family photos she had up were ones without me in them. I didn't know she had those. The place smelled like the dog. I checked her drawers, saw a package of condoms. That was new. The boys' rooms were in pretty bad shape, too. And the kitchen was a wreck, with spoiled food on the counter, unopened bills on the dining room table. Did anyone really live here?

The garage smelled like grass, even though no one had run the lawn mower in months. The gas can was half full. I lingered by the work bench. My old tools hung on the board on the wall. Some of them I had inherited from my grandfather. His last words to me on his deathbed were, "Think good thoughts." He was never a religious man. No one on that side of the family had any fear of God.

I picked up the can and twisted off the cap. Hansel and Gretel left a trail of crumbs to find their way home. I wandered around the rooms, then out the back door. What last words would I say, when the time came? Leave your mark? That one always had weight. And I had to ask myself, did I have the fear of God?

The moon blazed above. The surrounding homes shimmered with hope and impacted conflicts. The realtor of night was updating the listings. I lit a cigarette and took another shot. I tossed the match. It's all a sea. And the stars tumbled in the vast lottery of space. Then I caught that first scent of surprise.

A Memory of Hands

Michael Gray

I

The interview with Lace Watkins can still be found online, a one-hour CBS exclusive that originally aired on December 16, 1999. For a brief time it was fairly popular on the Internet—just a candid, unadorned conversation in a well-lit living room. The blunt sixty-eight year old with her dowdy bisque cardigan and resolute stare. The grandmother of Emmy Lester with a story to tell.

Not sure I believe them with most things, but I do that—about where they found it. I know that picture so well. There's a tack hole near the top edge of the original because I always kept it on the cork board, by the kitchen window there. Sun faded it in places, but look close enough and you can still make them out pretty clear.

~

In the photograph, the young girl is seated on a fissured concrete stoop with an infant balanced on her lap. Wild, peach-blonde hair, chalky-blue tee shirt, bare feet on the sidewalk with her toes in the sun.

Some have said it's not the innocence that stirs them, but the absence of it. The girl's expression—the weary, dutiful grin, shaded eyes fixed on the baby, or maybe gazing just beyond him. One columnist called the image "a still frame of depletion." It's an expression belonging to a worn life, though the girl was only twelve years old at the time.

This photograph was released to the media anonymously nearly a month after Hillsboro, and it helped redefine the capricious public perception of Emmy Lester.

~

A guest psychologist in the wings of a newscast weighed in on the relevance of the photo and Lace's interview. He suggested that "why is always easier once you understand where, and in the wake of the Burkhart crime wave that's precisely what they offer us."

For Emmy Lester, "where" was a dilapidated two-story house in East Dayton. It's still clear at a glance that the neighborhood she grew up in is just a step away from the poverty line. Many of the houses on Nassau Avenue have since doubled as low-income apartment buildings. They have bed sheets for blinds, squat porches without rails, awnings that bleed rust down the aluminum siding.

Emmy's parents, Stella and Greg, were never married. It's said that both of them openly kept other lovers in the house, usually from the pool of transient friends and boarders constantly streaming through. Greg worked on an assembly line packaging auto parts for thirteen years. A fourth-generation alcoholic, he was by most accounts somewhat grave and laconic, carrying a hint of hostility in the way he dealt with people, though no one could remember him ever actually losing his temper.

In contrast Stella Watkins, Lace's only child, served nine months for her part in a burglary when she was nineteen and never held a regular job in her adult life. She was histrionic and verbally belligerent, traits that helped sever the ties with most of her immediate family. She eventually had a total of four children, though paternity beyond Emmy is uncertain. Her first son wasn't born until the fall of 2000, so Emmy was the only child who ever lived in that house.

~

There are few reliable details about this early period in Emmy's life.

Several years later, when Emmy was first identified as Clancy Borden's girlfriend, the public craved an explanation. People couldn't help but speculate about the upbringing of a girl like that. It was easy to imagine all that could go unchecked in such a place as the house on Nassau, a young girl steeped in the irregular shuffle and clatter of adults, but until Lace broke her silence the media had to rely largely on partial records and imagination. They knew that like most of the local kids, Emmy attended Wynn Elementary. Neighbors said she was a common sight coming and going, but a scarcity of facts always plagued their testimonies.

Of course her mother, Stella, gave interviews when first approached, often passing herself off as a kind of neighborhood mother hen. About half a dozen clips from encounters with local reporters exist. In one of these Stella plays the parent of a martyr. Standing on the sidewalk in front of a neighbor's house, the inhalant addict, with her long nails and nicotine-colored highlights, rambles on incoherently about public schools and the economy, and all while holding a toddler (a friend's son) that's so heavy she can't even keep up a pretense of tears.

Aside from the age difference there isn't much to blur the physical similarities between Stella and Lace, especially the slight hook to the nose that makes them look secretive when they grin. But what's striking is the difference in sincerity.

Though Emmy's grandmother never says it directly, it's possible these early news clips are what inspired her to step into the public eye. When her interviewer suggests she might face criticism for justifying Emmy's part in the Burkhart crimes, Lace Watkins simply shakes her head. *Please don't do that. I'm not here to talk about those others. Their story's been told.*

II

Hers may be a name indelibly linked to Clancy Borden, but it's been argued that another man is responsible for Emmy Lester's fate.

Vern Anders: a tall, gaunt drifter from West Virginia with an eighth-grade education and nineteen arrests to his name, all for petty thefts and misconduct. He worked the line with Emmy's father at Dover Packaging that fall and reportedly lived in the house on Nassau for about a month during the winter, somewhere between 1995 and 1996.

No one knows where he wandered after that. Or what became of him.

He was forty-two at the time. Emmy was eleven.

She told me not to, so I never asked. But I knew. She was already living with me by then and she'd wake up screaming and kicking, quilts all over the floor, and I'd whisper it over and over—I know, honey. I know.

Police weren't called in time to do much. Emmy didn't tell until she couldn't hide it anymore. They say her daddy went hunting for the bastard, but he didn't go any further than route thirty-five. I was there. He came back that same night with a case of Budweiser.

Then about a month after Oliver was born, Emmy tells me about finding a man in their basement, sleeping face down behind the furnace. She was down there playing. Said it was dark, all the windows had masking tape on them. Took her awhile to get her guts up, but she started in close because she thought maybe he was dead.

Only he wasn't.

~

The move to Lace's home was supposed to be permanent.

Stella visited four times in those five months and each time Lace pushed the subject of legal custody. Even if she didn't make any progress, she said, it was a sure way to hurry Stella out the door.

Lace would later explain that she was preoccupied with the pregnancy and hadn't pushed hard enough. She was used to Stella's procrastination and unreliability, but she hadn't expected all the trouble that followed the birth.

Emmy carried the baby to term solely in her grandmother's care, and when she went into labor Lace kept the news from the rest of the family.

Oliver Alan Lester was born on Tuesday, September 10, 1996 at 6:21am. Pink skin, searching hands, a prominent lash of peach-blond hair curling up from his forehead like a question mark. Lace recalls how the medical staff called him perfect, though it had not been a perfect delivery. Emmy remained in the hospital another three days before returning to her grandmother's home. Lace had prepped an area in Emmy's room, purchasing enough furniture and supplies to last a long while.

However, Emmy and her baby only remained at Lace's home another four months.

By late January of 1997, Stella had still taken no official steps concerning the agreed-upon change in custody. Then in February she got the police involved and demanded the return of both her daughter and grandson.

Lace readied herself for a fight in court, but without any legal agreement, she was told, her case would likely amount to nothing.

~

When asked about Stella's motive, Lace has an answer ready.

As I recall it was coming up on tax season. In hindsight it's not so hard to see coming.

III

According to the faculty at Wynn Elementary, Emmy returned to school the following winter term and immediately became a target for ridicule from her peers, most of whom had advanced in the interim. The official story was that Emmy had missed the better half of fourth grade because she'd been severely ill, but it didn't take long for the truth to surface and there was little compassion once it did. In one case a sixth grade boy she didn't even know was suspended for misspelling "hore" on several pages of a textbook he'd stolen from her.

Emmy became a truant almost in self-defense, but the attention found her at home as well. It quickly became common to see a spare knot of kids hovering around Nassau, trying to get a look at Emmy Lester's baby.

Lace goes on for nearly two minutes about Emmy's maternal instincts and dedication, but she was still a little girl. It's anyone's guess who watched the baby on those days Emmy decided to attend school. Even though the reception was frigid, Lace said she tried to make it to the house on Nassau several times a week. She'd usually bring fresh supplies and look in on Emmy and Oliver, but the condition of the place disgusted her. One afternoon, after finding cigarette ashes in the crib, she decided to call child services. The only lasting result was that Stella locked the doors against her from that point on.

Lace continued sending care packages addressed to Emmy whenever she could, but she never got to see her great grandson again.

~

May 21, 1997.

It was quickly established that Emmy was not home that morning. Nor should she have been. As the child services agent told Stella, Emmy *should've* been at school.

However, she hadn't been there either.

In fact Emmy didn't return home until an hour after the regular dismissal time. She paused at the front door when she saw the official-looking group milling around the living room. There were burrs and bramble thorns stuck to her sneakers and pant hems.

Cleveland Park, she admitted.

A moment later, they told her that Oliver was dead.

For at least half an hour that morning, the eight month old had had free reign of the cluttered backyard. At some point he crawled into his blue kiddie pool, still full and murky from earlier in the week, and drowned.

Though the incident was eventually ruled an accident, Emmy was removed to a foster home for the rest of that year. In her absence, Stella sold most of what Lace had purchased for Emmy's baby, including his clothes, crib, stroller, and highchair. Lace tried to vie for custody a second time, but once again it came to nothing. She would never be able to understand or accept the decision.

By the time Emmy was shipped back to Nassau Avenue, it was as if her son had never happened.

IV

The story of Emmy Lester's early adolescence is largely unknown. Records show that she never completed another full year of school, at least not at Wynn Elementary. According to some, she became withdrawn and aimless. She lost interest in old amusements. Friendships stemming from before her pregnancy were allowed to dissolve.

It's not clear exactly how or when she met Clancy Borden, a recidivist six years her senior. He hailed from a nearby neighborhood called Burkhart, named after the avenue all the surrounding streets branched off from. Because of the proximity, some people suggest they met through acquaintances. Others say he was just another transient passing through the house on Nassau. What *is* clear is that by the time Emmy was fourteen years old, they were rarely seen apart.

~

Early in the interview, Lace is asked to describe her impression of Clancy.

Emmy brought him and those other two by for breakfast one morning. It was just a little visit. They were all real polite. Asked me about my lighthouses, cleaned up after themselves. And now I can say that I've known evil men.

There's nothing else worth saying about them.

~

53

At least part of what fueled Clancy's notoriety is that he *looked* evil, but not in the Hollywood fashion. He was fairly short and slight, weighing less than 150 pounds. The black hair he kept parted down the center contrasted with his pale complexion. When taken together these features might've suggested something of frailty, but not when you consider his eyes. When he was six, Clancy fell against a tree stump sticking just a few inches out of the ground. The wood cut into the upper lid of his right eye, which scarred and gave his expression a slant, impatient quality, like some emotion was always on the brink of surfacing. A former accomplice once said Clancy "never seemed to be frowning or smiling, but like he could do either one at any time."

Like many of the young men who would later join with him on and off, Clancy barely made it to high school. His police record began with an assault on a classmate when he was just eleven and grew steadily from there. For a while the local police were on a first-name basis with him, but at seventeen Clancy graduated to armed robbery and was no longer considered a petty threat. Back then he favored the small groceries and gas stations bordering Ohio, Indiana, and Michigan, passing between states in stolen cars. He used a semi-automatic handgun and carried a long, thin hunting knife in plain view on his belt.

The two who were most often with him at this time were Leslie Harrow and Travis Dane, friends from the Burkhart neighborhood. Together these three toured the border roads of the Midwest, stealing cars and holding up mostly small, isolated establishments whenever they ran low on money.

It's estimated that between April and June of 1999 these "Burkhart Boys" committed nine such robberies: three convenience stores, five gas stations, and one fast food restaurant. It was a difficult routine to trace because of the random nature of the group's movements. Then on a cool spring evening in Anderson, Indiana, when a twenty-three year old communications student left a bar to pull money from an ATM, the routine changed.

Clancy and the others happened by the student while looking for a place to spend the night. On a whim they parked and tailed the young man, holding him at gunpoint until he withdrew money for them. This task complete, Travis hit the student behind his right ear with the butt of his pistol and kicked him into a coma he wouldn't recover from for eight days.

Though they made off with over four hundred dollars, Clancy and Travis were later identified by the machine's surveillance camera.

It was a mistake they wouldn't repeat.

Veering toward individuals didn't always pay better than their traditional robberies, but there seemed to be less risk involved. The group refined their approach, only targeting people at free-standing ATMs, which allowed them to stand behind the units and avoid the cameras. They also established a pattern of kidnapping the men and women they robbed instead of assaulting them. With an often loud, collegial bravado they would drive their victims deep into rural areas and release them into fields or roadside thickets without their shoes. The steady, clerkish Les Harrow was clearly the designated wheelman who worked hard at keeping silent while Clancy and Travis tried to banter with their hostages, asking questions about their jobs or families or life goals. Even though none of these first victims were harmed, a number said Travis had produced a sewing needle from the brim of his ball cap and threatened to stick them if they didn't "sunny up."

~

In their reports these victims gradually started mentioning that there was a young girl involved. Not another victim—at least not that they could tell. Seated in the front passenger side, a small girl with a thin hook nose and light orange hair who would occasionally turn to glimpse beneath her headrest.

She never spoke, though several claimed to have seen her smiling.

V

When asked about the rapidity of her granddaughter's descent, Lace Watkins takes a moment to respond.

Happened the same way everything does, I guess. One after another.

~

September 8, 1999. Portage, Michigan.

At about 2:40am police responded to a call from a startled widow who said someone was tearing at her back door. Moments after they arrived, officers identified the suspect as Travis Dane.

55

He was unarmed, sprawled on the woman's back porch with a severe knife wound to his left side, a few inches below his armpit. On the chance that his associates were in the area, police began a thorough search of the surrounding neighborhoods, which turned up nothing but a station wagon stolen ten days earlier in Toledo.

Travis, often considered the strongest, most volatile member of Clancy's gang, survived for another two hours. When questioned in the Emergency Room at Spring Valley Hospital, Travis refused to give up his group's exact location, but did say they'd been drinking and playing cards. He admitted that he'd struck Clancy's girlfriend in the mouth after she spilled a beer across their winnings. Without a word, Clancy leapt and stuck him with his hunting knife, digging in straight to the hilt.

Though she would not be positively identified until after Hillsboro, this was the first time authorities heard the name Emmy.

Travis Dane took his last breath just after five that morning.

In the same moment, Clancy Borden became a murderer.

~

On September 12, 1999, four days after the Portage incident, Les Harrow and Clancy held up a small all-night diner called Perth's in Solon, Ohio. After they emptied the register and collected valuables from a handful of patrons, the manager tried to tackle Clancy.

It was a mistake. While on the ground, Clancy pushed the barrel of his semi-automatic against the manager's left cheek. Witnesses said he whispered something before firing. The forty-seven year old was dead before the gang's vehicle was even clear of the parking lot.

Less than an hour before dawn that same morning, the gang hit three gas stations outside of Akron, one after another. After the diner robbery, Clancy seemed to develop a fondness for the sound of his own weapon. In all three instances, he fired rounds through front windows and glass cooler doors. This blitz was answered by authorities, but they missed Clancy's newly-stolen minivan, which headed north, reportedly passing back through Solon before disappearing.

~

These events established the gang's tastes and methods during a serial robbery spree that held the Midwest hostage for almost two months afterward.

The only video footage of Emmy Lester that exists was taken during this period, from a gas station surveillance camera in Seymour, Indiana.

At first the footage seems fairly commonplace: gunmen storm the counter shouting muted commands; employees fumble with the register, empty their pockets. But then the front doors swing open and a petite young girl with light orange hair enters.

Your breath catches.

For a tense moment you expect the assailants to turn and see her— you watch for her reaction. But neither of these things happen.

Instead, the small girl in jeans and a plain yellow top strolls back to the wall coolers for a bottled soda, fills her pale, thin arms with chips and candies, then heads right back outside. Except for a sideways glance, she doesn't even look at the register.

VI

October 20, 1999. Hillsboro, Ohio.

A cold, gray dawn. Rounded clouds draped low over the countryside like spilled bearings. On the thread of road called Locust Avenue, hemmed in by browning fields and spare thickets, Clancy Borden coasted a steel-blue Maxima along at a calm pace. While Emmy slept in the passenger seat, Les Harrow, seated behind her, silently offered a length of beef jerky to the young brunette buckled in beside him. She politely refused.

During the last weeks of their spree, the only discernible pattern in the gang's behavior was the targeting and abduction of ATM patrons. At some point in late September, authorities in Indiana and Ohio started positioning small teams of undercover officers at some of the more remote ATM units as bait. It was a long shot, one the officers involved didn't particularly enjoy. But at about 5:30 that morning, just a few steps down from an old Colony movie theater in downtown Hillsboro, the unlikely plan succeeded.

The woman sitting beside Les Harrow was a Highland County Deputy.

~

Officers on this assignment followed a strict routine. They would take turns approaching their chosen ATM, trying to look casual as they repeatedly withdrew small amounts from dummy checking accounts. The nights were tedious and numbing. Deputy Ashley Coates had already been

57

through the routine twice that night, each time donning a different coat and hat. She'd just entered the PIN when Clancy struck out from behind the unit with a pistol leveled. He had her withdrawal her maximum, $200.00, then he forced her down the sidewalk at a trot.

The officers admitted that after weeks of uneventful tedium, the speed of the crime caught them off guard. Rather than risk a firefight, they held back as the Maxima pulled up at the far corner. Another figure appeared from the backseat and motioned Deputy Coates into the car. Only after the vehicle was out of sight did they begin their pursuit.

Locust Avenue acts as a kind of serpentine access road dividing the rear acreage of a number of surrounding farms. By 6:00am a formation of cruisers had the road blockaded at the intersection where it dead-ended several miles ahead. In the meantime, two other cruisers closed in from behind.

According to Coates, Clancy noticed the pursuit just after cresting a hill and accelerated. He shook Emmy's shoulder and told Les they were being followed. Coates played along, keeping still as Les dug through the mass of handguns and loose ammunition on the floorboard.

Deputy Coates would later explain her actions as stemming from a sudden understanding of the suspects' resolve. In short, she hadn't expected the assault rifles hidden under a lap blanket at Les' feet. The gang had never used such weapons in the course of their crimes and there is still no record of how they acquired them.

Les checked the weapons and handed one up to Clancy, who wedged his beside the center console. Les then rolled down his window, leaned into the brittle blast of morning air, and tried to steady his sights behind them.

Clancy was approaching a curve at high speed. The young girl, Emmy, buckled her seatbelt.

With Les busy out the window, Deputy Coates was free to reach for a bleary chrome revolver she spotted on the floor. She waited for Clancy to start into the curve, aimed the revolver at the back of his head, and fired.

~

The pursuing officers watched as the Maxima swiped a rainwater ditch and flipped seven times, finally coming to rest upright some distance into a field.

Les Harrow was thrown from the vehicle on the first rotation. He landed on the frost-hardened ground nearly sixty feet from the crash site and died there from internal injuries.

The gunshot to Clancy Borden's head had been fatal. His body wound up face down in the backseat, his feet hooked over Deputy Coates's lap.

Coates suffered facial lacerations and a broken collarbone. In her report, she claimed that when she regained consciousness, moments after the crash, she heard a thin moan from the front seat. Even though Emmy Lester had strapped herself in, the force of the vehicle's collision with the ditch caused her torso to slip beneath the upper strap of her seatbelt. As the car rolled, she'd been shaken violently from side to side.

Coates managed to reach far enough over Clancy's body to check the young girl's vital signs.

She found none.

VII

Emmy Lester had remained anonymous up until her death. Authorities had initially labeled her a possible kidnapping victim, then later as simply an unknown female accomplice, which added a layer of mystique to the group's crime spree. The story drew the attention of the local media right away, but when Lace's interview aired it ignited an unexpected surge of curiosity and coverage.

The local outcry drove Stella Watkins from Dayton within a month. After facing threats and at least one assault, she fled to Indiana. Her house on Nassau was emptied out by police and vandalized by just about everyone else. The structure was soon condemned, though shortly after the plywood went over the windows and doors, it was firebombed to the ground.

Greg Lester, Emmy's father, disappeared westward much earlier, having never been placed before a camera.

A few months before they killed her, Emmy came by on her own. I couldn't get her to sit down anywhere. She was so loud and jittery, laughing at every little thing like she got something you didn't.

Not sure what she was hyped up on. She followed me all over the house, smelling like scotch and ashes. Then we were standing in the kitchen and I remember she stopped laughing because she spotted that picture on my board, the one they found in her back pocket afterward.

I was making ice tea. Seeing her in that state got me sour, so I said I was surprised she even remembered Ollie.

It wasn't a nice thing to say.

Emmy didn't seem to hear right away. She took the picture down and held it awhile, then she said, "I remember those little hands."

A few seconds after that she was gone out the backdoor. I didn't think about her taking the picture until later.

Lace pauses a moment. It's the only time during the interview that she offers one of her knowing smiles.

There was this man on TV not too long ago and he was talking about people who do these things, and I remember he said something about the tragedy of it, how people like Clancy and them have these lives that are compressed into just a few acts of violence and crime and that's all they leave us with. And I guess that makes sense. But then I thought that that doesn't really apply here. There was another Emmy at one time and she had a life that lasted about twelve years. May not have been a great one, but it had nothing to do with those others. Nothing to do with crime. Whatever it was it belonged to her.

Justin Brouckaert

Charlevoix

It's easier for Daniel to start with tears—to imagine pulling a binky away, popping the head off a favorite doll. A simple denial: "Uncle Daniel doesn't love you." There are certain thoughts that trigger the brain's defenses, but sometimes the seeds slip by. Sadness shifts to pain: a yank of a ponytail, an outstretched foot lying in wait in the hallway for a pair of unsuspecting toddler shins. At the top of the stairs, a push from behind— just the slightest push.

It's only on the worst days that Daniel allows it to go further—only when the baby wakes at three in the morning and won't stop crying, not even when they hold him, not even when they give him gas drops or Tylenol or lay him out on the bed to let him stretch and roll. Days like these are when Daniel allows himself to forget which thoughts he's supposed to be blocking. When the fantasies bleed into one another, each more hateful than the last, mounting with the baby's constant screams into a single, glorious vision: Daniel gripping the fat thing by its haunches and punting it into the valley, watching it plummet into the tall grass, downed unceremoniously by the trees.

"Can you take him for me, please?" Daniel's mother snaps the TV off with her foot, quieting the clamor of voices he'd turned on to drown the sobs. "Just for one minute?"

Without waiting for an answer, she drops the crying baby in his lap, all wet cheeks and scarlet face and balled fists at his eyes. Daniel turns him around on his knees. He's as light as Spalding Pro.

~

Daniel and Claire had fought most often when Daniel was still wild and unfiltered, when Claire was old enough to defend herself but still boyish enough to tackle. Daniel, thirteen, would dunk his eleven-year-old sister in Lake Charlevoix or pin her elbows behind her back to get a laugh from his friends. Their fighting was common enough, but the wrestling matches ended the night Claire broke free of her brother's headlock and pushed him backwards into a bonfire, six of Daniel's eighth grade basketball teammates staring dumbly as he cried and flailed on the ground in front of the woodpile.

The look on Claire's face afterward wasn't one of triumph or celebration, but instead a lingering mask of panic—a frenzied look she got when she had escape in her sights, when she had made up her mind not to let anyone force her somewhere she wasn't already headed.

Years later, when Clare was in the hospital with her first child, Daniel recognized that same look. At first it was only a hint—a glance so fleeting Daniel told himself it must have been something that came to a woman with childbirth, some motherly change in his sister it wasn't his place to recognize. But after her second child, there was no mistaking it: when the nurse placed Claire's little boy in her arms, she held him like a cloud holds rain, showed the kind of smile that's only given because it's asked for.

Six months later she was on her way to stay with a friend in Sacramento. Daniel's mother had said yes to watching the kids too quickly, telling Daniel the way Claire had been working lately she deserved the break. Claire was living in Lansing then, a few hours south of Charlevoix, and it was true she had her hands full raising both kids without their father, a college boyfriend who lived out of state and didn't even make it back for the birth of his son. But Daniel had been watching Claire during the hand-off. He had seen enough to tell that this wasn't just a break, that she wouldn't be coming back to Charlevoix—at least not until coming back to Charlevoix was what she wanted.

Daniel bobs the boy on his chest while his mother plays puzzles with the two-year-old in the bedroom down the hall. They call the kids' temporary room the back room, but really the house is so small that the back of it isn't far from the front. From the kitchen, Daniel can hear his niece giggling, putting cat heads to duck bodies. With his free hand, he reaches into the refrigerator for a beer and cracks it.

"It's probably time for his bottle," his mother calls.

"Time for brother's bottle," the two-year-old echoes.

Daniel takes a drink and straps the baby into his activity chair on the kitchen table.

"Ack," the baby says, loud and punchy. "Ack!"

"Shut up."

"What's that?" asks Daniel's mother and her echo.

Daniel's mother used to ground him from the kitchen when she heard him swearing in his bedroom down the hall. Not once during the first eighteen years of his life did he sneak in past curfew; now she never seems to catch anything the first time.

The boy reaches out for Daniel's beer like a stupid drunk. Reaches so far that Daniel starts to think he might fall right out of the chair, hit the floor with a wet *smack.*

"I said what time did you feed him last?" he asks, sifting through the cupboard for a bottle.

~

Sounds travel a long way in northern Michigan—longer, at least, than any place Daniel's ever been. Boat horns, rifle reports and coyote howls rove in waves, dipping in and out of hilly pockets that ripple the landscape, trickling or flooding into Daniel's yard from five or six miles away. After Daniel feeds the baby, he sits outside and burns trash in the fire pit, drinking the rest of his six-pack and trying to pinpoint from what part of town the music is drifting, whether the car gaining momentum down the big hill nearby is roaring off to Petoskey, Harbor Springs, Indian River.

Daniel and his father built the fire pit themselves, like they did almost everything else on the property. Daniel's father did the digging while Daniel, only seven, got lost in the valley's tall grass picking out the rocks that now marked the edge of the pit. It had been more than three years since Daniel's father died, but it was still impossible to look at any part of the family's thirty acres without thinking of him. There was the pole barn Daniel had helped him put up behind the house, the garden he and Daniel's mother had tended for half a decade, the wooden fence that lined the property down by the road.

The house itself was the least impressive part of the land: a short, boxy thing that looked especially so surrounded by thirty acres of open green. In the sixties, Daniel's grandfather lost control of a fire in his front yard that ended up burning down half the county, including everything standing on his own land. The house he built as a replacement was only meant to be temporary, Daniel's grandfather's stubborn opposition to importing a cheap modular, but fifty years later it was still standing. Daniel's father had sketched out a blueprint for a new house—ranch style with sliding doors and a wraparound porch that looked out over the valley—but before he got a chance to build it, he took a twenty-foot drop off Bill Johnson's roof and died on impact when he hit the ground. It was that kind of freelance carpentry that had kept Daniel's father from working on his own land in the first place—everyone up north knew his reputation for good work, and it was his reputation that paid the bills.

Without him, Daniel and his mother get by on her pension and his paycheck from the dealership. Neither of them say a thing about Daniel contributing money; his mother never asks for it, and Daniel never makes a show about writing out a check for the water or electric bill.

"Oh they're fine, they're just fine," Daniel's mother's voice floats down to the fire pit from the porch. "But I do think they're starting to miss their mother."

When Claire left, she promised she'd call to check in on the kids once or twice every week. It's a promise she's kept so far, though she always seems to call late at night after the kids are asleep and Daniel's mother is exhausted from giving them both their baths, or quieting a tantrum.

"No, don't say that, you know that's not true," Daniel's mother says. "You know I love my grandbabies, even if they are a handful."

Daniel's mother sits slumped in her chair, but when the baby starts to cry, she snaps to attention. Daniel sets his beer on the ground and jogs over to the porch, but when he gets to the door his mother steps in front of him.

"Hold on, Claire, the baby's up again. Talk to your brother for a while," she says, handing the phone to Daniel before either sibling can argue.

Daniel puts the phone to his ear, still breathing heavy from the jog over. He waits to talk until his mother closes the door behind her.

"Claire."

"Hey, Daniel. How are you?"

"How the hell do you think I am?"

"I don't know."

"Havin' fun in California?" he asks.

"It's Oregon now," she says.

"Great."

"Listen, Daniel, I was just telling mom that if everything works out over here I'll be coming back—"

"You ain't coming back," Daniel says. "We both know you ain't."

"OK."

Inside, the baby's cries escalate into throaty screams and gasps for air. It's been a week since the boy slept all the way through a night.

"You got no idea what you stuck us with, do you?" he says. "You don't see what you're doing to mom."

"Daniel, she's their grandmother."

"They're *your* kids, Claire," Daniel says. "You forget that already?"

"I haven't forgotten anything," Claire says. "I call here every night to check in, and every night mom tells me you're all doing just fine."

"They're killing her."

"Daniel, don't freak out. You always freak out," she says. "I'm coming back. I told you I was coming back."

Daniel runs his arm across his forehead. He and his sister have the same conversation every week, and every week it leaves him with a sweat-soaked sleeve.

"What about me?" he says. "What am I supposed to do."

"Daniel, no one's saying you got to stay."

Her mother is singing to the boy in the kitchen, trying to keep him quiet while the bottle heats in the microwave.

"You always do this to yourself," Claire says. "You have an excuse for everything."

"That's not true."

"No? Then how come you're still in Charlevoix? How come you never took any of those scholarships? You're a big boy, Daniel, and mom's fine without you. Do you honestly think Daddy would have wanted to see you like this, after all he tried to do for you?"

Daniel's mother walks out with the baby in one arm and the bottle in another. Her hair, streaked with gray, is matted to her forehead.

When Daniel and Claire were young, their mother was always the one to put an end to their fights; even now, she doesn't let Daniel say a word against Claire. She meets his eyes and gives what he guesses is supposed to be an encouraging smile.

"I've got to go," he says, and, against his better judgment, swaps the phone for the boy.

~

The baby is not like other babies. When Claire first brought him to the house, he was rigid and tense, balling his hands into fists and striking Daniel on the side of his neck when he was angry. Even now he is beyond control most of the time, breaking through the makeshift barriers Daniel and his mother construct to keep him in the living room, pulling himself up onto couches and chairs. Though he has become more pliable in the past month, he is still too brutish—still stiffer and stronger than a baby should be.

On weekend mornings Daniel lies in bed pitting sleep against the baby's screams, the piercing "Ack" and retching growls that mean the boy is finding some new obstacle to climb, some new height to fall from. A couch or a chair or a step. A dumpster, a pit. A basket taken by nightfall to the coyotes at the edge of the woods.

Daniel lived for sports in high school, but he never loved the locker room humor, the farts and the rat tails and the dead baby jokes. Even now he cringes as his thoughts start to spiral—cringes at the relief he feels from orchestrating dismemberment, burial, drowning. He presses his eyes shut tighter and imagines walking back from the crest of the valley, wiping his hands clean at the lake.

In the living room, Daniel's mother drops the softness in her voice, sheds the practiced tone meant only for babies. Normally she is playful with the kids, giving voices to their toys or singing as she bakes in the kitchen, but on the mornings she is alone with them she is overpowered by the crying and grunting, her words lost amid the noise of screams and Disney movies and toys crashing off wood floors.

Daniel turns over in bed and puts his hands to his ears, digs his fingers into the skin around his temples. There are a set of small scratches there already. Any second, he's sure he'll draw blood.

~

Miles from the scenic strip of Charlevoix where land meets water, miles from the boat races, parades down Main and live music at the pavilion, the city's clean streets crack and turn to gravel. Open fields stretch wider, settling deep in pockets of land otherwise dominated by trees. Freeway centerlines fade as the roads split and narrow, branching into clusters of mobile homes, small ghettos of ramshackle housing peppered throughout the wilderness like rocks in a sandbar. Neighborhoods give way to "property," with "No Trespassing" signs linked across hidden paths and livestock keeping guard over acres of valley, deep and sprawling. Scattered like the rest of the structures in this wooded country are the community centers and schools, the post offices, gas stations, bars and diners, some buildings still in use and others split through the husk with weeds.

Daniel and Seth both grew up in this other Charlevoix, this city that wasn't a city but a constellation of gravel roads and abandoned houses. As kids, they memorized the city's trails and back roads, exploring with their bikes wherever they weren't allowed. Their best find was a basketball court they fast claimed as theirs, a thin blacktop with tall rims, surrounded so completely by brush that there was only one path leading into the clearing, nearly invisible from the road. The court served as part of the playground for an old school building down the road, but Daniel and Seth haven't seen anyone there for as long as they've been playing on it.

Seth is already tossing up jumpers when Daniel pulls up on his dirt bike. For the past week, Daniel's been riding over to the court after his shift ends to shoot around with his old teammate. They play for an hour, sometimes two if Daniel knows his grandparents are in from Pellston to help with the kids.

The court was already old when Daniel and Seth first found it, but it's decayed even more since then. The chain nets they hung have been beaten to only a few limp threads that slap at the rim with each make, and a series of cracks split the blacktop from one end to the other. Daniel kills his motor and watches Seth's miss clang off the rim.

"I hate to say it, but I don't think carving stone does shit for your jumper," Daniel says.

After Daniel and Seth graduated high school, Daniel applied for a job cutting, sanding and polishing cement floors for businesses on the east coast, three months on, three months off. Their landline was down around the time Daniel was expecting the call, so he gave the company Seth's number instead. When they called to offer Daniel the job, Seth accepted it for himself. A week later, Daniel picked up his job at the dealership and started putting in his forty hours. The two friends didn't talk for almost a year.

"Shit," Seth says, "between your shirt and that old bike, I smelled you all the way from Kring's. Threw me off so bad, I haven't made a shot in ten minutes."

Daniel grins and the two friends slap hands. Seth passes the ball to Daniel and they fall into their routine, jogging along the faded 3-point arc, feeding each other soft underhand passes around the key. Daniel takes a step in and shoots short jumpers until he finds his rhythm, Seth collecting rebounds and passing the ball back to him from beneath the net. The two stay quiet as Daniel heats up from the corner, hitting one shot, two shots, three. The fourth clangs off the front of the rim, and the two men switch roles.

In high school Daniel had been good enough to earn scholarships to a handful of colleges, both in-state and out, but the calls started around the time of Daniel's dad's funeral and there wasn't anyone, not Seth or Daniel's coaches or his mother, that could get him to answer the phone.

"You remember that game against TC Central?" Seth asks. "Senior year?"

"The one where you got dunked on?"

"What? No. Fuck no. That never happened."

"Sure it did," Daniel grins. "Kirby was too slow to get around the pick and you had to switch to his guy. I know it was TC because that big old boy ended up playing college ball at State."

"Screw off, man, I was hungover."

Seth launches a fadeaway three that knocks off the top of the backboard, forcing Daniel to chase after it in the tall grass.

"You were always hungover," Daniel calls over his shoulder.

"Yeah, and you never were," Seth says. "Always made the rest of us look bad."

"Look bad? I made you look good."

"Bullshit," Seth says. "If I'd been running point instead of you, maybe we would've made it past state semis one of those years."

"Easy now," Daniel says. "If your sorry ass had been starting instead of me, that team would've never even *sniffed* the playoffs."

Seth laughs and misses another three. Daniel collects the rebound and dribbles back out to the point.

"If I make this shot," he says, crouching with the ball in his hands and his eyes on the rim, "I say we go find Kirby and kick his ass."

"Hell yeah."

This was a game they had played since they were boys—equal parts fantasy, prophecy and skill. Daniel's shot clangs off the rim and bounces back toward Seth.

"If I make this shot," Seth says, "you finally take me up on my offer and we'll be watching Celtics games in the Garden before Christmas."

Seth fires, and the shot banks in off the backboard.

"There it is," he says.

"You know I can't."

"Come on now, Daniel, has this ball ever lied?"

"I can't."

Seth jogs over to where the ball settled and steps back out from the key.

"OK, how about this," he says, crouching again. "If I make this shot, we drive out to California and drag that bitch sister of yours back by her hair."

"Don't," Daniel says.

"And *then* you come out to Boston,"

"Man, don't."

"Don't what?"

"Just don't."

Seth straightens up, sets the ball on the ground and rests his foot on top of it. He pulls a tin of chewing tobacco from his pocket and sticks a wad under his lip.

"Seriously? She takes off the for other side of the country, leaves you with her dirty screaming kids and you won't even talk shit?"

Seth tosses the tin to Daniel, and Daniel tosses it back.

"Ain't as simple as that."

"Sounds pretty damn simple to me," Seth says. "Girl sleeps with half the guys in the state and then books it, lets her family deal with the mess she left behind."

"Stop it," Daniel says. "It's not your problem. *You* don't get to talk shit."

"Man, I'm not the only one talking."

"Fuck you."

Seth raises both hands above his head.

"OK, listen, let's calm down," he says. "I'm not trying to say anything. I'm just trying to understand why I'm the one that's mad and not you. I'd be furious. Hell, I *am* furious. After all the shit you been though, this is the thing that screws you over? After your—"

"Wait, wait," Daniel interrupts. "The thing that screws me over? Who said I was screwed?"

Seth shifts his weight and returns Daniel's stare. He raps his thumb against the tin in his pocket and spits off the court.

"You got two kids at home and their mom's two thousand miles away. Says she's coming back but let's be honest, she's not the type of girl who always keeps a promise. I'm not saying you're screwed. I'm just saying—a lot of folks thought you were going to take one of those scholarships, Daniel. Lot of folks thought you'd jump on the coaching job that opened up at the high school. Lot of folks thought—"

"Like I give a damn what a lot of folks thought," Daniel says. He starts walking toward Seth but then stops, raising a hand to point but clenching the gesture in his fist instead. "You're as bad as my dad. Always telling me to leave but you ain't ever gone anywhere yourself."

"Don't take this out on me because you're mad about what I got and you don't," Seth says.

Daniel grabs the ball in front of Seth's feet, holds it between his bicep and his side and keeps walking off the court.

"Hey," Seth says. "What are you doing?"

Daniel keeps walking.

"Where are you going?" Seth asks. "You can't be serious."

"Do me a favor," Daniel says. "Next time you go to Boston, just stay there."

He drops the ball behind him and swings a leg over his dirt bike. The ball bounces a few times and then settles in the grass. Daniel kicks at the starter until the bike sputters to life.

~

Daniel's niece is just waking up from her afternoon nap when Daniel pulls in. He puts on a clean shirt and then helps her eat her dinner while his mother changes the baby in the back room.

Daniel spoons a pear slice into his niece's mouth. She cocks her head as she chews, pointing at his elbow and resting her hand on his arm. Daniel isn't big by any means, but her fingers look like a doll's on his forearm.

"You gots an elbow?" she asks.

"Sure do."

She spears one of her noodles and drags it along the table.

"An' a teeth?"

"Right up here," he smiles.

She giggles and bites the noodle off the fork.

It isn't until Daniel makes the girl laugh that he realizes how rarely it happens. His sister made it look easy, but he often feels he's boring the child, that she is measuring him up against her real parent. If her life to this point has been a flickering of faces, some that are constant and others that come and go, he wonders if she has yet to classify him as one or the other.

"Hey," Daniel says. "You miss your mom?"

The little girl stares back at him, not smiling or frowning. Her eyes don't show panic, or confusion, or love—only the simple determination of trying to separate one thought from another.

Before his niece can answer, she's interrupted by a wail from the back room—a thump and two sets of sobs that bring Daniel out of the kitchen and down the hall so fast his chair freezes on two legs before crashing on the floor behind him.

In the bedroom, his mother is standing next to the changing table, rocking the half-naked boy to her chest. Both are flushed and wet with tears.

"What happened?"

"I don't know, I don't know," his mother says. "I must have closed my eyes for a second and he slipped."

"Shit," Daniel says. "Is he bleeding?" He walks over and scoops the baby off his mother's chest.

"It just hit me so fast," she says, one hand to her forehead. "I didn't—"

The baby howls in Daniel's arm. From the kitchen, the two-year-old echoes: "So fast."

"He's fine, I'm sure he's fine," Daniel says, pulling the binky from his mother's hand. "Just rest for a while."

"Daniel, you—"

"Just rest, OK?"

Daniel carries the boy out of the room and examines his head in the hallway light. He walks to the front door, wrapping the boy with a blanket from the couch along the way. The boy is tense again, his back going rigid against Daniel's hand, his shoulders jerking side to side.

Daniel walks him out on the front porch and then back around to the fire pit, shushing and bobbing as he steps. He takes the boy out past the pole barn, all the way to the edge of the valley, where a spectrum of landscapes sit just beyond the dipping land: a clump of rolling hills, a ribbon of forest, the lights from town perched just above.

"Out there is Lake Charlevoix," Daniel whispers to the boy, still twisting and sobbing on his shoulder. "Then Burt Lake and Walloon Lake, too, and then Huron all the way over on the other side."

A light from the kitchen illuminates a patch of the yard behind them. The back door creaks open, pauses as the phone rings and creaks again as it closes. Daniel glances at the house and then turns back toward the valley, bouncing the boy on his shoulder again and again.

"Shh," Daniel whispers to the baby, pointing out at the land. "Just look at it," he says. "Just look at how far it goes."

Free Swim

Kate Lister Campbell

We could do things in water we couldn't on land. We flipped our bodies like Easter eggs in bowls of vinegar and food coloring. We conducted orchestras with our toes. We begged our moms to take us every day. There were five of us that summer—me and Heather, my little sister; our neighbors, Emily and June Lee; and a smushed-faced boy from across the street, Matt, who we hated because he talked all day about science.

"Oysters and worms have three hearts," he told us. It was a Tuesday in July. Tuesdays were free swim at Swope Pool. Everywhere we went had to be free, even though it was only a dollar-fifty to get in on regular days. It added up, my mom said. We were economizing, she said. Our moms had a whole schedule of free swims laid out for the days left until Labor Day. School was far away—last year long gone, next year not even a tiny sadness yet. The cicadas weren't in the trees, though they would be in a week or two. My sister used to think the trees were breathing when the cicadas came to sing. She was little then, so we told her yes. Mom and Dad and me. We told her the trees breathed heavy at the end of summer because they were hot, like Sammy, our old panting dog.

"You've never even seen an oyster," said Emily Lee. We were in our station wagon, Matt and Heather and me in the way-back, where there were no seats. June Lee was in the backseat with her mom, Mrs. Lee, and Emily Lee all the way up front next to my mom, who was driving.

"Our dad eats tons of oysters," said my sister. "When he goes on business trips, he always gets them."

Our dad didn't really take business trips. He and Mom were taking a break and he lived in a hotel downtown. Heather knew this, too. But when Dad came to take us to dinner on Saturday nights, we'd play this game where he'd *pretend* he just came back from Aruba. *Do Arubians wear a lot of rubies?* Heather would ask. *Wear them?* Dad would say, with a look like Heather was crazy. *No, no, they catch fish with them! Would you wear a worm around your neck?*

We liked this game a lot. Our mother did not. She was a modern woman who could face the truth, she said. She wanted us to be modern too, she said, and sipped white wine from a big pink tumbler.

"Gross! Your dad eats hearts?!" shrieked June Lee, as we drove through the park's gates and wound through the roads toward the pool. The park was old, on land donated by a man, Colonel Swope, who wasn't a real colonel, but people called him that because he was so rich. He died under mysterious circumstances when his doctor gave him poison. I knew all this because I asked my librarian, Margaret. Every day that wasn't free swim was library. Margaret said I could call her at the library when I wanted to know anything. I liked how I knew all about Swope and nobody else did. You didn't have to run around telling all your good stuff, like Matt.

Swope Pool was far into the park, under the trees. It had an old stone building with locker rooms that smelled like pee. When we got there, we usually ran through it fast to get to the pool. But our moms changed in there, getting bare naked before they put on their one-pieces with little skirts. That Tuesday, when they were changing, I went into a stall and sat with my feet up on the toilet so they couldn't see me. I started snooping after my last birthday, when Dad didn't show up in time for cake and ice cream. We had to eat the cake, even though we didn't want it. Because you can't let what *he* does dictate what *you* do, Mom said. I ate two big pieces, to show how un-dictated-to I was. But I still felt bad, like my insides were a balloon getting squeezed hard until all the air was in my head. Later, I stood outside their bedroom door and listened to the yelling. Mostly Mom yelling. Mostly not about my birthday.

"This is the problem. Right here," Mom said, squeezing the skin of her stomach in both hands. "He told me the last time we did it to keep my clothes on. He said it all sexy, like it was some big turn-on. Should've known then, I guess." I looked at my own stomach, which was bare in my two-piece. It wasn't as big as Mom's, but I could grab it in my hands and squish it together around my belly button, like she did.

"Well, if you've got one problem, I've got two," Mrs. Lee said, and smacked her big butt with both hands so it jiggled. "Really, Jean, I don't think that has anything to do with it."

"Maybe not. But if Greg wasn't into it anymore, wouldn't you rather just know? At least have the chance to *do* something." Greg was Dr. Lee, who was also our dentist. Mrs. Lee was naked, bent over now, rubbing sunscreen on her legs. I imagined Dr. Lee in his dentist outfit, kissing Mrs. Lee's big naked butt through his mask.

"No. I wouldn't." Mrs. Lee said this soft, in a different voice than before. Mom stood up. She stepped into her bathing suit and wiggled from side to side as she pulled it over her hips.

"I saw Jim yesterday, driving," Mom said. "He drove down our street, on purpose. With some business woman with short hair." She ran her fingers through her own long hair. "She was talking on his car phone. He got a *car phone*. Didn't think to give me the number though."

Mrs. Lee got dressed fast, scooting into her suit and snapping the straps over her shoulders. Mom could get going, talking a lot. Talking so much she forgot who you were.

"Jess, though, when I see him, it's like seeing a part of me. Like a physical part. Like he's driving off with my arm or something. And he gets this whole new life and I get what?"

Mrs. Lee looked at Mom without saying anything. She had heard this before, you could tell. In the swimsuits, Mom and Mrs. Lee's backs were big white Us. Their stomachs were lumpy, with faded tropical flowers on them. Mrs. Lee gave Mom a hug, rubbing their flowers together. Then she wrapped a towel around her waist and went out in the sun. Mom sat down on the bench, hunched over. The U went up and down—slow, then fast, then slow again.

My dad was wrong, I thought, looking through a crack in the door. She looked much better naked.

In the water, we played Under the Sea. Emily and June were sea horses, Heather and I were dolphins. Matt was a shark who tried to eat us all.

"I wanna be shark," complained Emily, who had the teeth for it.

"You can't be. You're pregnant. In sea horses, the man gets pregnant. You're the man and your sister just got you pregnant." Matt grinned in triumph.

"Sick! I'm telling Mom!" yelled June Lee, who was always telling on people for things.

But Matt didn't care if you told on him. *What do you know about seahorses?* Matt would say to Mrs. Lee, like he was an adult. Mrs. Lee was the kind of mom who wouldn't say anything back. She'd just stand there with a mad look on her face and think about Matt's mom, Shanna. Shanna was a hippie in the sixties, but now she had a job downtown. Which was why Matt had to come with us. Matt was allowed to *call* his mom Shanna too, because of equal rights. I heard our mom say Matt's mom was a yuppie climber, but I didn't have a chance yet to ask Margaret what it meant.

Emily lunged at Matt. Matt went under the water and came up hard under Emily's legs. He lifted her in the air, then flipped her over his shoulder and dragged her head in the water. The lifeguard blew her whistle. Matt let go of Emily's legs and dumped her on her head.

"I can do that because you're a man, even though you're pregnant," said Matt, smirking. "It's okay for me to hurt you because you're a man."

June and Heather and I watched, excited. Matt knew he shouldn't mess with Emily. But some part of Matt *had* to keep messing with her. Like he didn't have a choice. I felt sorry for him. Emily blew her nose in her hand to get the water out.

"Do you wanna die now or later?" Emily asked, not looking at Matt as she wrung water from her hair, which was still blonde but would turn green from chlorine by the end of the summer.

"Everyone dies eventually," said Matt, shrinking down in the water a little.

"Okay," said Emily, "You can die later, but I'm not going to tell you first." She laid back and floated with her ears underwater so she couldn't hear us anymore. I went over to Matt, who was thinking about jumping on Emily's stomach. He didn't know it, but now she would be ready all the time.

"You should've let her kill you now," I told him. "Now you have to wait all day for it."

"She can't kill me," he said, looking at her with his little grey eyes that needed glasses at home. "I'm still the shark."

At the snack bar, during adult swim, we stood in line dripping water into pools around our feet. Water ran down our thighs and kept dripping from the crotches of our suits, where the material was thickest.

"Eww, you're peeing, you're peeing!" Matt yelled at us, as loud as he could. Other kids waiting turned around to see. June and Heather looked like they might cry and tried to step out of the puddles.

"You can tell when somebody's peeing," Emily said, "because it's yellow. Does this look yellow to you?" She swished her foot around in the pool where she stood. Then Matt shut up because that was science. I smiled at the ground. All the time, I wished I was Emily. Someday she would have a car phone and cut her blond hair short.

In line, I was in charge of the money for my sister and me. "We have to economize," I told Heather with my most serious face. "So just chips. No drink. Mom has water in the thermos." Heather thought our mom told me to say this, so she didn't fight me. I economized about every third day at the pool and any other time our mom put me in charge of the money. Sometimes I economized from a pile of fives and tens she kept in an ice bucket in the kitchen. She didn't notice if I did it while she drank white wine on the porch.

Some nights, though, I liked to sit with Mom out there. We rocked back and forth in these metal chairs. One night, I asked her if the break with Dad was really a break, like summer break. Heather was already in bed. Lightning bugs made little dents in the dark.

I needed to prepare myself for the reality that the break was permanent, she said. Not a break, she said, swirling the tumbler in the air. The end of the marriage. She had a funny smile on her face when she said that. She had *called* it a break in a spirit of hope. You should always have a little hope, she said. Part of life is endings, she said, but endings are just beginnings in disguise. She said it all dreamy, with half her lip twitching, in a voice like she was reading from a book.

After that, I started economizing on my own. I didn't know what I was saving for. But I knew I felt a little hope when I tucked another dollar inside my winter boots at the back of the closet.

When we got our food, we sat on the edge of the pool cross-legged, scraping our ankle bones on the cement. During adult swim, you couldn't even have your feet in the water. Mom and Mrs. Lee stood in the pool together, chatting and doing deep squats. Most of the adults looked lonely. Some of them swam very fast and straight, across the pool and back again. Other ones floated on their backs with their eyes closed or stood just looking at the space all around them.

"Dad's coming back on Friday," Heather said suddenly, to everyone.

"Where'd he go?" asked June, picking at a soggy Frito.

"I don't know. He doesn't tell us till he gets home." Heather closed her eyes, which I knew were getting blurry and sore from chlorine. "Probably Aruba though. He goes there a lot."

I wanted Heather to shut up. I didn't like her talking about Dad. I felt that squeezed-balloon feeling again. You don't have to tell everyone your business, Mom said. Besides, Aruba was just a game that made us less sad before Dad went back to his hotel. When Heather talked about it like it was true, all of a sudden, I was mad it wasn't.

I reached over and grabbed Heather's chips and dumped them in the water. She screamed like somebody was murdering her. All the adults, even the fast-swimming ones, stopped to look at us.

"Hey! I saw you!" our mom yelled at me from across the pool. She didn't care if everyone heard. Her whole face squinted up when she was mad, but I could only see half of it. The other half was underwater, swimming at me. Our mom was a champion swimmer in high school. She wore a Triple-A bra cup, which was terrible for life, she said, but perfect for swimming.

"What the poop, Erin? Seriously, what the poop?" Mom was yelling loud, hoisting herself out of the water next to me. She dripped everywhere, got all our chips wet. She started saying "poop" instead of "hell" or "fuck" when my dad moved out. Because those were was *his* words. When we told Dad about the "poop"-saying, he said he knew one bad word that definitely belonged to her.

"Why did you *do* that? Seriously?"

I knew why, but I couldn't explain it. Mom was giant, standing over me. The flowers on her stomach bulged out when she breathed. I looked up at her face, but I could only see her eyes and forehead with her stomach in the way. Red eyes, wrinkled forehead.

June and Emily and Matt scooted back from us like crabs. The chips were floating away, greasy and gross, making me sorry I messed up the pool. Mrs. Lee was still out there, up to her neck, watching. I looked down at the cement. I decided never to move from that spot again. Even when the sun went down and the bats came out. I didn't care what happened. Behind us, the trees were blowing in the wind, like crinkly paper. Like the only sound left in the world.

"I didn't do AAN-NEE-THING!" screamed Heather, making everybody turn around and look again.

"You're pushing it, kid. You're really pushing me today," growled Mom, in my ear. I didn't look up again. All I saw was her pruned-out toes. Her feet had these blue veins and skinny bones, like you could see her foot skeleton. Dad said Heather and I were lucky not to get Mom's feet. She yanked at my elbow, but I yanked it back down.

"Move or I'll move you," she said, still holding my arm. She grabbed my wrist and yanked again, hurting my shoulder. Somewhere behind me, the Lee sisters and Matt were watching—another thing I had to remember not to care about.

She should've given me a last chance. Usually, there was a last chance. Instead, Mom squatted down and put her champion-swimmer arms right under my armpits. She wrapped them around my chest then laced her fingers together like she was going to pray. She stood halfway up and grunted, pulled my butt off the ground. Her hands crushed the air out of me, palms against my chest. She pulled me an inch back, then two before I started to kick. But Mom was stronger. I tried to dig my heels in, but the concrete ripped at my skin. Her hands were near my mouth, almost close enough to bite, but not. She was dragging me, fast, the backs of my legs scraping the concrete. I could hear a heartbeat, mine or hers, I didn't know. We went backward past Emily and June and Matt. Past a bunch of teenagers who turned around to watch. Past the lifeguard, who saw us, but didn't say anything because we weren't drowning. All the way to our towels spread out on the concrete, next to the fence.

"You're out. Half an hour," she said, dumping me in a pile. "Put a towel on or don't complain if you're burned later." She walked fast back to Heather, who was still fake-crying.

I started breathing again. I wanted big gulps of air, but I could only get small ones. The breeze behind me was cool, the opposite of the hot feeling in my chest. Near the fence was always cool because it backed up to the park where the trees were breathing out oxygen. Matt explained that to me at the beginning of the summer. How what we breathe out, the trees breathe in and vice versa. I didn't believe it was true. How could the world work so perfect like that? That was science, Matt said. The whole world was one big puzzle. When it was solved, everything would make perfect sense.

Thousands of years still had to go into the perfect-sense-making, so we would be dead when perfection happened. But the important thing was our contribution. I liked him when he said that. I felt a little hope when he said that.

The backs of my heels looked like hamburger. I was hot in my chest, but cold and shaky in my arms and stomach. I pulled a towel around me. On the concrete, I could see little pieces of my skin. Mom would be sorry, I knew. She would put Bactine on the scrapes while I cried about the stinging, and maybe buy us McDonald's for dinner. But I wouldn't care. The not-caring was still inside me, only deeper, like she had forced it down with her hands.

"Hey, seriously, what the poop?" said a voice above me, not Mom's.

Matt plunked down next to me. It was forbidden to talk to me while I was punished. But Matt had his own things he didn't care about.

"Your face, that's what," I said, not looking at him.

He stuck his tongue out and crossed his eyes. His smushed-up face made him look like he was saying "so there" all the time.

"Are you out 'cause Emily's gonna kill you soon?" I asked him, wanting him to go away and not see my legs. It was getting toward the end of the day. I wanted to ball myself up in the towels and stick with my plan to never move again.

"No," he said. "I was coming to talk to you."

"You better get in there. Nothing worse than a chicken shark." I tucked my knees together and pulled the towel so it covered all of me.

"Shanna says she feels bad for your mom. Like sitting on the porch like that." He was trying to be nice, but Mom *and* Shanna could go die for all I cared.

"Shanna says maybe your mom should get a job," he said, quiet now, different.

"Oh yeah?" I said. "Should she be a yuppie climber like *your* mom?" I hoped Matt knew what it meant and that he'd be mad.

"Shanna is an *assist*ant. Like, to help people. Maybe your mom would like helping people." He said it so gentle I almost hit him.

"At least I know where *my* dad is," I said, turning to look at him, the hot feeling in my chest going into my head. Mom told me never to talk about

Matt's dad. He was a hippie, too, but stayed a hippie and did drugs all day in California.

"My dad is a musician! He sends us tapes all the time and they're GREAT." Matt looked at my ankles, which were soaking spots of blood into the towel wrapped around them. "At least my dad didn't leave me with a mom like your mom."

I wanted to kill him, but everything on me hurt. Even the parts where I didn't care.

"Uh, hello? *Your mom* leaves you with *my mom* every day. And at least I have a real dad with a real job. Saturday, he's taking us to Ocho Hombres for dinner." I made a "so-there" face. Some of the hot went out of my chest.

But when I said that about Saturday, something happened to Matt. All his face-smush fell down a little. Around his eyes and his cheeks and his chin. Half his lip twitched, like Mom's did when she talked about endings being beginnings. Matt's dad would never drive up in his Cutlass Supreme and take Matt to Ocho Hombres for virgin daiquiris. Even though I wasn't caring about anything, I wanted to fix Matt's face. I pulled one of the towels over his shoulders so he wouldn't get sunburned.

"Hey, you wanna know something cool?" I asked him. He shook his head no, but I kept on anyway.

"This whole park belonged to this guy, Colonel Swope, before it was a park. When he came out here from Yale, only Indians were here. He chased off most of them...but there's still a secret tribe somewhere in the park." I didn't plan to say that, but it sounded more hopeful than the real story. I hoped Margaret wouldn't be mad at me for changing it. Matt's eyes smushed themselves up again.

"Do you think we could find them?" he asked.

I thought for a minute, looked down at my legs, then over at Mrs. Lee and Mom. They were sitting on the pool steps where you get in, water up to their waists. They were drinking out of a Thermos that was different than the Thermos Mom kept our water in.

"I don't know," I said. "Maybe we could. That tribe is so deep in the forest, though, we might only ever find clues they exist."

"Cool!" said Matt. "Let's sneak out the front and go look." I shook my head. My legs were hurting now like they didn't before.

"Next Tuesday, okay?" I said. "Besides, you better go let Emily kill you now." Matt looked sad again, but not like before. He had a right to. Emily's killings were the worst—dunkers, pinches, Indian burns, stomach-fat twists.

"Or, you know, stay here. She can't kill you on land," I said.

"It doesn't matter," Matt said. "She'll just kill me tomorrow." He lifted his head. We pulled our towels around us. The trees were making oxygen behind us, keeping us alive. In a week, the cicadas would come back and we would yell over their noise while we played kickball in our yards. Everything should have been good, but it wasn't.

"Always get killed tomorrow," I said and closed my eyes against the sun.

At home that night after the so-so-sorrys, the Bactine, the McDonald's, I went up to my closet and got out my snow boots. I closed the door to my room and put a chair under the doorknob. When I turned the boots upside down and shook them over the bed, the money came out slow, all hot and stuck to the fabric insides. I counted a hundred and forty-five dollars. I took twenty-five out then rolled the rest up, tucked it back in the left toe—that was for librarian college, I decided. In one pile in front of me, I put five one-dollar bills. Flint arrowheads were a dollar at the Toy and Science store. I figured five scattered around in the park dirt would prove to Matt the secret tribe existed. In the second pile, I put a twenty-dollar bill, birthday money, not economized. I took a pen and wrote on it tiny letters: *Use only in case of.* Then I thought for a minute and drew a long line at the end of the sentence. When I needed it, I could fill in the blank. I folded the twenty and tucked it in a little pocket I carved in my shoe. Then I went downstairs and out to the porch, which was empty right then.

I sat down at the top of the concrete steps, the warmness of them burning my scrapes. When Heather was in bed, Mom came out with her wine. She sat behind me, in her metal chair. We watched the lights come on in our neighbors' houses—at the Lees' first, then Matt and Shanna's. Tiny red mites climbed my arms and I squished them flat with my fingers so they looked like freckles. When the sun went down, we sat in the dark. In Matt's house, the TV turned the living room walls blue and white. Two brown heads watched, shoved forks in their mouths. At the Lees', the blinds were closed everywhere but the kitchen where the just-washed dishes dripped in the dish rack. From the backyard, Sammy barked at something he couldn't catch. Ice popped and slid in Mom's glass.

When we'd been sitting a long time, eyes adjusted to the dark, a Cutlass Supreme drove down the street, slow. I waved but it kept going, red tail lights down the hill. I reached down my calves, felt the scab lumps on my heels. Tomorrow was free swim at Overland Park. The chlorine would sting, but I would jump in, like always. Tomorrow, those scabs might change into anything. Jellyfish stings on a deep-sea explorer. Close encounter with a shark.

When Trapped in a Car under Water

Landon Houle

These poems about mercy, these scenes of fathers and animals suffering on the road, remind me of my own dad and those nights he drove us grille-first down the boat ramp.

We couldn't afford a boat. Once, though, at Sandy Creek Marina, we played make-believe. He ran his chapped hand down a Stingray with a ruby-slipper stripe and played the possibility. I played like I believed him. I believed it was the salesman we were tricking.

To launch a boat, you drive in reverse. You ease down the ramp until the water is just above the trailer hubs. But without a trailer and without a boat, only a family of three in a rusted Chevy edges closer and closer still until the dirty lake—black at night—laps against the tires, and I'd like to believe he was a few in. I'd like to explain by saying he was drunker than a skunk and stoned out of his mind. If this were true, I'd tell you something besides the way the headlights shone on the water and how, if you could trick yourself, you might think something beautiful glittered there just beneath the surface.

But if I'm honest, I'll say he was never as sober as when the cab began taking in water, when the water came up to our ankles. He was never more clear-headed than those nights when my mother pressed my face to her chest, and when I remember, I remember her screams, but when I dream, I dream the truth. I was the one screaming. My mother was quiet. My mother never said a word, and through the pillow, through the soft flannel of her nightgown, I hear nothing but the beat and this as steady as ever.

In the poems about mercy, a father does what's best. He drags the hazard of a doe, unborn fawn be damned, off the road and pushes her into the river, and I don't know that the water is black any more than I know this man is a father, but there are truths you only imagine, realities you dream to understand.

The choice is never easy, and I wonder if it was more difficult for my father to drive into the water or out of it. I wonder which direction felt more like a kindness to a man whose face shone as dark as a night lake.

I'd like to read more poems about fathers who open their coats to bloody fawns. There, too, in the beat or—better yet—the caesura, should be a silent mother, a manual about what to do when trapped in a car under water. In my dreams, we bust glass with our fingertips. We reach out and touch something beautiful. All we have to do is wait. All we have to do is stay calm.

Swimming Lessons

Brenda Peynado

Your parents believed in infant swimming lessons, in pool water that cushioned you like a womb, smooth with clarity. Once a week, they held you underwater to see bubbles released from your nose, then brought you up to air, your arms and feet kicking like again you were born. Months later, you can swim like a little frog. They graduate you from the class with fanfare and baby-safe balloons.

Two years later, you remember none of it. Your parents throw a party, everyone grilling or swimming or running in the backyard. It is easy to forget you. When you fall in the pool, no one notices. In dreams you still have now, you remember falling like this: You walk on the bottom of the pool, adults' legs kicking in the blue in a slow ballet, mica ground into the walls glittering and pockmarked. It's like walking on the skin of the moon. The world hovers in a deep silence. The steps, shining aquamarine with tile, waver in front of you. A net on a long pole plunges into the water, extends towards you, lifts you towards the surface. You are smiling.

Your father tells you a different version. When they realized you were gone, when they saw your dark head underneath the water, he dove in, thinking you were already dead, grabbed you up by your arms. Everyone was yelling. Were you already dead? you want to know. Did someone have to use CPR? you ask. But no one remembers.

It will take you seven years before you relearn how to swim. Until then, you scorn arm floaties and instead hug a beach ball as you go into the deep end, twelve feet, deeper than any of your friends' pools. Once, you squeeze the ball too hard and it explodes from your grip. You flail harder than you'll ever remember moving, and you scream. For a moment, you rise out of the water like you're about to fly. Then you sink back down. That time, an uncle saves you. Once, you float on your ball around the deep end as the edge of the water by the tile begins to curl blackly. A water moccasin slides towards you. You kick to the steps just in time. Your father tells you to hold the screen door open while he brings the snake out on the grass, and then he lets you hold the pool net to shield him while he chops its head off with a rusty shovel, the gritty crunch of metal on the concrete walkway. The tail slithers wildly towards you without its head.

As a teenager, you run wild with a pack of other kids at a tennis camp. The green clay courts grind to dust under your pounding feet. Behind the courts and the clubhouse, a pool sparkles in the summer. In fall and spring, the pool grows brown-green, so milky with algae that anything could be living under its cover. Those school months, you pull up weeds with the other teens and tend the courts with wheels that uncover white lines of tape from under green dirt, blades that slice up chunks of mold, golf carts that run brushes in their wake. You remember a boy, skin the color of chocolate, eyes black and unfathomable. When summer comes, you all swim during breaks, letting the courts go wild. Once, the camp holds a swimming competition, categories in freestyle and treading water. You are not the fastest swimmer, but you and the boy—who you want to beat, who is also the boy you want to love—remain the last two treading water against each other. You both swim for hours. The other kids have long since grown bored and returned to the courts. One coach stays on as referee. Your arms stroking the water, their rippled reflection almost touching his underneath. Your secret is your breath, how you keep your lungs full of air. Finally, the boy pulls away to the ledge. You have won. The boy will turn out to be a sore loser and barely speak to you before he stops coming to the camp altogether. You want to keep treading for hours more, like you already know that water can be mirrors and you are the only thing standing in your way. The coach blows the whistle. Months later, the pool is murky again and impenetrable.

Your father signs you both up for scuba diving lessons as a peace offering, the summer after your first year of college. You resent him, for how safe he's tried to keep you all these years, when all you want is to fly into danger head on. The hiss of your breath in the regulator. Your faces in masks. You still blame him for almost killing you in a practice exercise while thirty feet deep, proving you could take the regulators out of your mouths, let them float and fill with water, replace them into your mouths safely. Your father pulls the wrong regulator, yours, putting yours in his mouth, keeping your air. Five years after that, he signs you up for diving with the sharks at Sea World. In the time between, you have backpacked alone in Eastern Europe, in India, in Latin America. You have gotten the danger you have always reached for. The sharks circle you, trainers kneeling in front of you with large metal pipes like tridents. A hammerhead shark seems unusually interested in you every time it swims round. The trainers keep pushing it away with the metal tubing, placed just behind the eyes with a slow, firm shove. The shark is fooled; it thinks it has hit the clear aquarium glass again, somewhere beyond which it cannot go. Your mother, on the other side of the glass, becomes hysterical, waving her arms. You stay very still, watching the giant groupers, the flash of teeth, the flare of sharks' gills. That moment is the quietest moment you remember.

In graduate school, you house-sit for a professor going up-mountain for the summer. You are charged with tending the pool, the yard, the dog and the cat. You feed the dog and the cat, forget about the pool. At that moment, you are struggling with your life, its deadening stability, how fast everything can change. Your mother is officially in remission from cancer, the occasion for going back to school. One rainy day, it is cool enough that you can walk out to the patio without worrying about sweltering heat. The precious blueness of the water has disappeared and gone to green. Algae forests cling to the walls. Snakes curl up against the ledges. Frogs and tadpoles lunge around the depths, mosquitoes and frog eggs frothing the water into a film. Two weeks later, you have killed everything, the eggs and the bugs, and beheaded the snakes. You can smell chlorine even in the house. Everything is still again, waiting.

When you dream of flying, the air is as thick as water. To rise, you suck in deep breaths. Hyperventilating, your lungs fill like balloons and buoy you up. You tread the air. Often, you dream you are living underwater in the mute of a pool, the churn of bubbles and the booms of cannonballs off the deep end. You have cut the heads off snakes, and their bodies, strung up on the walls, wave slowly. A shark lives in the deep end. Everyone is afraid and splashes out, but the water won't release you. Will the shark eat you whole? Will it circle you forever?

Their Names

Erika Kleinman

Right after breakfast, we told Shea about the twins.

She was sitting on the couch, her arms folded under her shirt. *Sesame Street* was on the television. "Shea, take your arms out of your shirt. You'll stretch it." She took her arms out, keeping her eyes on the show.

"Daddy and I have something really important to tell you about your friend, Cash." She looked dreamily away from the television.

I looked into her eyes. I wanted her to see me, to understand the gravity of the situation. "Cash's twin sisters died."

She tilted her head. Elmo's voice rang out exuberantly in the background. She stared at us. "Why?"

I looked at Michael. He was sitting on the ottoman, his hands folded in his lap. I said, "Remember how Lydia was in the hospital to let the babies stay in her belly for a while? And remember how Lydia was sick?" She nodded. She had been very interested in the babies. She had learned a lot about pregnancy and birth when her little sister was born. She was excited when she found out the babies were the size of peas, raspberries, the palms of my hands. "The babies," I said, "were accidentally making Lydia really sick and the doctors had to get the babies out right away." I hesitated. "They were born, but the babies were too small to survive; they didn't have enough time to grow."

"Oh," she said. "Okay."

Michael said, "It's really sad."

"I'm not sad," she said. "They weren't my babies."

Michael and I glanced at each other. "If you have any questions," I said, "you can ask me, okay? You can ask us."

That night she couldn't close her eyes. She said she kept seeing two skeletons, one with green eyes and one with red. The hair on my arms stood up. "Were you watching something on television with skeletons?"

"No," she said, her eyes watery. "I don't know these skeletons." She pulled the blanket up to her chin. "They went away now," she said, closing her eyes. I lay next to her for a while, listening to her breathe.

In the morning, she told me Cash was lucky the babies didn't live because now he wouldn't have to share any attention and listen to them cry. She said, "I wish we were a family of three again. I don't like having a baby sister. Phoebe is boring." Phoebe was moving a baby doll from the couch to the floor, putting a washcloth on the doll's back and patting it. "Nigh-nigh time," she said cheerfully. She had loose blonde curls at her neck and a tiny ponytail on top of her head, like a fountain. Shea looked at her and crossed her arms. "See, she's stupid. She can't even play right," she said, scowling. "I just want to throw her in the garbage."

I nodded. I felt a tightness in my chest, a surge of protection for my younger child. "Yeah," I said. "I get that. I felt the same way about my brother sometimes."

I put together a package for Lydia and her husband, John. Some books, some puzzles for Cash, and a bag of weed from the dealer of a local celebrity, so I was told. I didn't know if she and John smoked but I had a hunch she might partake. I had bought a glass pipe at the gas station. My husband made pumpkin pancakes. He wrapped them carefully in a towel and put them in a Pyrex container with a lid. "You'd better get going so they stay warm," he said. Shea had written a note to Cash for me to include. It said, "I'm sorry the babies died. Come to my house sometime." Flowers. Happy face.

She asked me: "What are their names?"

The names were given to them after they died. At twenty-five weeks gestation, Lydia and John had not yet decided on names. Lydia told me their names when I crawled into bed with her, right after she came home. Her eyes were hugely swollen, her eyes fleshy slits. "I cried last night until I fell asleep," she said. "There was salt on my face this morning." Then she told me their names. After a poet and a Dylan song.

"Their names," I said to Shea, "are Rumi and Isis." A murmur and a whisper.

The next day we left for a planned trip to Costa Rica. We were scoping it out to see if we wanted to move there. At a beach restaurant, Phoebe fell off of her chair and smashed her lip on the table. I soaked the blood up with napkins, dropping them on the table one after another, as both children screamed. My husband took her as soon as the bleeding stopped, holding her against his chest, smoothing her hair. That was going to be a fat lip.

Shea continued to cry long after her sister had recovered. Phoebe toddled away, looking for hermit crabs with her dad. "Hey, Shea. Come here." She sat on my lap, trembling. "Phoebe is fine. She just has a big owie on her lip. Your lip has a lot of blood vessels in it so it bleeds a lot. She's okay."

A look of recognition. "An owie?"

"Yeah," I said, squeezing her. "Did you think Phoebe was hurt really bad? Is that why you were crying?"

"I was crying because I thought she wouldn't be alive anymore."

We played at the beach the next day until sunset. Shea and I walked back to the hotel. As we walked around the corner to our hotel room, we saw a dead squirrel. He was brown and red like a fox, with a furry black tail. He was on his back, bloated. His eyes were black and shiny. His teeth were yellow and sharp. Shea knelt down. She reached out to touch his head.

"No!" I said sharply. "Don't touch it." I didn't want her touching something dead.

Shea covered her face in her hands, sobbing. "I hate it when people die. I don't want Phoebe to die. I want her to stay alive and I wish a fairy could make everyone alive again, even Cash's babies. Even this squirrel."

She reached for me then. I lifted her into my arms, and felt the weight of her, the tears from her face on my shoulder, the salt-sun smell of her hair. I breathed her in. We were quiet the whole way to the hotel, then she let go of my neck and slid down my hip. She ran toward her cousins, away from me. I watched her until she reached the safety of their circle. They were exclaiming over some tiny shells they had found. They stood together for a long time, comparing their treasures and holding them up to the sun to see their bumps and spirals, their chalky pastel colors and iridescent shine. For days, the children carried the shells in pockets, in palms; as if they were not charms, but amulets offering protection, delivered from a deep and ancient realm.

Flown

Karen Kasaba

Through the wall, the rush of water, my daughter's voice—singing the Decemberists' "Infanta." We've never been to Boston; we're here to look at colleges over Thanksgiving break. Not Harvard. She likes Rhode Island School of Design, in Providence. I'm glad she's an artist—I get the chance to understand her. We toured the RISD campus, which they call Rizdee. Smelled the turpentine in the day-lit studios. In the Film Building, I let my fingers rest on the edge of a take-up reel while I spun the rewind, just to hear it sing, like when I was in film school.

On the hotel television I'm watching a PBS show about turkeys. The show sneaks up on me. A man named Joe Hutto is incubating sixteen wild turkey eggs. He wants to imprint them—to be their mother—and raise them, to get a look into their world. Here is a close up of speckled eggs, with Joe in the background, making convincing turkey sounds. The eggs—*the eggs*—answer back, peeping, and I weep.

It's good to get my weeping done while she's in the shower. She thinks I cry too easily at the television. The eggs pip. Joe is so full of awe; he almost forgets to make his turkey sounds. The first poult cracks open its shell and stumbles out. Joe's gobbling sounds come from deep in his throat, soothing and welcoming. The wet poult pivots its tiny, pin-feathered head, searching for the sound. There it is. It's Joe! They lock eyes, and Joe says in voice over:

Something very unambiguous transpired in that moment.

Now it is not the television, it is not Joe and the hatchling turkey; it is my newborn daughter brought around crying from behind the C-section drape, straight up to my face. There she is—she is perfect. We lock eyes. I say, "I love you, I love you." She stops crying, her eyes wide.

Through the wall, the water stops running, her singing stops. The turkeys are seven days old and they can fly.

"Why are you crying?" She's wearing a hotel robe, her blonde hair turbaned in a towel.

"These sweet turkeys!" Onscreen, the young turkeys flutter around Joe, lighting on the fence he's sitting on, then his shoulder, his head. The scene is backlit, with glittery particles of dust orbiting around Joe and his brood.

She arranges some pillows and nestles next to me on the bed to watch.

The turkeys follow Joe everywhere. He doesn't have to teach them how to be turkeys. They know what to eat, which snakes bite or not, and where all the grasshoppers are. When he is with the turkeys, an array of woodland animals venture near. Deer, box turtles, rabbits and squirrels. Joe is full of wonder. He is an honorary turkey.

But Joe can't keep close tabs on these birds for long. They are becoming more independent. And he is hungry for a sandwich. By the time he returns to their pen, a corn snake that slipped in through the chicken wire cannot escape back out again, due to the large, turkey-shaped bulge in its middle.

"I can't watch anymore." She starts to get up.

"Raw nature," I say.

Joe shoos the snake away, chastened by the loss. My daughter settles back in.

The turkeys are birds like other birds. They fly the nest. Joe knows this, he does what he can to ready himself, but this whole experiment requires more emotional elasticity than he can imagine. It is gut wrenching—even for a man who is neither a turkey nor a mother—to watch the turkeys disappear one by one, until they are gone.

She's sixteen. We still have two more years.

Guitar riff. Montage: Joe remembers the turkeys in reverse. The bold young toms and inquisitive hens. The fledgling poults. This sweet chick, exploring the tall grasses, her eyes drowsing from all she's taken in.

By now we're both weeping.

Birdman

M. M. Adjarian

I was five years old when my father revealed that he had once been a birdman. In 1945 and just before Hitler's defeat, my high-flying father had joined the French Army to train as a paratrooper. His missions took him to North Africa where he jumped out of airplanes and sailed over the deserts of Morocco on wings of silk and rope. He showed me a bronze-colored medal with a star emblazoned on a parachute.

"Look at this," he said proudly.

I wasn't satisfied.

"I want to see how you flew out of the sky," I told him.

My father did, but not in the way I expected. One afternoon he beckoned me into the toolshed next to the corrugated metal building where he did the rare book restoration work that absorbed him during the day. He dug through tin coffee cans filled with metal odds and ends and poked in dusty corners until he found what he was looking for: a rusty iron ring that fit in the palm of his hand, four pieces of string, and a stained cleaning cloth that he cut into a neat, handkerchief-sized square.

He set to work. With slender hands—so like my own but made muscular, calloused and sure by years of moving, lifting and repairing heavy old books—my father wound and tied one piece of string around each of the four corners of the cloth. When that was done, he carefully attached each end of the string to the ring. What he made seemed so clumsy and makeshift. To me, he was nothing but a crazy foreigner with strange ideas. Why make do with what you had when you could maybe buy a parachute toy with a real little soldier attached to it?

When he finished, we walked together into the exuberant overgrowth of our Southern California backyard. My father wound the strings and cloth around the ring. In one swift, fluid motion, he raised his arm, flicked his wrist, and tossed the toy into the air. To my surprise, the parachute puffed opened and the iron ring paratrooper floated back to earth with the easy grace of a butterfly.

I chased after it, amazed that what my father had made actually worked. I threw the toy into the air several times after that, learning how to roll the string and cloth just right so that it flew and fell as lightly as it had the first time it left its maker's hand. My father in the meantime looked on in silence. His normally smooth brow contracted like an accordion into furrows that ran the length of his forehead. He seemed sad and I didn't know why. What he made had not only triumphed over gravity but all my doubts as well.

Leaving the backyard with my father, I soared higher than I'd thrown my toy. Now I had my very own birdman and I would play with it forever. But the iron ring paratrooper and his cleaning cloth parachute disappeared the next day. Still, the memory remains. That ugly and ungainly toy had me feel close to its maker, the kind but at times sullen man with a last name that did not suit his blue eyes and fair skin, and who spoke with an accent that untrained ears mistook for British.

Another memory remains. Early one morning a few weeks later, my mother rousted me out of bed. My older brother hovering beside her, she dragged me, still in my pyjamas and still rubbing the sleep out of my eyes, to where my father's station wagon stood idling at the bottom of the driveway. "Max!" my mother cried as she pushed me toward my father, who had climbed out from behind the steering wheel. His face was closed to me, an unreadable blur. Stumbling into the empty space between us, I felt my heart pound in fear.

My father did not go.

Somehow, my mother had found out her ex-birdman husband's intentions to leave the country. And on a day that should have been like any other but was really the beginning of the end of our life together, I had become a tether, the one thing that had kept my father from flying free of a marriage and family that had become heavier than the earth itself.

Cop Cars

Sharon Rawlette

It's seven a.m., and we're sitting in the living room drinking our Sunday morning coffee when the cop cars pull up. You have your back to the window in your favorite chair. The one from which you watch all your football games and DIY shows. The one my parents gave us as a wedding present three months ago. I'm on the couch facing you. Facing the window when they arrive. One. Two. Three four. Spraying gravel as they skid to a stop in our country driveway.

"Honey . . .," I say, and lift a stunned finger towards the window as four officers jump out and two of them, shotguns in hand, start to circle the house. This is one of those moments in which I know that one of two things is true: either there's been a huge mistake or my life is about to change irrevocably. Possibly both.

As you turn your head to look, I'm back at that night when we awoke to flashing lights outside the bedroom of our old house. You went to investigate while I stayed frozen under the sheets, unwilling to move a muscle. My hearing heightened by fear, I could make out the low sounds of your conversation with another man. Your voices were calm. But then there was the sound of machinery groaning. Clanking. Cranking. Finally, you came back into the house. You sat on the edge of the bed, hands on your knees. "They're towing my truck," you said. Apparently, there was a lien on it we didn't know about. It took us five hundred dollars and a day of bureaucratic hell to get it back. Now, I think maybe the pickup we just bought two weeks ago is stolen property. Even though the guy we bought it from seemed nice enough. He said he had kids.

You're still in the process of turning towards the window, just beginning to get a peripheral on our visitors, when I'm already onto a second, more terrifying scenario. A scenario in which the cops are not coming for our vehicle, they're coming for you.

We got married quickly. After less than a year. Didn't that book say you couldn't really know someone in under eighteen months? Here we are just scraping seventeen. Maybe these cops are about to reveal your secret life.

I know things can change this quickly. I know that this is how the biggest, most terrible changes always happen. With the man I loved before you, it was a telephone call received in a hotel bathroom. "I can't marry you," he said, and sent me sinking to the blue tile floor. After nine years. Maybe the eighteen-month rule isn't so foolproof. Do I have to wait nine years to be sure you'll never turn out to be someone other than the man I rely on you to be?

"What the—," you say, when your eyes finally focus on the cop cars. You, unlike me, head immediately for the front door.

I stand just behind you, peering around your shoulder, trying to shove the dog back with my leg as two police officers make their way up our cracked concrete sidewalk.

"Hey, Mark," you say. It's news to me you know a police officer in our county. Good news, I think. "What's going on?"

Mark recognizes you, and relaxes.

I relax. Of course you're not the guy he's after. You're my husband.

"We're looking for T.K.," Mark explains. The sheriff's office in the next county over gave them our address.

"I have no idea who T.K. is," you say. "I believe you," says Mark. You let him search the house anyway.

I sit on the couch while you open all the closets for them. You tell me later that, when you open the back door to show them the deck, you're startled by a gun barrel six inches from your face.

One of the officers comes back into the living room. "Not who you were expecting on your front porch this morning, are we?" he says good-naturedly. "No," I respond, and manage a laugh. I'm wondering if you, too, had a split-second when you asked yourself if there were crucial—felonious—things you didn't know about me.

How to Be a Grown Ass Lady

Helen Ellis

Compliment everyone. Take a compliment. Wear sunscreen on your face and hands even when it's cloudy. Dye your grey hair black, brown or blonde. Run the dishwasher half-full. Have company over and serve what you want to eat. When a guest says your meatloaf looks like a football, don't tell the woman that her husband is obviously gay.

Don't bite your cuticles. Get rid of a wart before there's a cluster. Don't sit on a toilet in front of anyone, ever. If your husband wants a bigger TV, for heaven's sake let him have it.

Go to the mall for your *Clinique* bonus gift. Buy three pieces of clothing twice a year at full price. Get refitted for bras on your birthday. Replace your tights every winter. Forget thongs. If your white shirt has sweat stains, throw it away. Tip twenty percent on the whole bill including alcohol and tax. When St. Jude's mails you personalized address labels and asks for a $45 donation, write them a check.

Get your pap smears and mammograms. Get your teeth cleaned. Join a book club. Join two. Never put your phone on a restaurant table. Don't tell your friends with kids that if they die, you'll take care of their kids.

If you don't like something someone says, say: "That's interesting."

If you like something someone says, say: "That's interesting!"

Don't brag about not going to church. Don't complain about your interior designer. Give flight attendants your full attention during their in-case-of-emergency routines. Talk to cab drivers. Engage strangers while waiting in line.

Don't reprimand people who call you sweetheart.

Don't reprimand people who call you ma'am.

Accept it: you're too old to drink more than one drink and sleep through the night. Face it: you're never going to get carded again, so quit asking bouncers if they want to see your i.d. Quit going places where they have bouncers.

Call friends you haven't spoken to since high school and tell them about your weird dream that they were in. Don't chastise your husband because he dream-cheated on you. When your husband is in the bathroom, don't knock on or talk to him through the closed bathroom door. When a young person doesn't get your reference, don't repeat, "Kiss my grits!" with the hope that they will.

Call people under thirty, kids.

Call people over sixty, young.

Listen to gangsta rap in the privacy of your own headphones. Listen to erotic audiobooks when you scrub the bathroom floor. Worry about cancer. Google menopause. Challenge insurance claims. Ask your friend who's a shrink if you should see a shrink. Don't look at your profile because it's not the mirror or the lighting or the time of day, it's you.

How to Love a Telemarketer

Diana Spechler

Be lonely. Be lonely as only an eighteen-year-old in a college dorm can be. At night, watch circles of girls eat pizza on the floor. Watch girls in tank tops and underpants shave their legs together at the sinks. Watch those girls join sororities for which you lack sufficient hygiene and social skills. Shave your legs alone. Bleed as though you're lying on a Civil War battlefield. Cry and call your mom. "Ouch," tell her.

Let go of your fantasy: You will not be best friends with your roommate. Your braces-wearing roommate from the Colorado-Utah border does not need friends because she has a twenty-three-year-old boyfriend who visits her in his UPS uniform. She burns so much incense, you experience life with her through a cloud. She blasts Enigma, the least enigmatic band of the 1990s: *Love. Devotion. Feeling. Emotion.*

~

Answer the phone in your dorm room one afternoon when you have nothing to do. Any afternoon, really. The telemarketer wants to sell you a long-distance plan. Tell yourself his deep voice is sexy. Later, tell everyone who will listen, "His voice was so sexy, I bought his long-distance plan." But you're too young to understand what sexy really means. You're a virgin, despite all the hand jobs. You can't even manage a tampon. You're still that girl who gets her period in her pants. You're still that girl who thinks Birkenstocks give her a certain je ne sais quoi.

Keep him on the phone. You don't know how lucky you are—you're among the last teenage girls who get to twist the cord around their finger. Pelt the telemarketer with personal questions. Wonder if you'll grow up to be a professional interviewer like Ricki Lake.

Wrench from the telemarketer an amazing coincidence: The name of his hometown in Oregon matches the name of the town in Texas to which your family just moved from Boston. You have heard, though you forget where, that nothing is a coincidence. Say, "Weird." (Say that a lot, in various contexts, to suggest your deep insight into the world's weirdness and your subsequent separateness from it.)

Invite him over.

Tonight?

Tonight.

~

Now get nervous. He is a stranger. What if he's armed? What if he's thirty or has a tear tattoo? Put on your denim overalls. Take them off. Put them back on. Put on your Birkenstocks. Wonder when they'll finally mold to your feet. Admire your reflection. You look very casual. You look like a girl who goes out with so many of her telemarketers, she can't keep them straight.

Leave your door propped open. Scribble a few hearts on the white board so he'll think friends write you messages. Watch him appear on the threshold, fill the space with his football player body, his amber eyes, his dimples that suck the air from the room. Offer him a root beer from your mini fridge.

"I'm good," he says.

"I know," you say stupidly.

Together, walk all over campus. Every now and then, his knuckles brush yours. Walk past the stone lions outside the dorm; normally they vomit a steady stream of water, but tonight they practice self-restraint. Walk past the library with the engraved quotation: "Who knows only his own generation remains always a child." The sentence is missing "He"—"He who knows." You're too young to understand how silly that omission is, how removing a word is like screaming it.

Count the number of times the telemarketer says, "my ex-girlfriend." Campus is beautiful. It's so beautiful, it's not to be believed. You can see the foothills of the Rocky Mountains, even at night. You've never quite registered all the beauty before—in Boulder, in Colorado, in the universe.

(Four times.)

(That's also like screaming it.)

When the telemarketer shows you the Taurus tattoo on his back, tell him, "I always date Tauruses." When he smiles, long to marry the b'jesus out of him although you're barely a legal adult and he's a stranger who's not even a Jew.

"You're funny," he tells you, bumping your shoulder with his.

After your walk, let him hug you outside your dorm. Vanish into his vastness. You've never been held by muscles before. Your high school boyfriend weighed one hundred forty pounds. Make out with the telemarketer and see sparks like the time you crunched Wint-O-Green LifeSavers in a dark closet. Run inside and up four flights as fast as you can. In the hallway, find your neighbor with the long blond ponytail, a girl you hardly know. Tell her, "I'm so in love. I just kissed this guy. I'm so in love."

She is kind and hugs you and jumps up and down while shrieking, *eeee*.

~

Be a girl whose boyfriend has to dial dozens of numbers a day, but calls her two to three times a week because he wants to. Be the only person in the world whose telemarketer doesn't call enough. Don't tell the telemarketer that you use the word "boyfriend." Do spread fun facts about telemarketers: There are business-to-business telemarketers and business-to-consumer telemarketers; the latter are more intimate. Tell people, "It takes a lot of charisma to turn a guarded stranger into a customer."

Enjoy this bit of your life. You're at that age when you're convinced by whichever opinion you voice. You're no longer so lonely that you try on every article of your own clothing to kill an evening. Boulder is always sunny; it boasts more sunny days than California. You love your poetry class. The professor looks like a poetry professor—his eyes twinkle, as if everything is funny because he's wise—and he reads your work aloud. You make the friends you'll have forever—three guys at the end of the hall, one of whom has a perfect glass bong flecked with colorful swirls. Get high always and daydream about the telemarketer.

~

On the days he doesn't call, wither like a neglected plant. Stay silent, curled on the Salvation Army couch with your new friends. Take sullen bong hits. When he calls, feel watered back to life. On days when you know you'll see him that night, smile so much, you'll need Burt's Bees lip balm, and pay people compliments that land in a unique way because you mean them. You *mean* them. You have enough love in your heart for all the world.

You are starting to gather intel: There was some muddying of things, a girl he loved fiercely who left him, a father who died while he watched, a dropping out of college in Oregon, a getaway to Colorado. He never sits down to tell you the whole story; he feeds you tiny pellets, plant snacks.

Practice telemarketer telepathy: Sit across from him on your bed and with as much force as you can muster, send the message *I love you* from your brain into his so he'll boomerang it back to you. Remind yourself that telepathy takes time.

~

When you get your first look at his apartment, feel unable to stop touching him. His kitchen is so cute. His Pulp Fiction poster is so cool. Your hands want to feel the shapes of his face. You don't have to be a virgin anymore, right? Eventually, everyone leaves their virginity behind, the way you left your Barbies, your childhood home with your dog buried in the yard, your family when you moved to Colorado; the way the telemarketer left Oregon, left his past with its jagged edges. Maybe together, you'll leave behind every person, place, and thing like a trail of discarded clothes.

In his bedroom, note the framed photographs all over his walls—the telemarketer and a girl drinking from a coconut, the telemarketer in a tuxedo with the same girl in a prom dress, the telemarketer and the girl laughing, buried up to their necks in sand. Look closely at the girl. She's you—dark hair, something similar in your smiles. But understand that she is prettier. Understand that she is much prettier. Understand that she has the body of Janet Jackson. Understand that losing your virginity to the telemarketer will mean sleeping with a guy to whom you are a low-rent Janet Jackson impersonator.

"Come here," he says.

In his arms, you would give him anything. Let him unfasten your overalls. His torso swells with muscle. He wraps your hair tight around his hand and looks back and forth between your eyes. Now you know what sexy really means. But his penis stays slumped over like someone sad.

"It's not you," he says.

~

The sound you will forever associate with the telemarketer's weeks of silence is the garbage truck that rolls up outside your dorm each morning. At 6 a.m., it lifts the dumpster off the ground, pouring trash into its mouth like a cartoon monster who eats handfuls of people. Then it slams the dumpster down so hard, you feel the vibrations in your bed. It is the worst sound you've ever heard. You can't believe that you're supposed to endure this soundtrack to your heartache.

~

Go ahead. Call the telemarketer's home phone. Why not? Didn't this whole thing begin because he called you? This isn't the 1950s. You can call a boy. Call him. Again. Call him again. Call him again and again and again and again and again and again and again. In a year, the first time you see a Caller ID box, remember these days and feel briefly faint. Call him. Call him. Call him. Call. Him.

~

You have felt a version of this pain before—three years ago, because of the boy from photography class who kept guitar picks in his pockets: You dropped acid together on a golf course and fell in love with him under the stars. Days later, he fell in love with your best friend. Holding hands, they said, "We would never do anything to hurt you."

And another version, another time—when a boy you thought would always love you talked on and on about a girl named Hannah. "But she's so ugly," he made sure to add, and you understood that you'd lost him to her.

You know this panic, this hollowing of the chest, this nausea. You all know it—information tucked into X chromosomes, passed through generations of women since the dawn of time like an instinct for danger. You will know it again when you lose your virginity in a fraternity house and then lose the fraternity boy, and again when Mike, the one you'll love best, plucks you like a tick from a sweater. And again when Peter—the glass bong owner, the one with whom you sometimes pass hours just sitting and staying quiet together—chooses opiates (over you?) and disappears for most of a decade. You will know the feeling at twenty-seven when an ex gets engaged. And again at thirty when a man says he tried; he tried to love you, but couldn't.

That time, you'll think, *something has been cut out of me that I'll never get back.* The thought will pass in a fit of melodrama, but you're right: You won't get it back. You won't notice its departure until it's a balloon speck in the sky.

~

Keep calling.

~

Have a real conversation with your roommate. Sit on your respective beds, barefoot and cross-legged. She's run out of incense. You're playing your own music, Sublime, Bradley's love song to the girl who sells oranges by the freeway. *You're not the only one,* she tells him, *but you're the best, Bradley.*

Your roommate says she's going to have sex with her boyfriend.

Think of him, his UPS uniform, how he always looks ready to deliver. "I thought you'd been having sex with him for years."

"No, but when I brush my teeth, I always brush my tongue, and one day, I realized I'd lost my gag reflex. So I can deep-throat. So that's kept him happy."

Be impressed.

Add "gag reflex" to your mental list of things that wouldn't hurt to lose.

Add "deep-throating" to your mental list of things that make men happy.

~

When he finally calls you back, run to his apartment as fast as you can. Say, "I missed you," when he opens the door. Throw your arms around him. His hooded sweatshirt is the softest thing your cheek has ever touched.

He tells you he saw a therapist about his uncooperative penis. "It's anxiety," he says. "That's all. I was worried it was me."

Sit on his bed. Note that he stays standing. Note that his muscular arms stay knotted across his chest.

"Now when I want to get hard, I imagine floating in a pool. On a raft."

Ask, "Inflatable or wooden?" and dip your toe in his laughter before you remember that he's dumping you.

"It works," he says.

Of course, all of this will wind up behind you—this moment, Sublime, your hymen, your colorado.edu email address, the Birkenstocks that will never get comfortable, your eighteen-year-old skin, your waitressing aprons, people who, as your heart is being broken in the telemarketer's bedroom, are such givens, so permanent, you don't even have to think of them; you know they'll always be there, like deep water when you dive.

"I'm sorry," he says, "about how things went."

Have the ex-girlfriend pictures multiplied? She's everywhere. She's laughing at you. Or maybe she's smiling, saying, "I am the other kind of woman, the kind who knows how to leave." Telling you, "Stand up, be strong." Telling you, "*Please.* You're eight-fuckin'-teen."

At the door, the telemarketer hugs you and says goodbye, and you say goodbye to the telemarketer, whose great love replaced him and vanished, whose father died without warning him. Day after day, he gets hung up on. Hello, I'm calling because. Hello, I'm wondering if. I want to tell you about. I won't take much of your time. I just want to tell you about.

Later, feel happy for that boy you knew who got to say goodbye.

"How to" Theme Contest Winner – 1st Place

How to Breathe

Ginny Hoyle

I.

I want to strip my life clean, reduce my stuff
to bare essentials—a tree in winter
at winter's end, a cliff above a white sea.

Make that a white cliff, swallows wheeling,
and let the high priest of morning
sing up the sun.

Make it Millay's West Country sun
with her lark in air and that song
clean through me

and Millay's West Country cry—
What have I done with what was dearest to me?
It is not here.

II.

Everyone gets a key to the garden,
a stone seat big enough for one
worn smooth by longing.

III.

Called to the window by petals leaping,
morning breeze. No words
soft enough to say
how this delicate infusion,

a teaspoon of violet dissolved
in an empty sky,
alters the intake of breath.

I bow my head
and look into my heart:

open door
patch of sky
and the wind moves through.

How to Know Your Heart

Ginny Hoyle

I saw my heart today, four valves, four tongues
lapping up the stuff of life, endless flow, insatiable thirst.

Don't talk, the tech said, so I lay still and let the world move
through me: footsteps in the hall, doors that open, doors that close.

Such a crude machine, this muscled pump,
it doesn't love, it works, one stroke over and over.

The bed is hard. The gown is thin. The room is cold.
I entered this world a mere child—a terrible lapse in judgment.

So don't expect me to be logical now, steeped as I am in memory—
scent of earth, mid-summer air, one finch

on a small branch, grooming. Behind a locked gate
a blue pool beckons.

How quickly light steals across the courtyard,
cobble by cobble, packing heat.

"How to" Theme Contest Winner – 2nd Place

How to Leave a Garden

Shirley Fergenson

"We must cultivate our garden."

—Voltaire

You may never need to know this. I certainly didn't think I would. But in the name of good sportsmanship, I pass this on.

First you cry, but not near the delphiniums. Their melancholy, stooped, blue spires in no way advocate for their tolerance of salt. Their downright finicky need for full sun, cool temperatures, high humus content, and a neutral pH, should argue against their presence in the garden at all. But it doesn't. You probably agree. Some things are worth fussing over.

The young plumbagos, on the other hand, wear their baby blue crowns like they're expecting to be stepped on, spreading willy nilly past defined borders, low to the ground and underfoot. The more mature plumbagos dare you to remember that their prickly brown seedpods were once as soft as the youngsters they replaced. A few tears won't kill them. Delicate and hardy, I leave them both to you, to fail or thrive without me.

For as many years as it has taken the wanton wisteria to overwhelm the stalwart silver maple, unlucky enough to have been planted too close, I have been friend, midwife, and undertaker to these four acres. If I had done half as well in the house with Richard, I might be there yet. Give me a chrysanthemum, and I know just when to stop pinching back to get the best bloom: a skill I never mastered with my husband.

So: I leave Richard; I leave the house; I leave the garden.

The boxwoods, thank goodness, can take care of themselves. Study them to see how well they manage: seventy years old and still able to regenerate after a hard pruning. The last time I cut out so many yellow and orange cupped-leaf branches—phytophthera infestans the extension agent said after I sent him a sample—I wondered if maybe it was finally too much. But it wasn't. The next spring tiny green fingers, sprouting everywhere there was a cut, tickled me back when I ran my hands over their innocent exuberance.

You can practically take the ferns for granted, but don't. Their brave fetal push through last season's seemingly impenetrable carpet of leaves defines hope. Every spring be amazed that their fiddleheads are tough enough to break through. They hoard their strength in tight rolls, and only unfurl to feathery delicacy when they are well past the hardship of their birth. Take note.

If the ferns aren't compelling enough, look to the peonies. Pale, fleshy tips break cover in early spring and break hearts: they are too pink to survive. An oblivious foot, an unrestrained rake or a too heavy hand at weeding reduces the potential of the most sanguine nib. But, like the ferns, they take their strength from their fierce self-centeredness. Only when their heads reach above foot level do they forgive their enemies, and unfurl with mitten-leafed optimism.

And, as if they wouldn't be invited back without a gift for the hostess, they offer up creamy, fat buds, so heavy they can barely lift their heads: certainly too heavy to open by themselves.

So they call for help. Ants.

Do not spray.

The sticky nectar is their reward for releasing a mille-feuille of silky petals. Be prepared when the sun-gold stamen draws you ineluctably down to inhale. There is no aroma, except maybe that of the lily-of-the-valley, which is more seductive. Tuck a bloom behind your ear. Richard does not like store-bought perfume.

I leave them to you because I cannot grow where they are. I thought if I nurtured them, they would return the favor. If I didn't cut the daffodil leaves until their bulbs resorbed the lifeblood for next year's flowers, they would shield me. If I cut back the bearded iris in the summer and carefully pulled dirt away from their rot-prone, tuberous chests, they would stand guard for me the following spring. If I divided the astilbes so their pink, red and white plumes had room to toss their pretty heads like young girls who know they are being watched, they would warn me, somehow. But they didn't. I may have been asking too much. It doesn't matter.

I have a confession: there's no excuse for what I did to the clematis. Up to the very end, I lied to myself. Why did I plant five new varieties on the sunny side of the fence, when I wouldn't be around to keep their feet cool with a ground cover? So what if I tied their frail leaders, oh so tenderly, to the uprights? They needed to be under-planted. I knew that. And I acted as if I had all the time in the world, that the searing sun was months away. And it was. But I was long gone by then—except for stealth visits when I knew Richard was out.

They burned. Like babies left out without their bonnets. Crisp. Brown.

I don't deserve to be forgiven for that. But somehow the cosmos and impatiens, one-season annuals, don't hold a grudge. A trick neither Richard nor I ever learned. They reappear on their own in heavily mulched beds, like forgotten deposits growing unexpected dividends. You may wonder why the rest of the annuals stay missing. In my own defense, I left before Mother's Day, the safe frost-free planting date. Weeds have filled in for the zinnias, ageratum and salvia, like unrehearsed understudies. I'm embarrassed to leave such a mess. If you don't mind a suggestion, think about sweet alyssum next to the volcanic rock border. It looks like fairy dust.

The beech was not my fault. The drought was so severe, no matter how many times I moved the hose, the hydrangea or the weeping cherry, or the kousa dogwood stayed too thirsty. The tree surgeon said it was already stressed, that the lindane, toxic as it was, could not recall the invitations the beech had sent out. The bark beetles feasted. There was nothing to be done but use the logs in the woodstove.

That should have been the end, but it wasn't. When the beech came down, the yellowwood scalded from too much sun hitting its previously shaded, forked crotch. And the pachysandra, like supplicants in a holy temple of dappled shade, suddenly destroyed, couldn't shrivel fast enough. A once lush bed shrank to a few hardy survivors. I've seen some new offshoots this spring. It may come back yet, if you're patient about weeding the vacated spaces; give the new life a chance to take hold.

Inasmuch as I chose to leave, I admit I'm surprised how quickly Richard has replaced me with an exotic variety. I wonder if you'll thrive in foreign soil. I hear you're an accomplished gardener in zone four, but I could probably still give you some pointers for zone seven: how to conserve moisture during the dog days—mulch deeply around the magnolia; how to send roots deeper and wider for nourishment—deep water the sunflowers until they refuse to be uprooted at the end of the season; how to plant next to a sympathetic, concurrently blooming variety—choose a bird-magnet mulberry tree, as a willing martyr for the sour cherry.

But you'll probably want to find out for yourself. You'd mistrust my motives, anyway, as if I'd leave out the secret ingredient in my anti-damping-off potting mixture.

Smell, feel, and taste the dirt, so if you ever have to leave, your nose, fingers, and mouth will remember. There is no substitute for torn-cuticle, broken-nail gardening. You know that. You'll worry holes with your index and middle finger through every pair of gloves you buy, no matter how durable the label promises. You'll grind through the knees of your pants. And don't become too attached to your tools. You'll lose your trowel in a frenzy of finishings whenever Richard calls you away from your seedlings to tend to him.

Let it be the morning glories rather than the delphiniums that draw your tears. A bit of salt won't hurt them. Their frail blueness belies their tough, sweet potato vine ancestry. Maybe you already know that the seeds require a twenty-four-hour soak and nicking of their hard seed coat before planting, that their jack-in-the-beanstalk growth pattern is splendid for covering up eyesores.

But there is something else. Someone should warn you.

The most dangerous time will be mid-morning when their pale throats are open so achingly wide, as if their honest vulnerability could stop the inevitable. In an hour their heavenly blue bells will be twisted shut; in a day they will be litter off the vine to be gathered for compost.

Gardeners learn best from experience.

A final tip: it was never Eden. And you don't really need four acres. Window boxes planted with dusty miller, trailing vinca, and blue salvia can be quite lovely, viewed from a dining table set for one.

And if you add lantana, expect hummingbirds. Call it a party when they sip nectar from their tiny, ruby and amethyst pitchers.

"How to" Theme Contest Winner – 3rd Place

Fall 2014

On Learning the Year Used to Be 410 Days Long

Moriah Cohen

When the first warm day broke spring open, you waited
for sounds you could believe in to wander
through the screen, waited for a clean-shaven

magician to pull your father from a hat
like the rabbit he was. When that was over,
all you were left with were oyster shells

and a balloon-sword that couldn't cut
the sun in two. Your whole life it continues,
this process of being opened just to see

what the rings inside you tell about time.
Yesterday, your son turned two, and I told you
it's not that the world is any less

distant than it used to be, but that it's found
something to savor. Now, this close—the scratchy
patch of your chest pressed to my back—I can see you

will never leave her. I wonder if all parents
realize they are small gods plucking our dark
bodies from a curve and crashing them

one bright moment into another.

Green Hole

Elizabeth Langemak

I give my students a quiz and they fall to the bottom of a green
hole where answers might grow anywhere.

One student looks at me. Another stares out the window, where it
is greener, a wild flowering. Some cast their hope toward the door.
What they should know wraps the room like fingerless hands
choking the air.

When I took quizzes myself, I too kept my eyes where I wanted the
answer to be. I watched my hand and I learned

that a quiz is a way of looking inside oneself. A way to practice
what action to take if you find nothing there.

Jesus's Lambs

Elizabeth Langemak

I skim both arms under our cat's belly and raise them like a
forklift. This cat, I say, likes to be held like one of Jesus's lambs.
The cat exhales

between my elbows. You look up from your paper and say, I don't
think Jesus did a lot of lamb holding.

The cat's legs hang fixed as furniture. His black hair suspends a
constellation of dust and he does not sigh again. He has devised an
expression

for waiting, eyelids in half-sleep like the patient Jesus in all of
those paintings you don't remember. In each, Jesus doesn't look
up but holds only a lamb

in his view. Like the cat, he understands that if he can persist my
attention will shift. Soon I will turn and leave him to his sleep.

The Moment of the Fall

John A. Nieves

Autumn awakes the night mouse
avoids snake, its strike

made sluggish by the cooling
air. The branches hear

the victory squeal, the slow
recoil, a tongue flicked

in hunger. And how could they not
change? The reds and golds

seep subtly into the edges—a slight
tint of things to come, of a forest

stained with setting sun, poised
to shake itself naked

across the lengthening nights'
lingering chill. One small

escape, one tiny failure: a life
spared to bury itself, a yearning

born to fan small fires in houses,
in windows waving summer

away, lapping up the coming cold. Already,
we are pulling closer, together.

Proposing to Dickens

Sally Rosen Kindred

> *[Little Red Riding Hood] was my first love. I felt that if I could have
> married Little Red Riding Hood, I should have known perfect bliss.*
>
> —Charles Dickens, *A Christmas Tree*

I want to be your Little Red.
I want to meet you in a wood.

We both know you were a flea-weak husband.
I don't want your hearthstone, your whining ring, spoon

unfolding the thick Christmas pudding
in the same cellar basin where I'd need

to stir the children's wash.
No dusk. No prone spoon.

Instead, our bodies tall between alders
(their thin leaves shaking like ghosts) and yours

in fur's smoke fury, asking
which path I'll take.

I want to find you in a bloodied blue dress,
grandmother, triumph-lined cheeks, saying *Guess*

what? and *The better to feed you with!*—
slinging for me your knife's wild story, a full bowl

of wolf stew.
I want to wait in my red child-

hood, wine-dark
as a closed book—

wait wolf-belly hard
for you to come with an axe,

blade eighteen chapters wide
to cut me out

of that mistaken house
as you did when I was twelve:

your Copperfield, wired on a shilling's worth
of whelks and pippins, lifting me away

from the mother spooned down
on the black den couch

and into the noon grit of your market streets—Southwerk
to Blackfriars, Hungerford Stairs—your mouth's dirty light

telling me
through, in sickness

and in hood, till death do us bread-
in-the-basket, death do us

teeth, my huntsman, my
alder, my Charles: your words,

my wolf,
first bliss.

It is Raining and the Planks on Lewes Pier Bleed

Mark Lee Webb

mackerel, striper, rotten skate. I have nothing better
to do when it rains, so I take holidays and crab,

scrounge chicken necks for bait from the Co-Op,
stop at Derrickson's for a cold cola, walk past

Saint Peter's Episcopal Cemetery where irises bloom
on Miss Henrietta Stotesbury. Tomorrow, if it stops

raining, I will rise before dawn, slip on overalls,
and climb two-story ladders to ice gingerbread

in Salmon and Sea Green. My strokes are not savageries
inflicted on complicitly-stretched canvas, my palette not

Van Gogh's Mediterranean Saintes-Maries brushed
in mistral winds. I work with my son at common labor

and together we walk scaffolding, lacquer Victorians
on McFee in Anemone and Bay Breeze. But if it rains

again I will slip away, stay on holiday pulling my pots,
sorting black fingers from rocks, blues from greens –

the females laden with eggs I will throw
back, the males destined for a scalding.

Another Man They Think I Am at Heart

Jeffrey Morgan

I feel like I was born angry, and all my life I've been sliding
out of orbit. Nothing is on fire, but everything is,
you know? The uncleared table, the dirty cups and plates
like a city abandoned quickly, crumbs and buttery smudges, ghosts
where they touched their dinners with silver. The world is loud.
The stove's elements, red as four embarrassed faces—
like a family of them—is loud in its way. Four is a family.
Sometimes I get a little confused.
They burn and feel nothing. We do. You have to
cover them with tea kettles to hear their screams, right?
Gas is better—the blue hiss of even heat.
But that one was electric. I remember.
I cut a large garbage bag up with kitchen scissors
like one night becoming many, the past stumbling into the present
then back again as if it had forgotten something
in the other room. Why would a hero need a mask?
Elton John said it right: *It's lonely out in space*. I kept the fire
extinguisher close like my best girl. I was a bit of a tease.
I showed her off, the hard red tongue of her,
so stingy with her blizzard of kisses.

Scientists Film Inside a Flying Insect

Amy Wright

"If we can reproduce it . . ."

–BBC News

An x-rayed blowfly
in action wheels inside, buckles,

a mid-stride Derby horse
pleasuring itself

against the air. Slowed
for the human eye,

miniscule muscles
bend the whole rower

the way a neck
rocks a wooden horse

or a girl
on the swings

pushes her arches
to the sky.

The pull
of life

recognizable
now by fried

mother boards, one
hundred little deaths

attempting to lift
a tiny electric

aeronaut, buzzing,
from the earth.

Flight Path

Damon Barta

Will was too young to remember the vacuum-cleaner salesman, but he remembered the roar of his product as it sucked dust from the deep-pile carpet. He remembered the sour odor, badly masked by aftershave, of a desperate man whose livelihood depended on door-to-door demos for housewives who didn't wait for their husbands to get home to sign checks. Will's father was home that day, laid off the day before. He let the man clean the carpet, but he did not sign any checks. The roar stopped, but the smell lingered. Will remembered looking up at his father, who watched through the living-room window as the man who smelled like fear trudged back to an old Cadillac, a dilapidated artifact of better fortune, his back crumpled around a mute vacuum.

Will was twelve years older when a different man came to sell World Book. This man smelled like mild soap and wore stylish eyeglasses that framed soft brown eyes. He carried a small briefcase, within which was a thick, crisply-bound book with gilded pages. He opened the book as he had opened his briefcase, with one fluid and magisterial sweep of his hand. He watched Will's mother carefully while he did this. He was not a hopeful beggar like the vacuum-cleaner salesman. He would leave quickly and politely if he did not see what he needed to see. He stayed.

The book opened at "Anacard," and a large, glossy picture of what both Will and his mother had always thought of as a cashew opposed a terse paragraph on the next page for "Anachronism." Will's mother flipped pages. The man watched her eyes. She looked down at the pages of the World Book then looked out the living-room window at the world. This world began and ended for her at the edge of town, a gulch with steep walls, a sunken spot where fetid lives collected.

"Keep it for now," said the salesman. "I'll come back in a week, and if you don't want it, I'll take it with me. If you do, we'll talk."

She kept it, but she wouldn't let Will touch it.

"Wait," she said. "Just wait. I don't know if we can buy it."

She delicately set the book on a shelf near the living-room window, where worlds had always negotiated between themselves. She watched the World Book man make his way, with a weightless gait and an empty case, to a car that few in the gulch would consider a luxury but most would agree was very reliable.

Will waited until she was asleep, then he took the book down from the shelf and opened it. By morning, he had not slept at all, and he knew of things he had never imagined. He had learned that there were living things in the world that did not need oxygen, that memories could suddenly and irretrievably be lost, and that there were people who didn't pretend to know what caused anything. Concepts were born and named in the same moment, and questions ensued.

Anaerobes, Amnesia, Agnostic. A collection of matters bound only by the spine of the World Book, or were they? Did the letters they held in common constitute some secret shared meaning? To complicate things, the image of the new words would sometimes dislodge themselves from the new concepts and float free in Will's mind, where their mysteries deepened.

Will's mother woke and found her bleary-eyed son staring out the living-room window, trying to reconcile the soot-stained shingles in front of his eyes with the silver sheen of Anthracite behind them. Anthracite burns slowly.

"Have you had breakfast?"

"No."

"You'd better have breakfast. It's almost time for school."

"I don't want any."

"Have something anyway."

His mother produced an Apple.

"What kind is it?"

"What kind? It's an apple."

"There are thousands of them."

"Probably a lot more than that."

"No, Mom, *kinds*. There are thousands of kinds." Will started to cry.

"Red Delicious. I think it's Red Delicious. Did you sleep?"

"No. I couldn't."

"Why not?"

"I had a dream about Dad," he lied. He was thinking of the word "Anabaptist."

Will's mother swallowed. "Do you want to tell me about it?"

"No."

"Do you need to stay home from school and rest?"

"Yes."

"Okay. But then you rest. No TV. Are you sure you don't want to tell me about it?"

"No."

"You're not sure?"

"I don't want to tell."

Will did not like to lie to his mother, so he tried to think of ways that what he'd said could be true. He *did* have dreams of his father sometimes, and they *did* upset him. In one of them, his father was a mangy cat who clawed his way up the bluffs of the gulch and was killed immediately by a truck on the highway. The dreams were usually bad, but they were his only ways of bringing his father back into the world that he knew. That world had seemingly gotten bigger in a single night. He could now imagine his father in Argentina, the Andes, or Antarctica. He decided that this, too, was a sort of dream. He'd dreamed about his father. He had to stay home and rest.

"I might not be home until five," his mother said. Her shift usually ended at three. She wanted to buy him the World Book. "Get some sleep."

Will did fall asleep. He dreamed he was an Archeologist.

When he got up, he went straight for the World Book. He marveled at the benefits of Acupuncture as he tried to imagine a world without Anthropic interpretation.

Archeologists study what people who are gone have left behind. Acupuncturists use pins to relieve pain. There could be any number of unbeheld worlds.

~

Will had the book open in his lap when he heard the car pull up. Thinking it was his mother, he marked his page with a long strand of hair he had found on the carpet before putting the book carefully back on the shelf. He waited for the heavy crunch of the front door, his mother's voice, the thud of grocery bags on the table. Instead there were three loud raps, then the doorbell. There was a woman at the door, about his mother's age.

"Hello, Will." She knew his name and felt comfortable using it. There was even a hint of maternal authority in it, though he was not sure who she was. The factory next to the river produced these figures as prolifically as it did zinc, lead, and arsenic: village busybodies who knew some things about their neighbors and, under the pretense of "concern," were determined to know more.

Will's mother had been rushed to the hospital, the woman at the door told him. An Aneurism. Will tried to let this word float away, but it tethered itself to a full-page glossy photo of a distended artery.

"When will she be home?"

The woman squinted, and her furrowed brow seemed to push the corners of her mouth down.

"When will she be home?" he asked again.

"An aneurism is very serious, Will. Is your father here?"

"Not right now."

"Do you know how I can get a hold of him?"

"No."

"Do you want me to take you to the hospital?"

"No."

"I think you should let me take you to the hospital. She's in the city. They had to airlift her to the city."

"For Angioplasty?"

The woman blinked several times. "Maybe. How did you know that?"

Will looked at the living-room window and saw a translucent World Book reflected back at him, superimposed on the smokestack outside. His father, and now his mother, were out past the boundaries of the known world, but he wanted to stay here with Astronauts and Amazons.

"I'm going to stay," he said. "I'm going to wait for my dad."

The woman blinked again, more rapidly this time. "Where did you say he was?"

"Out of town. I'm going to wait."

The woman shrugged. She seemed vaguely offended by his decision, but she did not protest. She walked back to her car and drove away.

Will went back inside and opened the World Book. He read the entry on Astrology. Astrological signs could supposedly be seen in groups of stars, but when Will closed the book that night and went outside, where no one had connected these stars with bright white lines, he could not imagine scorpions or bulls or goats. He thought it looked more like some spastic child had thrown handfuls of thumbtacks at a black canvas. He went back inside.

~

Not everything inside had a correspondent outside. This was true of the World Book especially. There were Argonauts. There was Algebra. There was Absolute zero. Things he could not touch. Things he could never see with his own eyes. But then he'd never encountered an Aardvark or met an Archbishop either. What was the difference? There were only a few things that Will thought he could know for sure: the deep-pile carpet on which he now woke every morning, the book open on his lap all afternoon, the waning light in the living-room window as evening approached. All else was hearsay. Still, there seemed a difference between the murmured rumors of gossip-mongers in the gulch and the glossy pictures of Athens in World Book. Some accounts of the world seemed more plausible than others. Your father lives just down the road, in the city. The Parthenon still stands.

The light faded and Will went to sleep. He dreamed that he had unearthed the round table of Arthurian legend. He found it just underneath the petrified remains of a dead cat.

~

The World Book man came back the next day. He squinted at the check Will handed him.

"You're sure your mom wanted me to fill in the amount?"

Will nodded. "You never told her how much. But she wants the whole set."

"She can pay in installments. Does she want to pay in installments?"

"No, she'd like to pay for them all right now."

"I see. Well, that's perfectly fine too. I will bring her check to my boss and we'll ship World Book right away."

"Ship?"

"Yes, it shouldn't take more than a week."

"You don't have them with you?"

"Not a whole set."

"What do you have?"

"I have an N-O, for demos, and a special volume that contains world maps."

"How much for those?"

"Well, we don't sell individual volumes. But you'll get the maps for free when you buy the set."

"Then you can leave those two and ship the rest?"

The man looked at the check again. "Can I get your phone number on here?"

"Sure."

"I'll leave the maps."

"And N-O."

"Your copy of N-O will come with the others. I can't give you two."

"Okay."

~

The world map folded out from the middle, many times over, until it nearly eclipsed the carpet. The flattened globe looked like the giant rinds of a peeled blue-green fruit. Will took a pencil and made a mark where he imagined his town was. Now he had a point of reference. He used the scale to measure out the distance from there to Tokyo. Eight thousand miles, give or take. London: 3500. Philadelphia: 2000. Los Angeles: 1750. He tried to make a pencil mark at the place where his mother was. The scale of the map would not allow it. On this map, any distance between Will and his mother was negligible. In theory, his father could be anywhere. He made marks with his pencil as the impulse struck him, like the half-wit who'd made the stars. It was easier to believe that his father had fled to Madagascar or Spain, Greenland or Laos, than it was to believe that he had simply settled into the city just down the road--that on a world scale they occupied the same place.

A police car pulled into the driveway. Will went to the window and wondered what would happen if he did not answer the door. Would this uniformed man with the sagging jaw lower one of his hulking shoulders and force his way in? The man knocked loudly and waited. He knocked again and waited. He came to the living-room window and tried to look inside. Will stepped back and looked at the man looking. The day was bright, but the house was not. The cop was struggling to see past his own reflection and that of the smokestack behind him. He pressed his face to the glass like a capricious child. Will half-expected his tongue to come out. His cheeks adhered to the glass for a moment and left steam cloud jowls that shrunk slowly as he walked back to his car.

Will sat back down in front of the map and began to cry. How could there be so many people in so many places, so far from each other? Why did almost no distance feel the same as eight thousand miles? He drew lines between the pencil marks he'd made on the map and tried to find the shape of something he might recognize. Nothing. The word "aneurism" suddenly abandoned its place and drifted like a hitchhiker through Will's mind watching potential vessels pass it by. He tore the world map out of the book, and beneath it he found another map, this one of a single landmass, snugly condensed onto one page. It was labeled "Pangaea: the supercontinent." Here was the one from which the many had sprung. The place before the drift. Will folded the world map as many times as he could and put it in his pocket. He left Pangaea lying in the center of the floor.

~

Will felt the fact of distance, the consequences of drift, in his weary legs. He had gone about twelve miles before he began stopping to look hopefully behind him at oncoming cars. He couldn't bring himself to use his thumb. As soon as he'd reached the rim of the gulch, he could see across it to the highway on the other side. A few steps further and there was only horizon, the only trace of the town below a black plume of smoke from the factory smokestack. Or maybe it was the breath of a sleeping dragon from an Arthurian legend, torpid after a feast of flesh. Some accounts of the world seemed more plausible than others. The living room he hadn't left for more than a week now seemed as hypothetical as his next step. He walked on the loose gravel between the paved highway and the grassy ditch, kicking rocks to one side or the other, listening alternately to chirping birds and rumbling engines.

Will had stopped looking back at cars, and he could now only hear the sound of uninterrupted velocity as they approached. His plaintive gazes had not been able to penetrate these wind-shielded little worlds. Not even here, twelve miles from a place where everyone was curious to a fault. Cars kept emerging from the ground, mirages that moved closer, made sounds, moved away. It occurred to Will that he had brought nothing to eat. He sat down on the roadside and watched the horizon behind him. Another mirage emerged, and Will waited for it to evaporate. Instead, the World Book salesman pulled to the side right behind him.

The hazard lights flashed an invitation, and Will came to the passenger-side window. Nothing happened. He brought his face up to the glass, careful not to let it touch. Still nothing. He put his forehead to the glass and peered. The salesman's face was dimly discernible now, and Will could see his lips moving. "Winter donut worms," he seemed to say.

"What?" said Will.

"We know Disney World."

"What?"

Finally, the man reached over and opened the door.

"Window doesn't work," he said. "Would you like to get in?"

"Sure."

The inside of the car smelled like new vinyl and warm meat.

"Headed home?" the World Book man asked, not waiting for the answer before swinging a wide U-turn across the empty highway.

"No, I'm going the other way." The man fluidly followed his U-turn with another, making an elegant circle as if it had been his intent all along.

"Where to, then?"

"The city."

"Me too. I've sold as much as I can back there. Time to move on. Does your mother know you're out here?"

"No. She's in the city. At the hospital. An aneurism."

"Jesus. Why are you walking there? Where's your dad?"

"The city."

"At the hospital?"

"No."

"Mm." He seemed to understand something Will had not told him. "My father has been gone a long time."

"Mine too. He left when I was little and he didn't come back. I barely remember him."

"Jesus. I remember my dad, but he's dead now."

"When someone is not there they might as well be dead."

"That's true. When someone is not there they are only a story that you tell yourself." Will thought about the marked-up map, hopelessly crushed and dampened in his pocket, and Pangaea, back at the house on its pristine page.

"When people aren't missing things, they don't need stories."

"What happened to your dad?"

"He hung himself with the cord from one of his vacuum cleaners. He sold vacuum cleaners. Or didn't sell them. That was part of the problem."

"Why couldn't he sell them?"

"He did, for a while. But things changed."

"What changed?"

"The stories people told themselves. When my father first started, he sold a lot of vacuums. He would go to a house, show the person inside how well his product cleaned the carpet, and walk out with a check in his hand. This worked for several years. It worked because for these people inside their houses the world was their houses. And who doesn't want to live in a better world?"

"People still vacuum their floors, don't they?"

"Sure. But when enough of the people in their houses started believing in worlds beyond those houses, they stopped trying to make the known world better, and started dreaming about another one. These dreams did not involve vacuum cleaners. This required an adjustment that my father was unable to make. He was unable to make it because he thought he was selling a product."

"You're selling a product."

"Do you see any products in here?"

"You ship them. I have some of your books at my house."

"What house?" Will did not have a good answer for this. He had all but forgotten the house once he started walking.

"You're not in a house, and you aren't carrying any books. I found you on a highway with nothing in your hands."

"I'm hungry," Will said.

"Lucky for you, I wasn't." He reached behind his seat, pulled out a brown paper bag, and handed it to Will. Will reached inside and found something still warm in a sheath of tin foil, which he began peeling away. "I sell a different story than my father did. It's about worlds that are far away.

134

Some people want to hear this story right now. Think their children can live in one of these worlds if they read about it. Maybe not in five years. Maybe their kids have gone then. Maybe they can't remember their faces, or which of those hypothetical worlds they disappeared into. Maybe in five years they want their homes to be the only place again."

"What will you do then?"

"Sell them a different story."

Will bit off the tip of what turned out to be a rubbery hot dog in a soggy bun. The highway stretched out on either side of them, like a line someone draws between two points and calls a snake.

~

Road signs started appearing as they approached the city. Signs of green aluminum, signs with substance. They passed "51st Avenue," "Business District," and "City Center." Then there was a sign with two symbols: a large "H" and a tiny white airplane bearing the caption, "Next Right." They took the exit, where they found the H and the plane on their own signs, arrows pointing in opposite directions.

"I'm on my way to the airport," said the salesman. "But I can take you to the hospital."

"Why are you going to the airport?"

"I'm flying to Hawaii."

"What for?"

"Just to be somewhere else."

Will had never been to Hawaii. Or an airport. "Where else can you go from there?"

"Just about anywhere. Sometimes you have to stop somewhere and get on another plane, but you can go anywhere."

Will tried to visualise an infinity of lines radiating from the first pencil mark on his world map. A profusion of flight paths. The thought felt like a thousand pins in his skull. Not the kind that acupuncturists use to relieve pain, but the kind that made holes in the sky. He started to cry.

"I'm sorry about your mom, Will. I know it's not much, but I'm going to tear up that check you gave me and ship you World Book anyway."

"I don't want it. It's just a story. You said so yourself."

"Okay. I'll just take you to the hospital."

"I don't want that either." If Will's mother wasn't there with him now, she only *could* be dead, but it didn't work the other way. If he knew for certain that she *was* dead, she could never be there. Not unless he was dreaming.

"What do you want?"

"To go to the airport."

"Have you never been?"

"No."

~

There were more signs as they approached the airport. Blue ones now. "Arrivals," "Departures," "Short Term Terminal Parking." They followed one that read "Rental Return."

Inside, still more signs: "Security," "Customs," "Information." He walked with the World Book man to his gate, where they sat down together and waited for the boarding call. "I feel really strange about this," said the World Book man. "Leaving you here. Are you sure you don't want me to take you to the hospital? I could get the next flight."

"It's okay."

"Do you have money for a cab?"

"Cab?"

"To get to the hospital."

"I was going to walk."

"Don't walk. Here . . ." He reached inside his pocket and pulled out a warm wad of bills. Will took them, clutching them tightly to preserve the warmth. He pretended they were a promise.

Will and the World Book man watched the jet bridge unfold and extend.

"That thing always reminds me of a strange vacuum attachment that my dad had trouble explaining to people. Another reason he didn't fare well as a salesman. Also, he refused to fly. Limited his range."

"When will you come back?"

"I don't know. I haven't booked a return flight yet."

Will started to cry.

"Oh, Will," he said. "I know." He opened his briefcase and took out N-O. "Hang on to this for me. I'll come and get it from you when I get back."

Will clutched the book to his chest and felt his heart bounce back at him off the stiff cardboard cover.

~

Will wandered the airport with wide eyes. He counted the number of destinations on the screen of a large monitor. Two hundred and four: a finite number. Will found this comforting until he realized that all these departures would arrive at other airports, from which another two hundred destinations, maybe more, would become available. These were what the World Book man called "connections." The options may not have been infinite, but they were exponential. Pins in the skull.

Will walked from gate to gate, passing restaurants and bookstores and newsstands and cafes and gift shops. He looked in from the corridor at hundreds of different people, each doing one of the same few things. He thought of a salamander he'd once had in a terrarium, moving from rock to plant to water to rock. He wondered if the salamander conceived of these as "options."

Will came upon something like an escalator, only flat. He could stand still and it would move him through the airport. Some people walked on it. This seemed redundant. Will stood sideways, and now the shops were like comic book frames, and he tried to imagine the story this book might be telling. He couldn't figure it out. Sometimes people came out of the frames. A young woman brushed by him as she ran towards a gate, desperate to make a connection. Will had just seen her in the gift-shop queue, buying a sweatshirt with the city's name on it, though she had not been in the city for more than an hour, and she had only arguably been in "the city." He averted his eyes when a white-bearded man with not enough buttons on his shirt looked out of the frame and directly at him, grinning conspiratorially as he sipped foam from a glass that had the name of a beer on it. Will wondered whether the beer on the glass was the same as the beer in the glass. He wondered whether potential discrepancies mattered in these cartoons at all.

Will found an empty bench in a quiet alcove and went to sleep with N-O under his head. He dreamed that he was back at the rim of the gulch, looking over the top at the other side. The World Book man stood on the other side, shouting at him. When the man opened his mouth, Will could hear no sounds, but the shapes of the words themselves sprang forth from his open mouth and flew towards Will. Before he could see what they were, they dropped into the gulch and disappeared. He knew, somehow, that among these lost words was the man's name.

When Will woke, he was hungry. He hadn't eaten anything but a soggy hot-dog in two days. He fumbled for the warm crumpled bills he knew were in his pocket as he lurched towards a kiosk that sold giant pretzels. He felt their pulpy warmth, but once they were in his hand, he reconsidered. He was hungry, but this hunger had given his dreams new dimensions, and he had begun to believe that if he kept dreaming, he might catch a glimpse of a world that had been there before people had to tell stories about who and what was not there. Also, he no longer had to sleep to dream. He let the damp wad drop back to the bottom of his pocket. Will hadn't even considered opening the N-O. It was just a hard weight against his ribs that slowed him down. He set it down on the pretzel counter and kept walking. "Thanks," said the pretzel vendor, as if yet another ordinary transaction had been made. "Have a good day."

He dreamed as he walked. His mother was lying on a table, Will standing by with a skull full of pins. He plucked the pins from his head and put them in his mother.

When he came upon a pay phone, Will called intensive care at the hospital and asked for his mother.

"Who is this?" said a sharp voice on the other end of the line.

"I'm Will. I'm her son."

"We've been trying to contact you, Will." The voice softened so quickly that Will almost hung up the phone. "Can I put you on with the doctor?"

"Okay."

He tried to flee into the space that he knew existed between the sounds that came out of the doctor's mouth and the things they described, but the words she used made it across before he could get there, and they hit Will like a blizzard of pins or a handful of hurled tacks. He started to cry.

He went back to the gate where the World Book man had vanished. There was no one there now and no plane outside. The jet bridge had been retracted. It looked like the withered stump of an Amputee. Will curled up next to the door and went to sleep.

He dreamed he was in an airport, one in which there were only arrivals. The planes touched down tentatively, wheels skipping before gaining the runway for good, while the jet bridges reached out eagerly and without doubt to touch them. People poured through the gates and out onto the terminal plaza, where there were no restaurants, no shops, no kiosks, no telephones, no signs. Just black walls embedded with millions of shiny pins and Will lying on his back in the center of the floor, surrounded by a swelling mass of humanity. His mother emerged from one of the gates. His father from another. The World Book man from yet another. Each of them plucked a pin from the wall and, just like everyone else, approached Will at the center of the plaza. No one made a sound. One by one, the billions came and pushed their pins delicately into Will's body. With each one, Will felt the pain ebb from his skull. With each one, it became more and more difficult to distinguish between the body that accepted the pins and the hands that pushed them in.

Will awoke to the sound of a boarding call. The gate was jammed with people hurrying towards a queue for departure. Some of them even laughed as they pulled away from outstretched arms and shuffled towards what the World Book man thought of as an inexplicable attachment, and what Will couldn't help but think of as a phantom limb.

Starfish

Danielle LaVaque-Manty

A starfish spins on the ceiling in Sheila's father's bedroom. Pulling the chain makes it go fast, faster, fastest. Sheila likes to sit in the breeze it makes but worries that the starfish will get dizzy. Her father made it for her mother, wrapping an old fan in layers of paste and paper that he molded until they looked alive, painting them in shades of cream and brown and gold until they shimmered like wet sand. He said it would be the best present ever.

Sheila's parents met on the beach. Her father told her the story while she watched him make the starfish in his workshop: he was collecting shells for a sculpture when he noticed a woman in waders poking around in a nearby tide pool. Her mother, who had been some kind of student back then, was collecting sea cucumbers for research. She wore her hair in a braid, thick as a rope of seaweed, to keep it out of her eyes when she studied in her lab. When Sheila was born, her mother dropped out of school to take a real job as a manager at the aquarium. Sheila still isn't clear on the difference between real jobs and fake ones.

Sheila's father installed the starfish on her parents' fifth wedding anniversary. "Five is the luckiest number, isn't it, Sheil?" he said, while she watched him twist the wires. He'd learned earlier that day that a gallery downtown would be taking five of his works. The kind of gallery, he said, that could sell absolutely anything. Which meant that her mother would be able to go back to school again soon.

Sheila thought the fan was beautiful. So real! But when her mother came home she said, "Starfish live on the ocean floor, you know." She bent over and looked up at it from between her legs. "You've turned the world upside-down." She gave Sheila's father an upside-down smile.

The day Sheila's mother moved out, her father sprawled on the bed like a four-armed starfish while the fan whirred overhead. On the Discovery Channel, Sheila learned that starfish can grow almost anything back as long as they haven't lost their centers. She's been watching her father closely since then, but she still can't tell for sure how much of him is missing.

Arrows

Jordan Farmer

When I arrived, Edmund was already out on the front porch haloed in the light coming through his screen door, smoke billowing up from his beard as he puffed his pipe. I parked the Mercury beside the gate and waited while he descended the steps on his cane. For a moment, I thought he might trip in the yard where the grass had grown high. I hadn't been over to mow it in a few weeks, and the leaves had collected in deep piles. The gold and crimson shriveled by several nights of frost that froze them off their branches. Edmund stumbled around them, his body swaying as if the ground shifted under his feet.

The scent of cherry tobacco filled the car as he climbed inside. From the dark half-moons under his eyes, I guessed he might have managed an hour of sleep.

"What did Sally say?" he asked as I drove out of the hollow, the mountains opening wide and the curving road leading to better asphalt, a straighter route as we approached the dark ribbon of the interstate.

"Just that they called family in."

"What if they don't let us see him?" he said. There was a sort of wide panic in his eyes I could make out even in the minimal glow from the dash lights. His hand rubbed his lower thigh, traveled down to scratch at the place where I supposed he ended and the prosthesis began. I wasn't sure how exactly it worked. I'd been driving Edmund to his appointments at the VA hospital in Charleston, but he never let me inside the exam rooms. He'd become protective of his new stump, refusing to allow anyone to even see him in shorts, so I found myself wondering what the fake limb looked like, if whatever polymer they constructed it from attempted to have the same bulge of calf muscle, maybe even the dark mat of hair the IED must have incinerated.

"They'll let us inside," I said.

Edmund took a pill bottle from his jeans and shook a capsule into his palm. He dry swallowed it and rolled the window down to feel the night air.

"They better," he said.

~

Warren sat cranked forward in the hospital bed, the sheet falling away to reveal the distended dome of his stomach. His arms had gone thin, the veins moving to the surface like worms unearthing to escape rain. His breath smelled like wet leaves and the whites of his eyes had turned a color not known to nature. Warren barely noticed us when we entered, but Sally was on me before we cleared the door, her arms around my waist as she laid her head against my shoulder. I held her at arm's length to take a look at her. She'd applied a bit of lipstick, tried to fix her mascara no matter how much she knew she'd just cry it away.

"I think he was ready a time or two," she said.

Edmund stood over the bed. Warren's eyes opened and he tried a smile, but it looked wrong on his face, his teeth more bared like an animal too wounded to be touched.

"I'm glad to see you," Edmund said.

"I'll give you a moment," Sally said. She kissed Warren's cheek and the lipstick smeared supplied his only color. The beeping of monitors filled the room's silence.

"What can we do?" Edmund asked.

Warren's dry tongue stuck to the bottom of his mouth. He swallowed hard.

"I'd burn in Hell for one last drink," he said.

A brief anger flowered in me, a moment where I wanted to point to the machines attached to him and rant, but Edmund took my hand.

"We'll be back," he said and led me from the room.

In the hall, Edmund chewed the end of his pipe while passing nurses gave him nervous glances. I hoped none would stop and tell him he couldn't smoke inside.

"Your house?" he asked.

"Not a drop."

"Ok." He nodded as if he were convincing only himself. "Let's go."

~

As boys, the three of us were always close. Edmund lived next door to me in one of the former coal company houses where his father had been born during the days when his grandfather still worked for scrip instead of currency. Edmund's father, a second generation coal miner, bought the house from the company and never lived in another home until he died. Warren came to Lynch County at three when his father moved to West Virginia from Harlan County, Kentucky, deciding that rather than stand the picket line he would just mine coal elsewhere. I guess he felt comfortable with a boss' boot on the back of his neck. My father was the only man I knew who wasn't a miner. He avoided underground by working as a clerk at the Mt. Gay Market where he bagged old ladies' groceries and stuck price tags on cans.

No one in our camp had money. Most evenings my father brought home food near its expiration date to cook that night, discount lettuce with browned leafs and hard bread. The cabbage was the worst. He claimed it didn't matter as long as we stewed it, but I could always taste the wilt. My one luxury came at Christmas when every year my father put away a bit each week to buy me something special. As a boy, I had no idea the amount of sacrifice involved in this. I'm sure I would have felt guilty if I'd put enough thought into the cost of each gift. One year I received a model train set, the next a pair of leather cowboy boots with gold threaded patterns stitched up the leg.

"Maybe you didn't get anything this year," Dad would say. "Money has been tight."

I got this answer so many times I steeled myself for disappointment. The mines were cutting down, and that meant fewer groceries for my father to bag. It wouldn't be impossible for me to go without. Plenty of other kids I knew did and not just for toys. Most showed up to school in their older brother's patched slacks with the long hem folded into a makeshift cuff, or in shoes so beaten they looked as if they have survived brutal marches during combat campaigns. So when Christmas morning came without a present under the tree, I stifled my tears and climbed out of bed.

My father waited for me in the living room. He sat on the couch, his lap covered by an old quilt. I stepped in ready for a speech, apologies and embarrassment about how bad work had been. I tried to make myself hide the disappointment, but as I came closer I could see a smile creeping across his face.

"I know I've been telling you I didn't have anything for you this year, but I didn't want to let the secret slip. It was too special."

From underneath the quilt on his lap, he produced a bow carved out of some dark wood and a leather quiver full of matching arrows. When he handed it to me, I felt the warmth trapped in the grain, the curved wood sanded down until it fit my grip perfectly. I drew the string back until the coarse braid brushed against my cheek.

"It ain't a toy," he said. "Men used to kill each other with these things. Don't shoot it anywhere near anything living. Best to set up a target on the hillside. Arrows travel further than you'd think."

"I will," I said.

"Promise me," he said.

I promised and he let me take it next door to show Edmund and Warren. I found them in Edmund's yard, huddled in the melting snow and shade created by the shed where Edmund's father kept his carpentry tools. He built cabinets and hanging swings for rich women from town, but the work was never steady. I think it was mostly something to do on the days he wasn't underground.

The shed was only large enough to fill with some rough lumber and a few saws, but he had electricity wired to the building. Edmund had lifted the keys to the padlocked door and ran a severed extension cord outside. He and Warren huddled over a frozen bull frog, the exposed copper wire from the cord inches away from the amphibian's still chest. Edmund stuck the live wire to the frog and its legs gave a few strong kicks until black burns charred its chest and Edmund cut the wattage. The frog continued to convulse while Warren shook his head.

"Told you," he said.

"Doctors can do it," Edmund said.

I wouldn't realize it until Edmund and I were much older, not fully until his National Guard troop got news about their deployment and he showed up at my house to tie one on, crying and telling me being sent to Iraq at forty-five was a death sentence, but Edmund was beautiful as a boy. His cheeks sharp and his hair coiled in curls most girls envied. There was a softness about him the rest of us didn't possess. Warren was nothing like that. Even prepubescent, his voice came harsh, his glares reminiscent of feral cats.

They turned to see me with the bow and the frog was forgotten. I let Edmund hold my new weapon. He gave it a dry fire, the string thrashing the air.

"Bad ass," he said.

"Really great," Warren said. I could read some jealousy in his eyes and it brought out some type of satisfied cruelty in me. Warren's clothes deteriorated as the seasons stretched on. He ate a lot of dinners with me or Edmund and always finished, never complaining on the same dishes of too much pinto beans and cornbread. Even if he was a friend, it pleased me to see someone worse off than myself. Sometimes I just needed the reminder that it could be worse.

"I need a target," I said. "You help me with that and I'll let you learn to shoot with me."

"Just shoot it at the hillside," Edmund said. He pointed towards the end of the yard where the ground sloped and a small creek separated us from the mountainside. "Stick it in a tree."

"Break your arrows," Warren said. "We need something softer."

We stood passing the bow back and forth, looking down the shaft of each arrow as if our eyes could imagine the damage they might inflict. Warren hunkered down over the dead frog and poked at its soft belly with the blunt field tip.

"I can get us something," he said. "But I get to take the first shot."

It felt like a victory over me, but I knew it was necessary. If my father caught me shooting the bow somewhere unsafe, he'd carry it to the railroad tracks and leave it for a coal train to roll over.

"Deal," I said.

The next day I was sitting on the front porch when Warren arrived dragging a wagon filled with several large Styrofoam cubes. The front of each one had a three ring bull's-eye painted on it, the center ring a dark red. He parked the wagon outside our rusted chain link fence and spread his arms wide in presentation.

"Where'd you get that?" I asked. I knew he had no money, but I didn't much care. This meant a chance to finally shoot.

"Don't worry about it," he said. "Let's set it up on the creek bank."

We hauled the wagon behind the house to the sloping bank of Cow Creek and began to unload the target, stacking each cube until they covered a wide enough area to accommodate any poor aim.

"Should we get Edmund?" I asked.

"Nope. I wanna take my shot." Warren stepped through the weeds and over the hillside until he reached the bank of the small stream. We were around twenty yards away from the target. Warren nocked an arrow, drew the bow with three fingers the way we'd seen archers do in movies with castles. The arrow flew too fast for me to track it with my eyes, but it found the center of the target, the red fletching on the end barely emerging from the bull's-eye.

"Where'd you learn to shoot like that?" I asked.

Warren ran his hands over another arrow before he nocked it.

"My daddy had one like this," he said. "He taught me."

"Go get it," I said.

"Can't," he said. He let another arrow fly and it buried deep in the foam beside his first.

"Why not?" I asked. "What happened to it?"

He didn't answer, but I learned years later they pawned it.

~

Cheap Charlie's Carry Out sat in the hard curve on Switzer Street, situated beside a parking lot where the old K-Mart burned down six years ago. The locals had taken to setting up stalls on the lot, small yard sale tents where a man could buy anything from antique furniture, shotguns and pistols, even moonshine with a trusted recommendation. The vendors who'd been there longest left their tents and canopies up year round, sometimes the merchandise sitting inside unguarded on the pretext of trust or notorious reputation. The place looked like a sort of frontier trading post where unwashed pioneers would negotiate with pelts and fresh flake. I thought it suited Lynch better than any real store could have, and made the Pizza Hut, which set in the lowest part of the curve and took on water with every hard rain, seem out of place.

Cheap Charlie's definitely fit in. The rough lumber of the exterior, the wooden front door that stood in place of the usual convenience store glass, even the drive through window that had once simply been a normal pane that Charlie knocked out one evening on inspiration, felt more like a saloon in an unsettled town than a grocer's. I read the closed sign hanging in Charlie's window and closed my eyes.

Edmund parked the car around back of Charlie's and we sat with the engine idling, contemplating what we were about to do. Nerves had my legs trembling, but I knew I'd go through with it. I owed Warren at lot more than a last drink. Besides, Charlie was the type who might understand even if we had to break a window. I promised myself it would be all right, that I wouldn't even take anything I couldn't lay money on the counter for, but I tried one last attempt to convince Edmund we had better options.

"Let's drive on," I said. "We can buy somewhere off the interstate. Just explain it to the boy at the counter. Slip him some extra."

"We ain't got that kinda time," Edmund said.

I looked at the absent way his fingers drummed the synthetic material of his shin. I thought about the other men in the cab during that attacked convoy, wondered how many of them sacrificed pieces of themselves and how many died without even understanding what happened. A momentary flash, then the sudden eternity of non-existence, of short life shifting into a constant nothingness I couldn't fathom. I imagined Edmund bleeding into the sand, lying with his leg missing and waiting on that change.

"What's it gonna be like?" I asked.

Edmund shrugged. "Can't say."

"I just thought . . ."

"It won't be anything like what I saw. In a hospital with Sally..."

I tried to think of that as a comfort, but I couldn't manage to close my eyes and not see the machines and tubes inside Warren as invaders.

"He got cameras?" I pointed towards Charlie's.

"It really matter?" Edmund said. He climbed out and began hobbling toward the back entrance. He bent and plucked up a small rock, busted a pane from the back door, and reached inside. I stood scanning the empty lot, the only movement the abandoned vendors' tents billowing in the lazy wind.

Edmund led the way through the back aisles stocked with chips and beef jerky toward the coolers and bottles on the far side of the sales floor. I'd never been inside a store after hours and found myself surprised by the long shadows even without the florescent lights overhead, the way each foot step echoed. Edmund opened the cooler and the seal hissed as the trapped cold air touched his body. He held up a case of Heineken, turning it in his hands.

"Just get some Miller," I said.

He pulled a few tall boy cans from the rack and shoved them into his pockets. I walked about the aisles, looking over the glass bottles of bourbon and gin, the foreign names of delicacies I'd never tasted.

"Grab some Turkey," Edmund called.

I stopped in front of the high shelf, my fingers tracing the label on a bottle of Irish aged twenty years. I reminded myself only what I could afford to pay back and picked up a plastic pint of whiskey. It hid easily inside my coat pocket and I figured it would be better than sneaking up to the eighth floor with a fifth bulging like I had a chicken under my coat. I took the beer from Edmund so he could concentrate on walking and we moved towards the exit. Then I remembered my promise and ran to leave a twenty dollar bill on the counter.

~

I found the target gone first thing in the morning, the daylight so new it wasn't even worthy to shoot in. I stood looking at the flat and dead patch of grass, the imprint left in its absence the only sign our target had ever existed. I didn't feel much, maybe a little relieved not to be seen struggling to make progress while Edmund seemed to improve his shooting every day and Warren was already a God. Mostly, I felt afraid to tell Warren. The target hadn't meant anything to me, but it was an obsession with him, the only thing he talked about and the reason he came over first thing every morning.

I didn't hear Warren crossing the yard. He was never quiet, his boots always heavy on the frozen blades and snapping twigs as he trudged along, but I was so fixated on the emptiness in front of me I must have been in a daze.

"What the fuck?" he said. He paced in the hollow place where the target had been.

"Just came outside and found it gone," I said.

He sat down on the grass and I could hear something inside him tightening, his shoulders sagging as he began to weep. Despite how close the three of us were, we'd never cried in front of one another. At that age, I couldn't even contemplate something worse than crying in front of another

149

boy, but Warren didn't seem capable of keeping it in. He let it come, knees tucked into his chest and arms wrapped tight around his long legs.

"Goddamn," he said. He whipped his eyes with his coat sleeve and snorted deep. "Awful lot to carry out even if it doesn't weigh much. They'd have to haul it." He turned to me. "Which of them Bradshaw boys could have a truck?"

Bradshaw was on the other side of the mountain, a couple miles down creek and twice as poor as our part of Lynch County. I'd only driven through once or twice with my father, but Bradshaw boys carried an almost mythic amount of rumor. Bobby Blankenship said that the only Bradshaw boy he ever met carried a pig sticker knife in his belt and had homemade tattoos, patterns cut into the ham of his arm, the wounds rubbed with ink from a broken pen until the scars were dyed blue. I didn't want any trouble with Bradshaw boys.

"It's gone, Warren," I said. "Don't matter who has it."

Warren shook his head. "Go get Edmund and meet me at the tracks."

The tracks were the last sign of civilization before the roads ended. Anything further along turned to game trails or outlaw paths cut through the hills by marijuana farmers and hill folks.

"Shit, Warren," I said.

"I'll get him then," he said. "Meet me at the tracks."

He walked off before I could protest, and I knew that with or without me, he was going to claim something that had never really been his. I hoped that Edmund might be able to talk some sense into him. I had no desire to go start a war with Bradshaw boys, no wish to watch Warren ambushing kids from the brush, putting arrows into children poorer than us, but I knew that I would follow.

~

I parked the Mercury illegally in the Doctor's Parking. The small section of the hospital's had spaces placed right up against the bald rock face of the mountain. The stone looked perpetually wet, as if constantly sweating, and small tin signs had been fixed in front of each space that read DANGER: FALLING ROCKS. I wondered if any doctor ever came outside to find their Mercedes with a boulder through the roof.

Edmund took an old fleece jacket from the backseat, shrugged his shoulders inside, and began to fill the pockets with cans of High Life. He

150

raised his arms to expose the sides of the coat. "Can you see them?" he asked.

It was at least one size too small on him, the pockets bulging from the weight of smuggled beer, but I knew it wouldn't help to tell him that. We'd gone too far to alter the plan.

"Looks good," I said. "Let's go."

We walked in through the ER entrance, passed the admissions desk where a man stood with his mangled hand wrapped in a bloody t-shirt, yelling at a nurse who just gave him a steady nod. The waiting room chairs were filled with tired women holding kids hacking a croup cough. Men sat with jackets stuffed behind their heads for pillows. Three unattended boys, smeared with gift shop chocolate, ran circles after one another, receiving disapproving looks from the old women.

"What do you suppose the penalty is for something like this?" Edmund asked.

"None like earlier," I said.

We rode the elevator up with a group of nightshift nurses who rested against one another. They made me wonder what it was like to enter a stranger's room and have to steel yourself against the fact they may have passed.

The eighth floor was a living pulse, the combination of all the staff moving and the hushed sound of patients trying to survive. The false smell of bleach tried to fool us into believing everything was sterile, but I could sense the sickness under it, the recently mopped blood or vomit. Edmund looked uneasy, his stride slower and his body leaning hard on his cane.

When we rounded the corner to Warren's room, Sally was standing in the hall. Her hands covered her mouth and her back pressed against the wall as her two sisters tried to wrap her into an embrace. A gaggle of nurses stood nearby, and further down the hall I could see the preacher coming from the First Baptist Church, his blazer rumpled and some of his shirt buttons missed from hurried dressing at the late hour. His Bible was tucked under his arm.

Edmund stopped. His eyes seemed to be pleading, his fingers drumming the fabricated leg again as if enough touching could end the farce of flesh. I took another look towards Sally and watched the priest unsheathe his Bible. His finger slipped inside the pages to find the right passage.

"Let's go," Edmund said. "Now ain't the time."

We rode the elevator down beside a boy with his arm in a sling. He wore a death metal t-shirt, a busty Valkyrie brandishing her sword next to a throne of skulls. The boy kept eyeing Edmund, so he pulled a beer from his pocket and handed it to the boy.

"Keep it quiet, son," Edmund said and we started towards the parking lot. The automatic doors opened wide as if in greeting. Out in the lot, a few men slept in their pick-ups, more comfortable in a Ford than a hospital chair. At the ambulance park a few paramedics laughed and smoked cigarettes. Edmund struggled to sit on a nearby bench, so I got a hand under his armpit, helped him down before taking the space beside him. I took the whiskey out of my coat pocket, swallowed a long snort and passed it.

He drummed on his leg again, and before I knew it his hands were reaching up inside his trousers, trying to unlatch whatever kept the prosthesis attached. He struggled for a moment and then pulled the fake limb from the cuff of his pants and set it on the bench between us as he rolled up his pant leg to expose the nub. The doctor's cut looked fairly level with his knee, but the scar tissue was too fresh, the skin too much a patchwork of swollen raw purple to know just how much of him was lost. The end of his leg looked like something that might be growing, the red bud of a flower near bloom or a head of cabbage about to sprout open, and even though it had no business not continuing on into a real leg, somehow in the low lamp light of the parking lot it seemed a proper part of him, as much an organic thing in dismemberment as it had been when he'd still had a muscular calf.

"I couldn't take that itch any longer," he said.

~

When we reached the other side of the mountain, I was drenched in sweat that stung my eyes and my muscles ached from the hike. Edmund looked ready to drop, but Warren didn't have any of our fatigue. He stalked ahead, my bow ready with a nocked arrow, the quiver hanging by his hip. A Daisy air rifle, something Edmund's father used to kill squirrels in season, was strapped across Edmund's back by a piece of twine. He said he brought it for protection.

We came down the hill towards the valley and stopped to look at the row of squat houses that made up Bradshaw. Small buildings with dirt yards and the remnants of tiny gardens overtaken by weeds. Wooden stakes stuck out of the ground in a row, pieces of cloth tied around them to hold the dead tomato vines. They looked like grave markers for infants buried on a forgotten trail. Chickens scrapped the dirt and wash hung heavy on slack lines. All the signs of life, but I saw no one outside on porches, no boys out to create mischief.

"This is stupid," Edmund said. "Let's go back."

But Warren was already sliding downhill, moving quietly towards the camp. I looked to Edmund to see if he was serious about turning back, but I knew he would follow with me. Warren led our party forward, hunkered low through the high weeds as we approached the dirt road. Two vehicles sat by the road, a pickup and a dented Camaro with its backseat full of parts not yet replaced. We took cover behind the truck, and Warren moved to the end of the tailgate to watch the houses. He looked into the truck bed and turned back to us holding small bits of Styrofoam. Edmund took it from him, rubbing it between his fingers until the particles began to disintegrate. Warren stepped out into the road, moving around toward the back of the houses, chickens scattering as he crossed the yard. I tried to follow by hiding myself behind the stained sheets and other garments hung to dry. Behind the house, I could hear the voices of the Bradshaw boys, laughter that made my stomach clench.

There were five of them, three old and large enough to develop their first dusting of new beard. The other two were younger and recognizable as brothers from the same heavy brow and dark hair. The brothers stood looking pleased to be involved while the older boys leaned on a tree beside our target and spun stories to one another. The largest of the group gave wild gestures with his hands that brought more laughs.

"Too many," I said to Edmund. I was already in retreat, stepping back into the shelter of the sheets and skirts, but I saw Warren was on one knee and ready to draw. I wanted to shout out to him, but knew the Bradshaw boys would grab us before we could hit the hill. I watched him draw the arrow back and consider the shot for a moment, his cheeks puffing as he breathed before his release. The arrow would fly true, and at such a distance, I knew at least one boy would die before anyone could stop him.

Behind me, Edmund began to head back up the mountain. I felt rooted in place. Something in me needed to watch it happen, to see the arrow strike something more substantial than our target. For a moment it seemed inevitable, then he slowly let the string go slack and snuck back towards me.

We were back along the hillside, near the overgrown game trail before any of us spoke again.

"I thought you were going to do it," Edmund said. "I thought you were gonna drill one of the poor bastards."

Warren stepped forward and fired an arrow down the path into the rear tire of the pick-up. He nocked another as the air hissed out and shot the front tire. He screamed and nocked another arrow.

"Holy shit," Edmund said.

The Bradshaw boys began shouting from the backyard, the group coming around the side of the house and through the hanging wash. Warren dropped my bow and we ran up the mountainside, the arrows jostling in Warren's quiver, the sound of the boys close behind us and tearing through the thicket. We were moving hard, losing the trail as we crashed through the foliage, the path farther behind us and the only thing recognizable the sound of the boys chasing us. I remember wondering how we'd find home, if it might not be better to just crouch behind the tall ferns and oaks and hope the group passed me by, but I kept running. At the time, it felt as if I was running for my life, moving swift to avoid getting my guts stomped out, but now I know we were simply hurrying towards the inevitable. All of us rushing into a future where limbs would be lost in desert wars, a liver pickled by breakfast beer and, eventually, each of us severed from one another by the slow erosion of time.

Nebraska, This One's for You

Claire Seymour

I'm sick of dreaming about these trailer-park children that dart around in the golden dust and the limp trees that bend like wounded spines. I sit out back by the clothesline where the dirty sheets billow in the breeze, stare up at the sun until I can no longer see their thread-bare shirts that unravel at the seams, their filthy fingers that grope through fallen trashcans. I can no longer see them, but I throw rusted pennies at their ankles anyway.

They haunt me, these children, because I am one of them, only older, with patches around the elbows of my sweaters. I hide the poverty embedded in my skin with the drops of vanilla I dab behind my ears, by biting my lips so hard that they bleed drops of rubies, my own homemade lipstick.

~

In early September, my mother hand-washes laundry in soapy water that spills down the rusted buckets behind the trailer, leaves the clothing to dry on scraggly tree branches when the wind blows the clothesline down. I help her gather blueberries and peel the skin off apples, and when our oven breaks down, she cooks the tart over an open fire. I cough up summer and ash in large doses, and we sleep hungry that night, the smoke lingering in our lungs.

~

Airless September becomes smoky October becomes silent November and the gravel begins to frost over, the wind whipping at the windows, shaking the trailers so that the metal trembles. My younger sister learns how to curl her eyelashes using sewing needles, and a boy makes her promises in his red pickup truck. He pulls her apart like Clementine skin, and I pick dying sunflowers that reach my hips from the field behind the trailer park, spread them out across the kitchen table and pray for an early spring.

~

January shakes up Middle America as if it's hurricane season, and next door, Wyoming spits out her ghosts and old mistakes, which dance across the border. The trailer park children try to skate on lakes with clear ice, but the glinting metal blades break the surface before they can even push off the snow bank. My younger sister comes home at dawn in a beat-up Camry with cracked leather seats and climbs into bed with me, nicotine and snow clinging to her dress. My mother slits the throat of a rabbit in the sink when the fridge is empty, and I allow my eyelashes to cover up something like murder. Her hands are stained rusty red for hours, and I pretend it's anything but blood.

~

I have this dream where I feed golden coins to vultures, and their glossy black wings grow between my shoulder blades so that I can leap off the chain-link fence that surrounds my home, so that I can fly over rocky beach cliffs, shanty towns, lobster shacks in Maine. I have this dream where my younger sister and I put on mix tapes in an old stereo system and learn how to waltz while my mother claps her hands and takes a blueberry and apple tart out of the oven. I have this dream where the trailer-park children clean off their skates, lace them up tight, and glide across the ice like dancers, laugh and tumble while their breath swirls white into the air like smoke. I have this dream where I swallow dozens of fireflies, and when I cough, I'm the sun for one fleeting moment, wearing the sky all around me like a coat. When I wake up, my sister is crying in her sleep, cheeks stained with mascara, and my mother is watching the news in the living room, the female anchor describing a kidnapping in California, a shooting in a mall in Louisiana, a murder in an Arizona apartment, and she turns hope into a misdiagnosis. Outside, the trailer-park children are rummaging through a fallen trashcan, stomachs empty and hollow. The moon spills hot and angry through my window and onto my chest, and my lips burn when I wet them.

Dear Nebraska,

Your stars are dimming now.

Kentucky Pisser

Terrance Manning, Jr.

I found my best friend dead in his bathroom a week ago. He spun an Immortal Cry tee-shirt into a tight rope and hung himself from the towel hook on the door. Maybe a joke, I thought. Evan did shit like that. I laughed at first. "C'mon, asshole," I'd said, "I have the worst story."

He was twenty four.

I met Evan in a bathroom, of all places, in the 7th grade. Walked out of Math and only wanted to piss. I remember standing and counting purple tiles on the floor when this scrawny bastard, tight black jeans and one of those shirts with real-looking pictures of wolves on the chest, comes sliding in beside me. A dozen urinals in the whole place and he jams up next to me.

"Couldn't wait any longer," he said.

"What the hell," I twisted my body away, trying to keep piss in the urinal. He leaned in closer as I leaned away.

"What grade are you?"

"Are you gay?" I asked. I was the closed-up type—not that anyone would open up to a stranger with their dick hanging out.

"I just moved here from Kentucky," he said, still staring.

"You have piss buddies in Kentucky?"

He was quiet for a moment—then he laughed. Dropped his head back, hands at his crotch and laughed. I don't know what it was. Something beautiful really, this kid's laugh. And for a long time after that we told people the story—his side of the story—jamming up next to me pissing and starting an awkward conversation, how I damn near knocked him in his teeth and ran for help. I never mentioned that he'd struck something in me. Like suddenly I wanted him to laugh and keep laughing.

Last week, when I found Evan on the hook, I was sure he'd prop himself down, let the color back into his purple face. I sat on the tub and stared. "Evan," I said, like he could hear, "Evan, why'd you do that?" Couldn't bring myself to call 911. I talked to him. I know what you're thinking, but I had questions. Like the answers, for instance, to his stupid

157

riddles—like the guy standing in the rain, no umbrella, but his head never gets wet—and I'd boil over them for weeks. He'd smile when I tried to threaten the answers out of him and say, *Forget it, man...just forget it and a few years from now it'll hit you like, Bang! Just like that, man. It'll hit you and you'll thank me. I promise you, you'll thank me.* But I might never know and that shit scared me. Scared me more than his hanging on a bathroom door. And instead of asking things I'd wished I'd known, like why he'd come to Pittsburgh, or never talked about Kentucky, I kept asking in the bathroom, again and again, *Why'd you do that?*

~

In high school, Evan used to sit in his room all day and listen to Ride. Had "Time Machine" on repeat and I'd get to his place just as he had his knees looped around the pull-up bar in his room playing air-board to the middle of the song. He'd fall to the floor and pop up red-faced, laughing. He was tall and skinny, but strong-looking—like a basketball player, though he sucked at sports. Couldn't catch a beach ball if you tossed it to him. Still, people liked him—type of guy you told your secrets to.

I was different. Not that I couldn't keep secrets, because I could. People never opened up to me. I'm the guy you pat on the shoulder when you walk in the room, that you call your buddy, not your friend, that can hang in conversations about stupid things, like early nineties movies, or how John Cusak's not the coolest guy of our generation, our own Steve fucking McQueen, but beyond that, I've got retarded emotion. That's what my grandfather told me when I was young.

"You've got retarded emotion, kid." We were standing out back of his house on the wooden deck surrounding his swimming pool. My mother was arrested and my father shot and killed in a motel room north of Pittsburgh when I was a baby. They were buying drugs.

When my grandfather called my father a low-life and a prick, told me the man corrupted my mother, his precious daughter, I told him, "Okay, Grampa, can I have a fudge sickle?" And it pissed him off, I guess, that I didn't hate my father. Wasn't in me. So my grandfather said I had retarded emotion, took to saying that for a while until it got too burdensome to say in conversation, or when, to friends, or relatives, he'd have to refer to me, and he just started calling me *retard*.

By the time he died, grandma was slipping from the Alzheimer's and Uncle Barry put her in a care facility. I went to live with him after that. He treated me like a toy, a boxing buddy to throw gloves on and spar with his friends. So I spent as much time as I could at Evan's, at his mom's. We'd hardly even see her. She worked but I couldn't say where. Funny I've known the guy all these years and couldn't tell you where his mother worked. She had that shaky-blonde look, hair pressed flat, nearly disappearing or falling out. Had a cigarette in her mouth every time I saw her. Smiled like a growl. Had that deep-bread Pittsburgh, called us "yunz" instead of "yinz."

Once, I'd gone to Evan's after he hadn't shown up to school and the door was open. I could hear the drone of a television inside, mumbled words, dishes chattering.

In the kitchen, Evan sat on the table in his underwear eating a bowl of cereal. His mother sat beside him, smoking, one hand holding the paper, the other rubbing Evan's naked back. They looked up at me when I walked inside.

"No school," I said, bowing, as if some ceremonious gesture might make me more welcome in the kitchen.

"I'm not feeling well," Evan said. His mother's cigarette smoke curled around his body, looping down his pale chest.

She stood and grabbed her purse. "I'll see about that address," she said and kissed Evan on the lips.

I felt suddenly like I should leave, too, wondering what his mother was thinking as I watched, wondering what address. I felt like we were all naked in the kitchen as the wind tumbled in from outside, pulling leaves inside.

"Shut that damn screen!" his mother shouted.

They were unpredictable. Some days, he'd hug her around the shoulders, kiss her neck. Other times they'd stand in opposite rooms throwing picture frames at each other—her calling him a cunt, him calling her a dickhead.

Evan's dad left when he was a kid—some asshole, I guess—and most of the time, when Evan's mother wasn't around, we imagined we owned the place. We pumped iron in his bedroom, though our bodies never changed; we grew stronger, never bigger. And I joked that soon I'd track down his father and beat his ass in the street. Evan liked that, said things like, *That's my boy*, and *Fuck my dad*, and I think we felt closer because of it—though sometimes, when we talked about his dad, he'd get all weird and put Ride on again, turning it up loud, and I'd be yelling, *What's your problem; turn that down.*

~

I don't think I noticed a change in Evan. Like to think I did, but I didn't. If anyone had changed, it was me. Evan knew that. Before last week, we'd lived together nearly three years—since we'd turned twenty one.

Evan worked at Computer Goodies in Olympia shopping center. He sold obsolete computer parts and floppy discs. It was tucked away in the corner. Never sun spilling in through the showcase, cooking up the place. Never customers. When the manager wasn't there, he could read in the back—smart-assed books like Twain and Faulkner, shit I'd try reading and put down after every sentence, grab a bite to eat.

I worked at Subway near two weeks before they canned me. Told a customer the seafood & crab smelled like wolf pussy. Evan laughed as I outlined the details: the way the manager stood there, the way I tried not to smile. That customer must have thought I was going to pull out a sawed-off, shoot up the place. She backed out the door cringing, like turning away from a snake. I said, *I won't bite, bitch.*

Evan might have told you I had no patience. He'd tell you how we'd be eating somewhere, and if someone looked at me, I'd ask if they were alright—stare at them until their face grew red and they'd go back to eating their Smokehouse burgers and chicken fingers. I might stand up and say, *How about I shove that straw down your throat.* When Evan brought friends over, they'd do the pat on the back thing and I'd ask why they fucking touched me. Most of the time, I was kidding. Evan had gotten good at recognizing when. Like the night his buddy Ryan, from work, said, *Fuck you*, like we were old friends. Evan took him outside and left.

~

In high school, we had a number of friends. Might even say some weren't bad, that some of them were good guys, even fuckhead Joe Bard, who called Evan a faggot in tenth grade and I punched him in his mouth, dragged him into an empty classroom and told him I was going to make him suck my dick. He cried, told Evan he was sorry. Two years after high school,

Joe Bard drowned at college, a seizure under water. I would think about him crying that day and feel sorry for him.

Mostly though, Evan and I steered away from groups. We'd hang out on his roof nights talking stupid, like whether we could steal the grass from the neighborhood and store it in his basement. We'd have to plan well, use up the darkness between twilight and dawn, making sure to peel back the grass like scalping the entire place. We'd keep it stored away. Everything green and growing gone and we'd be the takers. And other times we lay quietly, looking into a neighborhood overflowing with night.

I could've watched him, paid closer attention: a trail-off in his story, insinuations. Conversations he might have tried saying something. Like the argument, years ago, over Pipedream vs. Jezzball.

"It's an exponential thing," he said.

"You capture balls." I laughed.

"It's complicated," he said. "Pipedream's one dimensional. Great game, but one dimensional: get to the other pipeline, drain your water."

"Yeah," I said. "And the water chases you. Starts draining before you've made a path. That's complicated. That's conflict."

"Who wants to be chased by toxic water?"

"Who wants to catch fifty fucking balls on a tiny screen?"

"That's the point," he said. "It's an exponential thing. They're everywhere. Like red eyes rolling around in a box and the better you do, the more advanced you get, the more complex the challenge. Don't you get that? It's brilliant. It's infinitely more and more complicated. No end game."

We had a thousand of those conversations: which was a cooler jacket, Simon's in *Seven Types*, or Charlie's in *Perks*; which made more sense, buoyancy or inertia. They were games. But I've been seeking clues, trying somehow to solve them like Evan's goddamned puzzles, like whether or not his idea of *infinitely complicated* had anything to do with his life, or what he meant when he said *end game*.

But all that was years ago. Long before, I'm sure, he decided to stand up on the tub and wait for me to get there.

~

At home, the neighbors beneath us were always playing country music. I liked the shit: old Hank, '80s George, Merl Haggard. Evan hated it. He asked them once to keep it down and they played Randy Travis's "On

161

the Other Hand" on repeat. Maybe that's why he spent more time at the computer store—to find quiet. For the last year, it seemed, each of us had been seeking a kind of quiet. Evan read. I had to get outside and move. I'd take a day and fish on the Youghiogheny with my uncle. The place had its own silence: river flies buzzing, cars honking through Christy Park, the sound of a train thumping through the trees across the river. We'd cast our lines and drink beers and listen to the radio until the sun went down.

I'd gone fishing a few days before I found Evan in the bathroom. I told him, *See you later* and he flipped me off as I walked out the door. Not unusual. He smiled when he did it and I smiled back.

I met my uncle in the morning, sat on a crate in his garage while he took his time packing the tackle box. I brought my seven-dollar rod, the one I'd gotten from the flea-market in Olympia, where Evan and I went sometimes on Tuesday or Thursday, looking for used DVD's, where we stopped to talk, nearly every time, to Flipper, the guy selling hotdogs.

It had started as a joke. Evan asked him for advice about coming out of the closet to his parents—load of smoke, but Flipper went for it. I don't know if it was Evan's sincerity or my grave but encouraging nods, but he went for it. I remember Evan had the guy telling him it was okay and it wasn't his fault. Flipper listened, replied with all the concerned *does-that-piss-you-off's*. We'd grab a bite and bullshit and the Flipper took a liking to us. Called me Bluto. I don't know where he got the name. I assumed one of Evan's jokes. But I liked it—my own confidentiality. I went back to the flea market and bought a tackle box, bobs, sinkers. Anything I needed for fishing. Each time I stopped and talked to Flipper.

Now thinking of Flipper, the river, the fishing, I feel like a prick. Like maybe, in the quiet, I'd stopped listening. Maybe I'd missed a sign, a fucking symbol. If anyone knew Evan, or might've recognized a change, it would've been me. And I didn't.

At Evan's funeral, I stood in a corner and watched his mother shake hands with people. They shook mine too, nodded, darkly, like I was the one that died. No one knew I'd found him. Evan's friends and family were there, aunts, cousins. Kids ran around. People came all the way from Kentucky. My uncle wore a flannel buttoned up to his neck, stood near me, and neither of us talked. When I left, Evan's mother was smoking a cigarette near the dumpster. I thought of walking up to her, but what would I say? *I know you two haven't talked? I know you kicked him out.* I didn't have time for talking, and more people arrived, people we'd known in high school. They were standing out front catching up and laughing and all I wanted was to leave before anyone else showed up bumping elbows and smiling and telling me that they were *sorry, so fucking sorry.* Maybe his mother was looking for her own kind of quiet by the dumpster.

~

I could be cold sober and talk to Evan, spill out like a pig's gut. I'd even told him once I thought I remembered my mother. Normally, I told people, *She died in jail, never knew her.* But I told Evan of an image, a curly-haired woman, crooked smile. In my memory, she leaned toward me. Behind her: a plaid couch and a window, pale winter light falling through. I told Evan it must have been her, that I must have been a year old. I didn't tell him what it meant to me, the image of her, that woman against the light. Evan was the "feelings" guy. He didn't have retarded emotion. He'd say he wished he'd known his father, too, wished he could have met him. And uncomfortable with the "too," as if I'd said something similar, I'd laugh and say, *He didn't wish he'd met you.* I feel bad about that now, but we gave each other shit. Friends did that. We'd be in a bar somewhere, piss drunk and drinking ourselves drunker, and he'd lean over telling me he loved me: *you're my best friend*, he'd say. I won't lie; that embarrassed me. We didn't even shake hands—too formal, too strict.

But you have to listen. The night before I found him, he was on the porch sitting in the dark. I've known Evan for years. Sometimes, he likes to sit in the damn dark. I almost went outside, but I'd been dropping apps at Radio Shack, Candy Warehouse. Put one in at Giant Eagle. I wasn't in the mood for Evan telling me I needed to find work, for another one of his conversations about purpose and meaning and what it meant to drag. I didn't need a lesson. Neighbors played music—steel guitar shit. Hank Two. George Jones. Conway Twitty. I knew Evan must've been pissed, but through the glass, he had his feet up on the railing. I'm telling you, I almost grabbed the handle and went out. I keep thinking how he looked through the sliding door, his face foggy, eyes blurred. I couldn't tell if he'd seen me. His mouth moved, like he was talking, telling me to come outside; *tomorrow I'll be gone.* He could've been singing. Evan did that—in the shower, cutting grass; he'd sing. But he hated the neighbor's music and I keep thinking of him through the glass, that moonless night as dim as the light inside, trying to tell me something: answers to his riddles, to open my eyes, my ears, to become aware.

Evan hadn't changed; I knew that. He was the same asshole from the bathroom all those years ago—only older, a beard now, taller. He loved obscure things, playing Jet-Star Bomber in the back of the computer store on an old monitor—the one that played five-inch floppies. He still collected rocks at night, or lay in a field somewhere to watch the hillside, still shoulder danced to music when he heard it—in an elevator, the market—or played his stupid jokes, pushed me to find work, offered me a job at Computer Goodies, though they were going under, still told his riddles, like infinite supply, still laughed a lot, still cried too much, still spilled on the bar when he was drunk, cheeks brightened red, talking about how the music always sounded so good, *so beautiful. Isn't everything so damn beautiful?*

~

People called me after the funeral. Mutual friends, guys we drank with, people from high school, a cousin from Kentucky that I'd met at the funeral. She left a message telling me that Evan was a good guy, that he had a contagious laugh, as if I hadn't already known that. She left a number, said, *Lets get a drink while I'm in town.* I couldn't answer. Why should I? I could be a jaded son-of-a-bitch and I'll own up to it. Evan never talked about these people, these aunts, uncles, cousins. He never talked about Kentucky. Who was this woman to tell me what I already knew? I'd known him twelve years—as old as he was when I met him. I needed time to figure out what to do with myself after finding him. How to stop thinking of the steps, how I'd carried him down to the street eventually, how his head bobbed a little, bumped into the wall, and somehow I thought I'd hurt him. You'd think you'd want to pull down the shutters, kick the lights, and disappear for a while. Not me. I had to get out, keep moving. I walked through streets, slowly. I'm not the kind of guy to rush around. I don't mind a little sun on my back. I thought about what I had left of Evan, what I'd collected.

Old tee-shirt, a few used pairs of Vans shoes, Hemmingway book, a USB drive with nothing on it, pack of Marlboros still wrapped, piece of limestone shaped like an arrowhead. Evan had found it in the woods behind his house, *right there in the hillside, man, just poking out of the ground, you believe that?* Found a coin collection in his bedroom, buried under tee-shirts in his top drawer, pennies left missing. I folded his unfolded shirts stupidly, set them in a pile on his bed. I sat back on a coffee table and flipped through his wallet, pulling credit cards out, feeling his name printed in thick capital letters with my thumb. He had a receipt: a candy bar and an iced tea from CoGo's. I held his ID. He was twenty-one in the photo, smiling. I stared into his young face, his teeth suddenly unusual, his eyes nearly mystic with what he may have been thinking—if he'd known he'd be gone in three years. I left the cash and took the receipt, the ID. I slipped them into my pocket.

I searched the rest of his room, making sure to touch anything. I looked through a stack of papers, a pile of computer games, a photo album, sketches, any scrap of paper he'd kept in a junk drawer. I held his pencils in my fingers looking for clues, feeling angry. He must've left something. Evan would've left something—an answer, a note. Evan would've wanted me to figure it out—a game, a challenge, a fucking riddle. I knew it was ridiculous. He couldn't prop himself down. He couldn't take back the puke, the shit in his pants. There was no damn game, I understood that.

Yet, for some reason, it was a postcard that got me—untouched by ink, wordless. There was a picture of rocks on the front, piled on top of each other, half in the sun, half darkened by splashing water. I stared at it for a time and lay it on the dresser, picked it back up, feeling suddenly guilty standing in his bedroom, naked, like I'd felt the day his mother kissed him on the lips in the kitchen. I could take it to her, the post card. Fucking silly, I know, but right then, in the bedroom, it seemed right that she should have it. Might mean something to her. Maybe she'd cry. Maybe she'd remain strong, tell me something profound, speak to me of Evan. Maybe we'd finally have the conversation we'd never had over the years, and in the end, I'd give her the postcard, hand it over like handing her Evan's life. If she wasn't home, I planned to hold onto it, come back every day until I encountered her in person. I wanted the action of it: my hand and hers holding onto it for just a second. And I'd leave—never have to see her again.

When I got there, she *was* home. I could see her from the street, could see her on the back porch, looking into the yard. Hell, I almost turned around, but I could have sworn she saw me. And what would that look like:

me running away, up the street, with a postcard in my hand? I walked around the side of the house and stood at the bottom step.

Sunlight poured over everything—the porch, the yard, glowing white from the shingles of the house. She was sitting in a chair, tucked away in a slip of shade. I had to put my hand on my forehead as I looked up into the light, squinting.

"Day's hot, isn't it," I said.

She had a cigarette in her mouth, unlit.

I turned and looked behind me into the yard, where she'd been looking since I got there. The grass was patched, overgrown, balding in spots. A plank-wood fence wrapped around, pointed at the tops like dry-rotted arrows toward the sun. I looked back to her, my hand glued to my forehead by my index finger and thumb.

I wanted to say I was sorry for her loss or some shit, that I missed him, too. But I didn't know how to talk to the lady. All those years, I'd smile in her presence, dry out and harden like a fucking wart in her kitchen. She'd ask Evan to help her pull cans from the cabinets, organize and restock them again. I'd help, awkwardly, getting in the way, and I never talked to her, always past her, toward Evan. She was miserable all the time, or miserable-*looking* with those cigarettes sticking out of her face like whiskers. I waited once for Evan in the same place, the bottom of the steps, while she picked weeds along the sidewalk. I asked if she liked Pittsburgh better than Kentucky, and she shook her head, smiled up at me and walked inside. Evan told me that I was lucky she didn't stab me with a gardening shovel and we laughed. Maybe she remembered that.

"I brought this," I said, pulling the postcard out. "I brought this for you." I had it all planned: my hand reaching out, her face filling with tears. But what had I brought, really? He hadn't even written on the thing.

I wanted to talk to her. If only for that day, in the sunlight, in the yard. I wanted to tell her everything I knew about Evan, all that I'd learned over the years, as if somehow that might make it better. And maybe I wanted her to tell me what I didn't know, like what his father was like, or what she and Evan had fought about, or why she'd kicked him out. I wanted to tell her what I found.

Hear me out, I'd say. The front door was open when I got there, swinging. There was music playing from the neighbors. Maybe wind, traffic flying by outside. I'd taken my time, already telling my story to the living room. *Evan*, I'd said. A plate sat on the table, bread crumbs dried, stale. A fold of crust with brown mustard. *Evan, where are you, I have the worst story*. Though it wasn't. I'd stepped in dog shit on the walk home. I laughed. *No, not at him; I hadn't found him yet*. I'd seen him just the night before on the deck. He'd tried to speak. I stood on the other side of the glass, my hand on the knob. *No, I walked away instead. I went to bed and slept*.

But the frame fell away, dissolving. In the yard, I wanted Evan's mother to stand up—just stand the hell up and say something. But she sat there in her chair looking past me, or through me, like I imagine she might have looked at Evan all those years after fighting, or rubbing his back, or calling him a dickhead, like she was looking *for* Evan.

I climbed the steps and walked to her. "I brought you this," I said again.

She looked at me like I'd disturbed her, lips curling away from that cigarette, a snarl. "The hell is that?" she asked.

"A postcard."

"Of course it's a damn postcard," she said.

"There are rocks on it," I said. "Evan collected rocks."

She snatched it from me. One second, I had it pressed between my fingers and the next it was in her hand. Made me angry. Frustrated. I thought of asking for it back, thought of asking for a fucking do-over. We were supposed to transfer the thing and there she was, holding it in her hand and staring down at it like I'd handed her a goddamned turd.

Then she lifted her ass just up off of the seat and threw the post card in a trashcan on the porch. I nearly reached out and slapped her. I would have pulled it back out, but how could I? You tell me what that would've looked like, brushing past her, grabbing the thing and holding it like some child with candy. No, to hell with that woman. I thought, *You want to put your baby in a can, that's fine*. So I stared back at her, stared right into her face, flooding everything I had into that silence, that quiet. I stood near a minute like that, leaning, peering down. And I left.

~

Now stay with me: people called. They called *me. Call his mother*, I wanted to say. *He has a mother you know*. She should deal with it, with the messages: *I'm here for you; I'm here*. And maybe they were. Maybe they called and she didn't answer. Maybe she ripped the phone off the wall and tossed it in the trash. My uncle called and said he wanted to take a drive, that we'd go anywhere. We could fish, drink a beer, listen to the radio. We could drive along and listen to the wind if I wanted.

"Not today," I said. Not any day, really. Maybe we'd pretend it didn't happen. Maybe we'd try to get back a year, a month. We only needed a day. Maybe people had figured out that I'd found him, and they wanted details. People always wanted details. And what would I tell them? *Yes, I found him. No, not a gun.* Or maybe the smell. *Like salami.* I'm sure from a sandwich he'd eaten; everything smelled like salami. How, in the bathroom, it was worse—like he'd thrown up. Like he'd shit his pants, which he had, in fact, shit his pants. Maybe they wanted the important stuff.

This is important: I talked to him for a while, I told you this. I sat down on the tub and talked. I'm sure he was dead. His face was dark and pale at once and something dry was on his lips, something imperfect, arced so little it's nearly impossible to recognize as a smirk or a frown. As if he'd still held his breath, still attempted to speak, and I wonder if he *had* spoken—what he'd said to himself, to the empty bathroom. Knowing Evan, he probably sang a moment, took his feet from the sink.

I wish I could tell you how much time had passed between my finding him and calling an ambulance. But after a while, I was quiet; I leaned my head forward and closed my eyes. The salami magnified. *Why'd you do that?* I kept asking. I pulled him down from the hook and laid him in the tub. That was hard because he weighed so much. I laid him there and leaned my back against the back of the tub, dropped one leg over the side, and we faced each other, crossing—the way we'd lay in bed when we were young and we'd stay at each other's houses. I might have fallen asleep. I know what it looks like, but Evan would understand. I don't feel bad about laying him down. He might have liked that, to be laid in the tub, in the pale afternoon light, the sound of summer outside in the streets, a lawnmower, a plane flying over the house, Willie Nelson singing softly through the floorboards, kids laughing somewhere in the neighborhood, far away from us.

~

Yesterday, I went to the flea-market to see Flipper selling hotdogs. It had rained in the morning. People held down tablecloths. Some vans had boxes half-packed, while others were setting back up. I saw Flipper standing at his kiosk, tarp above his head, smoke rising from the back of his grill and blowing out into the wind, a little thicker in the after-rain cool, no one talking to him—as usual—and I thought, *How could anyone miss this treasure?*

"Flipper, make your day's rent?"

"What summons yee?" Flipper changed his voice and I smiled. I felt like he'd waited all day, or weeks, just to change his voice for that greeting sentence.

"Actually, pal," I began and as I stepped up close to him, his eyes bulged, not too much like a cartoon, but enough to literally see them protruding from his face. He reached for my hand and I paused. I wanted to shake it and couldn't. Did I really come to tell him Evan was dead? I had the receipt, the ID. An extended Evan folded in my wallet. Maybe I could pull it out and instead of my hand, I could shove it all into Flipper's chubby fingers, his pink and shaking palm.

Instead, I wanted to leave. I couldn't bear to touch him, couldn't bear to see him. But before I turned, a gust of wind ripped through the market, pulling people's tablecloths off, knocking vases and rustic lamps to the asphalt, and Flipper's tarp turned inside-out above his head. I watched the wind tuck under the tarp and fling a splash of stored water into the air above him. Just as the tarp reached its highest point, it froze for only a second. And I could hear cars in the background, buzzing and beeping, humming and roaring. The sound of kiosk runners, early morning discount shoppers and children merged into a static noise, blowing through the market, laughing on the wind. I could smell Flipper's hotdogs just starting to burn in the center by the flame. I could smell the mustard on his stained apron as it dried. I could feel the heat in my face, taste the warning in my mouth, as just then water came down down over Flipper like rain, like one tiny cloud had burst open over his head and soaked him. He stared up, arms out, water dripping from his face and clothes and smiled as he reached up, grabbed the toupee from his head and rung it out.

A toupee! I thought. *He's wearing a toupee!* I didn't know whether to laugh or cry or scream or run but I stood and finally smiled and though I missed the bastard so much it hurt, I thought of Evan—how he might have looked, knowing more than me, knowing all that time that it was always a goddamned toupee, and how he might have laughed with me, again, for a little while, smiling a smile that said, *Didn't I tell you? Didn't you trust me?* and waiting for the right rock to poke up in the dirt, for some peculiar moment, like purple lightening in the sky, or a mudslide, and he could say, *Isn't that beautiful, man? The way it seems to fall away like that?*

The Flying Man

Michael Compton

In my mind, the only appropriate reaction to seeing a man fly is wide-eyed wonder, the look of awed delight that turns every face, no matter how old or hardened, into that of a child. It is Bobby's look—my six-year-old—those times on the front lawn when we spotted the Flying Man, flitting and swooping in the starry shadows just above the glow of the streetlights. That expression on my son's face, that upwelling of his pure spirit, is so wonderful to look upon that I forget the Flying Man and just watch Bobby's eyes, soaring on the updrafts of his imagination. This, I think, is my purpose: to introduce—but not just to introduce—to shepherd, to witness, to cherish my son to the marvels and mysteries of the universe. This is what I am here for.

It is a strange thing—to me, at least—that not everyone reacts to the Flying Man in the same wide-eyed way. If someone pricks a finger, for example—or tastes chocolate, or sees a newborn baby—we expect a certain reaction. And one would think that the sight of a seemingly ordinary man taking to the air without the aid of wings or wires or balloons or rockets on his shoes would elicit a common response. None of the rest of us can do it, after all, and to see the Flying Man glide above the rooftops as casually as a neighbor out for an evening's stroll is to see a miracle. But the truth is, if one only observes people's behavior with even a bit of scientific distance, it becomes obvious that we do not all react the same way to seeing a baby, or tasting chocolate, or even to pricking a finger. Reactions evolve. They can even be learned. But between the stimulus and the reaction is the feeling, the elemental sensation. Do we learn—or unlearn—those as well? A flying man is a strange thing. But to me, even stranger, is indifference to the miraculous.

By my observation, the most common immediate response upon spotting the Flying Man is the exclamation, "There he is!" followed by an emphatic jab of the finger at full arm's length and a whipsawing of every head in the vicinity to get a look. His appearances are not few, but they are fleeting, as he habitually flies low to the treetops and is almost never glimpsed in full view, suspended in the naked air. Like an enormous partridge, he keeps close to ground cover, and he has yet to be flushed into the open sky. When he is spotted, one rarely sees more than a half-obscured torso, or a leg or a foot, disappearing behind the foliage. But as he progresses amongst the treetops, glimpses of a leg here, a foot there, a hand, a shoulder—even that face, with its rapt eyes and wan line of a smile—create a collage of images in the mind that coalesce into a singular whole, much as the persistence of vision creates the illusion of a moving image from a series of static frames.

And someone will say, "Where's his cape?" or some such remark, which itself elicits a variety of reactions. Many just ignore the question, since, by now, they have heard it so many times before. Others laugh that obligatory laugh one uses to acknowledge a joke as a joke, without necessarily endorsing it as truly funny or original. Many roll their eyes, as at a tired pun, and yet some guffaw with thoughtless abandon, to be shushed like children by those who see the Flying Man as no laughing matter, whether he is an object of their sincere reverence or heartfelt outrage. Others, equally parental in instinct, perhaps, but following the dictum of patience rather than severity, take the question at face value and acknowledge that the Flying Man does, indeed, confound expectation.

In short, the Flying Man is no costumed super hero, no angel, no bat-winged demon or vampire, no gryphon dredged up from our mythological past nor alien horror conjured out of our collective Hollywood unconsciousness. He is just a man, and a seemingly ordinary man at that, dressed in khakis—or jeans on the weekend—with a neatly tucked-in polo shirt of a dark blue or black, and running shoes with silver reflectors on the soles. He is everyone's next-door neighbor: Dark hair, medium complexion, medium build, indeterminate ethnicity, the kind of fellow one could picture working behind the counter at some local retailer. Or, like me, the Information Desk at the public library. By now, everyone knows this. They've heard the stories, they've seen the blurry photos and shaky smart phone videos. And yet, they are still surprised, even those whose pop culture allusions come automatically, who wear their postmodern, ironic sensibility as casually as they wear their T-shirts and jeans.

Personally, when I hear such sarcastic quips—and I have heard them many times—I wonder what is real to such people. Are their minds so chock full of projected shadows and colored-in line drawings that they have no room in them for the plain light of day? For it is clearly the plainness of the Flying Man that shocks them. He is unreal because he is real, and to the many who would scarce raise an eyebrow were they to see some over-muscled titan in a shimmering suit zooming across the sky, the spectacle of an apparently ordinary man gliding through the air is not a thing of wonder but of smug mockery.

Children and the elderly seem to have the purest reactions. Their eyes sparkle, their mouths gape, as if they are ready to lap him up like ice cream. In those early, quiet days, when the Flying Man was strictly a neighborhood phenomenon, it gave me a great sense of joy to see the faces of the old and the young among my neighbors lifted together to share in the wonder. My most cherished moment came on the evening I had my dad and my son together, standing out on the front lawn, their two faces mirrors of childish delight.

But the time for fathers and sons to enjoy quiet moments watching the Flying Man from the lawns and back porches of their peaceful homes was brief. Once word spread beyond our neighborhood, the gawkers began to stream in. There was a story in the local paper. Then a spot on the news. When the national networks picked it up, the frenzy began. For weeks afterward, our sleepy little enclave was overrun by a mechanized cavalry of camera trucks, police cars, and out-of-town SUVs, spilling out hordes of invaders bristling with their peculiar armaments: cameras, lights, microphones, satellite dishes, and in the case of the city's SWAT team—called to the scene for who-knows-what contingency—even automatic rifles. For a brief time, images of the Flying Man appeared on every news broadcast, in every paper and magazine, around the world. The shaky video clips were ubiquitous. The face, captured in one fuzzy but indelible image—eyes rapt and far-seeing, lips spread in a gentle, god-like smile—became iconic, hallowed in that most extraordinary place of contemporary honor, the T-shirt. He was everywhere and yet nowhere, for no one could get to him, no one knew who he was, no one stepped forward to identify him.

This elusiveness, at first, only amplified the public's urgency to know, and the spillers of words, both professional and amateur, filled every form of media imaginable with their speculations and pronouncements. A great deal of energy was expended in deciding what to call the Flying Man, as if "The Flying Man," which is what nearly everyone actually called him, was too pedestrian. And yet, it was the Flying Man's very pedestrian nature which every nickname seemed designed to poetically evoke. Among the names tried out for him—most of which were quickly drowned in the flood of media chatter—were "The Soaring Suburbanite," "The Neighborhood Nighthawk" (since he flew mostly after dusk), "Polo Man," "Khaki Man," "The No-Cape Crusader," and "The Winged Wal-Mart Greeter." It was also tediously common to hear him alluded to as "Your Friendly Neighborhood Flying Man" (or worse, "Flying Dude"), but when the mayor once referred on national news to our neighborhood as Blair Heights—a name few in our town under forty even know—the Flying Man immediately became "The Blair Heights Birdman." Now, it is as if some irresistible worldwide authority has decreed that every story regarding the Flying Man must refer to him as "The Blair Heights Birdman" at least once. Most preferably, this is done in such a way as to imply that the phrase has been coined on the spot.

Fortunately, the frenzy has long since passed, the cavalry has retreated, and most mentions of the Flying Man in the media these days are of the "Whatever Happened To—" variety. The media can feed on unadulterated speculation for only so long, after all. Eventually, they must have someone to talk to besides themselves, and it is to the Flying Man's everlasting credit that he denied them this. The more they sought him, the scarcer he became, until he disappeared completely. With nothing to see, the media people and gawkers did an abrupt about-face, from breathless credulity to utter cynicism. The Flying Man began to be referred to as a hoax, and the fact that hundreds of hoaxers had indeed created their own images of "flying" men and posted them on every form of electronic media only seemed to reinforce that conclusion.

By disappearing as he did, the Flying Man, whom we proudly claimed as a neighborhood man, proved that he was exactly that. He gave us back our neighborhood by removing himself from it, thus starving the media beast until it slouched its way to another Gomorrah. And he doubly gave us back our neighborhood, in a way, by allowing us to be reminded that we had a name, and a character, too; that even after years of trespass from chain stores and city planners, Blair Heights had maintained its uniqueness;

that one could see it in the quaintness of the brick and stone bungalows, in the narrowness of the streets, in the ages of the trees, and in the sufficient friendliness of the people. And when the Flying Man slowly began to re-emerge, we returned the neighborly favor and kept news of his comings and goings to ourselves.

Like my neighbors, I was grateful, once the frenzy had subsided, to be able to walk outside my house again without being accosted by reporters, to have the streets uncluttered by satellite trucks, to have my lawn and my roses safe from trampling feet and churning wheels. But I was doubly grateful because Margaret, my ex-wife, who lives with my son in another town about an hour away, no longer had an excuse for withholding Bobby's weekly visits. Margaret is not a rigid or vindictive person, but she has strong opinions on what makes a suitable environment for children. The day after the news of the Flying Man broke, rather than having me pick up Bobby at her house as I usually did, she insisted on bringing him to me. As she entered the city limits that Friday evening, the waves of out-of-town vehicles must have buffeted her little Prius like a storm surge, because she did not make it within a mile of the house before she phoned to say she couldn't get through, and, in any case, she thought it best for Bobby not to visit again until things "calmed down."

So for over a month, I only saw Bobby on his mother's turf, taking him on brief, desultory little outings that reminded me of the early days of the break-up, when I was only allowed the briefest unsupervised visitation. Once things had "calmed down" I did not immediately request a return to our old arrangement, but rather gave it an extra couple of weeks, hoping she would be the one to suggest it. That didn't happen, so the next time I called to say I was coming, I casually mentioned that she should pack Bobby's overnight bag for the weekend.

"So this flying person is gone now?" she said, referring to the Flying Man in her usual way.

I told her that things were back to normal, but I did allow that the Flying Man wasn't quite gone. She listened as I explained that he only appeared once or twice a week now, and only just after sunset or just before dawn, and no one was taking any more notice of him than they would any other neighbor out for a stroll.

She may have sensed that I was exaggerating a bit, because I could hear the gathering resolve in her voice as she replied that she would be bringing Bobby herself. "I want to see," she said.

When they arrived, Margaret wore a look of exasperation, having spent an hour in the car being regaled by Bobby with everything he knew about the Flying Man. He especially liked to tell of the first time we saw him together, acting out his own comic double-take of amazement. Bobby's enthusiasm at that time was such that Margaret immediately expressed concern, citing news reports of children—and even some grown men—injuring themselves in attempts to fly.

"I don't want Bobby tying a blanket around his neck and jumping off a roof," she had said. My reply that the Flying Man didn't wear a cape didn't seem to mollify her.

She was in a better humor on this occasion, however, looking glad for adult reinforcement as she followed Bobby in the door, dropping her bag as she used to in the chair, and just catching herself before greeting me with a side-swiping kiss. I covered the awkward moment by offering them lemonade, which they enjoyed on the back patio as I grilled hotdogs. When she saw the bright red links sizzling over the coals she said, "Oh—" and nothing else, but in my mind I filled in the blank: "Oh, we're still eating processed meat?"

The construction, "We're still," uttered in a questioning tone, followed by the appropriate participle and noun to describe whatever thing or activity I happened to proffer for the family's enjoyment, had become a pet expression of hers. Since the divorce, only two years ago, I noticed that she had taken on a whole array of new interests and tastes, but what was remarkable to me was that she never seemed disposed to simply add on; instead, she must erase and replace. It could not be, for example, that she now simply preferred a veggie dog or a Kobe steak—it must be that she was mistaken to have ever considered a hot dog to be edible in the first place.

"They're kosher," I said, punctuating the quip with a smile.

"That's a strange thing to say," she replied.

I was grateful, at least, that Bobby was too young to follow the exchange, because he would have agreed with her. His ears were not yet attuned to the deeply encoded dialogue his parents shared, nor was he old enough to remember, that first time my then-fiancée had asked me about my preferred brand of franks, my lame joke about "keeping the 4th kosher." I felt barely capable of keeping up with her inferences and allusions now, and fairly cringed at the multiplying levels of play that lay ahead of me in Bobby's maturing years, especially with the inevitable addition of new mates, step-children, and half-siblings. I was not looking forward to that fast-approaching day when my own child would respond to some innocent remark of mine with a cool look and a roll of the eyes shared with another, even if the sharer was his own mother.

After our meal, when we had settled on a blanket on the front lawn, Margaret asked how I could be sure the Flying Man would be out that night. Bobby replied, "He *always* comes out on Friday night." She glanced at me as if she knew I was the source of that bit of information, and it bothered her, I suppose, that there were things that Bobby and I shared now that she was not privy to, just as the reverse bothered me.

"Most people think he's got a regular nine-to-five job," I said. "After the work week is over, this is just his way of blowing off steam."

"And he never comes out in the day time?"

"Not any more. It's always last light, like now, or early in the morning."

The last sliver of sun had just dipped below the horizon, and as the scattered clouds slowly turned from red to gray, I became nervous. Since the Flying Man's return, his route was much more variable, and there was no guarantee that he would pass over the house that night. I both wished he would, and wished he wouldn't.

To fill the minutes while we waited—or to cover my nervousness, perhaps—I recalled something I'd heard at the library's Story Hour. It was the old African American folk tale in which the slaves, coming into contact with new arrivals from Africa, are reminded of who they are and where they come from, and with a few words in the native tongue from a forked-bearded old man, they recall their innate power of flight, spring into the air, and sail away to freedom and back to the motherland. That story reminded me of my own flying dreams, in which I realize that I had always had the ability to fly but had somehow just forgotten. The Flying Man was running later than usual that night—if he was coming at all—and I found that I kept talking, tying the notion of forgotten flight, rather pedantically, I suppose, to

Plato's *Timaeus*, in which he describes the soul as that pure part of our being that lies within us like a deeply buried memory. That, I conjectured, was what accounted for the Flying Man's faraway, fixed expression. It was not a mask, as some had suggested, to conceal his identity, but rather the overawed projection of his inmost soul.

It was just as I noticed Margaret's eyelids fluttering wearily that the Flying Man made his appearance.

"There he is!" Bobby whispered, but so suddenly and with such a jerk of his outstretched arm that he gave Margaret and me both a start.

He was difficult to see at first, just a shadow undulating above the trees.

"I see him," I whispered back, just as he breached the gap between two poplars.

"Do you see him, Mom?"

Margaret said nothing yet, although her eyes seemed to be tracking his flight. And then the Flying Man did something unprecedented in my experience: he hovered. Directly above the street, in the widest space between the trees that lined each side, he paused, like a bumblebee rising above a flower. It was just a moment, but there he was, suspended in full view, his body angled about thirty degrees above the horizontal, his knees bent, his hands held out before him, palms open, as if testing the air. He was not quite silhouetted against the pale quarter moon above, not quite illuminated by the glow of the streetlights below, but every detail was clear. His eyes seemed to turn in our direction, though in that far-away expression of his I can't say that they actually looked upon us. In his rapt, almost beatific demeanor, I could imagine that he was indeed a man in deep contemplation of the soul, one who had found the connection that enabled the material body to release its earthly burdens and join in the soul's joyous flight.

"Oh my God—" I heard Margaret say, and then he was gone.

"He waved at me, Dad!" Bobby exclaimed. "I waved and he waved back! Did you see?"

"Yeah," I said, not so sure, but giving his shoulder an encouraging squeeze.

Margaret was still staring at the spot above the streetlights, as if she could still see him.

"He's so…"

Fantastic? Marvelous? Miraculous? My mind's thesaurus provided a dozen words to complete that sentence, but I knew I couldn't anticipate the one she would choose.

"Creepy."

Bobby was oblivious to her mood. "Did you see him, Mom? Did you see him?"

"I saw him, Sweetie." And to me: "I noticed you still keep that upstairs window open."

"Just in summer. It's good ventilation."

She lowered her voice. "Did you know there are two registered sex offenders in this neighborhood?"

"No," I said. "I didn't know that."

"You should look into these things. Come on, Bobby, it's getting late. Time to go."

Bobby raised objections, but Margaret answered/ignored each in her practiced, motherly way, managing to get him ready to leave as she continued talking with me.

"I really don't think it's a good idea for Bobby to stay overnight as long as that man is on the loose."

"No," I agreed, determined that this discussion would continue another day. "No, I guess not."

And so they left.

I was tired, but I didn't want to go to bed. The night air was warm and inviting, buzzing with the songs of crickets, cicadas, and tree frogs. I lay back on the blanket, the lawn's Bermuda grass making a prickly cushion between me and the hard earth. Sadness pressed down on me, but as I stared up at the gap between the poplars I pictured again the Flying Man—hovering unsteadily, his hands outstretched, daring a quick wave to Bobby—and it made me smile.

Some people mock the Flying Man for what they see as his timidity in keeping so low to the ground, but I find that this trait only further endears him to me. He does not soar like the eagle of poetry and song, lording it over all that he surveys, reducing us, from his perspective, to the realm of crawling insects even as we exalt him to the angels. At one hundred feet or a thousand, the air rushing in his ears, the giddy weightlessness, even the feeling of detachment from earth-bound cares must be the same. By staying so close—close enough to exchange friendly hellos, if he were so inclined—the Flying Man seems to be saying, not "Look at me!" but "Follow me! You could do it, too!" And I confess, I have tried, lying on my blanket, watching the stars wink out and reappear as the Flying Man passes between on his irregular flight, imagining my body becoming weightless, levitating, leaving the ground by millimeters, feeling the Bermuda grass stiffen beneath me, the blanket peeling off my back like a shed skin, the air growing cooler as I rise faster, foot by foot, meter by meter, until I am up there, soaring with him, looking down at my blanket, my yard, my house—all my earthly remnants—as they shrink from sight.

Many a summer night I spend lying out on the lawn that way, sometimes not getting up again until first light, with the morning's dew in my hair and eyes. I'm not the only one. All throughout the neighborhood, the old and young, fathers and sons, mothers and daughters, will sit or lie on their front lawns and back patios, finding that gap in the trees, that wedge of sky on which they can fix their eye, seeing the familiar, glowing bodies of the firmament, but looking for something else, something mysterious and wonderful, on those long, empty nights of the soul when the moon and stars are not enough.

The Trouble with Harry

Victor Walker

Let's suppose:

I've taken to looking over at her much more than I ever did—even when we had just started going together. Then I seemed to look at her all the time—her hair, her eyes, her nose, her mouth, the way she moved or sat still. I couldn't stop looking at her, even when she wasn't there. I would think about her. All the time. This sounds obsessive, but it really wasn't. It never got in the way of my work. I never stopped eating. Or lost any sleep. I never spied on her or called her up just to check on where she was. What she was doing. I was never jealous of her friends or the men she knew before me. I never asked her to tell me about her old boyfriends or imagined any to compare myself unfavorably to. Everything was always in the now. My past, her past, didn't really matter. It was as if we were invented just to be with each other.

There is a painting by Marc Chagall of a man and woman, a married couple, and instead of them holding one another or just standing side by side, the one is floating up over the other's head, but attached like a cartoon thought-balloon. That's what it's like, how she is with me.

But lately, I also find myself looking at her and noticing things I had not noticed before. The way the light filters through the folds of her ears or how her knees don't exactly match.

Sometimes I watch her sleeping. Nothing untoward. I don't pretend to sleep only to open one eye and spy on her while she's asleep. However, sometimes after I have gotten up in the middle of the night to pee or when I've gone into the baby's room and then come back to bed and my eyes have adjusted to the dark, I will just lie beside her for a while watching her sleep. I don't think she has ever actually watched me sleep in that way, although she has said I snore.

You might be surprised when I tell you that I don't think she's pretty. Not in a conventional way.

Nina (I'll call her Nina for the sake of privacy.) is smaller on the top than on the bottom, that is to say, her breasts are modest while her thighs and hips and buttocks are substantial, and she is self-conscious about that. I sometimes notice her stealing glances at herself in store windows when we are out walking.

She's a very bright woman, but she's insecure. I'm sure that's part of what attracted me to her. As well as her intelligence. I have read that it is the flicker of a flame as much as the light itself that draws the moth.

Sometimes when we're out, she'll stop in front of a clothing shop and gaze at a dress in the window, and I'll pause and look, too, and though she's ostensibly looking at the dress, I also know she's unconsciously comparing herself to the figure in the window as well. In some ways, I've always thought that the mannequins (elevated as they are in their dioramas) were like statues of figures in Greek mythology, the ones just below the gods, looking past the passersby, their gazes aimed into the distance. Oblivious of us, our mortal coil. There is something eternal about them, and I think it is their self-possession, not their 6-foot statures or their size 4 figures, that Nina longs to possess.

"They could use better glass," she says.

"Better glass?" I say.

"Glass that doesn't reflect so much."

She waits for me to catch up. She is patient with me. We have talked of trying to have a child again.

"A better quality would cut down on the street reflection."

I look at Nina's pear-shaped figure in the glass, at my bean-pole one.

"What exactly do you see?"

"I see the most beautiful woman in the world."

"I'm serious. Look at me. What do you see, really? *Who* do you see?"

I am determined not to be bullied.

"I see you, and to me you're beautiful."

"Don't take this the wrong way. I don't want to hurt you. But I don't want to *be* beautiful just for you."

I don't know exactly what to say. How to respond. It's as if I had just proposed only to be turned down. We were, in fact, not married, although many times I had asked her to marry me in the heat of lovemaking (when it did not count, of course), and she had said yes (which, of course, did not count either).

"I just once want to see who I really am on the inside on the outside looking back at me. And smiling."

"That's who I see," I say.

"And I love you for that."

Reflected in the window, I imagine her taking my hand.

"But it's not enough to see me through your eyes. Maybe it should be, but it isn't."

I feel her squeeze my hand as if it were a phantom limb.

"I need to see me through my own eyes—and I don't."

Maybe this is what has precipitated my looking at her more, as if I could sneak up on her and catch a glimpse of who she really is and nobody has seen—even her—that has yet to come out.

At times I feel like a cat waiting for a mouse to peek out of its hole. And pounce on it.

Sometimes I think about the baby we almost had.

The other day, I was sitting in the park. It was a nice day, and it was lunchtime, and I had taken my lunch to the park with me and sat down on a bench.

I had put my lunch on the bench beside me and was just content to sit and watch the sky and the other people in the park. I don't often take my lunch to the park. The park is a fifteen minute walk from work, but the other day I felt like walking and before I realized it, I was across the street from the park, so it just seemed like a good place to stop and have my lunch. I wasn't the only one to have had such an idea. The park was active with people, but in a relaxed way, not the purposeful way people belly-up to the lunch counters and crowd the outdoor tables along the streets that box the park.

I had gone just far enough that it was like being in another world, one where I could catch only a glimpse of a few tall buildings that rose above the treetops like the towers of distant castles. That there was a horse path that smelled of manure rather than bus fumes, that the walkways wound rather than crisscrossed, and that the grass rolled rather than flattened out in a city as flat as a bathmat was so relaxing that I did not begin to eat right away but rather sat on the park bench as a boy might sit on a dock watching boats go in and out of a harbor.

A squirrel climbed onto the lip of a trash receptacle perhaps ten yards from me, hesitated, then plunged in. I opened up my bag lunch, took out a sandwich, and listened to him rustling about. Nina, who was always watching her weight, always took care to prepare me cold chicken or turkey sandwiches seasoned with salt and pepper, or leftover salmon dressed with lemon juice but no mayo, and topped with a tomato slice and leaf of lettuce. For crunch, there were usually carrot and celery sticks, sometimes snow peas. Leftovers from take-out. Occasionally there would be a radish included. Like a rose.

Nina had the carrots, celery, and snow peas, too, but substituted yogurt for the sandwich. She never lost any weight; still she continued with the lunches.

"I want to be healthy when we try again," she said.

I tried to adopt this attitude myself. After all, wasn't what I put in my body equally as important?

"Of course," she said, "You have to supply the protein."

However I sometimes found myself bagging my lunches for a hot dog from a local stand and a bag of potato chips and soda. Unfortunately whenever I did this, I would come home after work feeling as if I had cheated on her and, in a strange way, on the baby we didn't have as well.

I took the radish out of the bag and tossed it in the basket. The squirrel scampered out of the trash (sans radish), jumped down to the ground, and stood for a second on his hind legs, his forepaws pointed back toward his chest in that *Who, me?* posture city squirrels seem to hold the copyright on, and looked at me before bounding away.

Maybe he thought I was trying to hurt him. Maybe radishes are too peppery for his taste. Maybe he was just being a squirrel.

I took out the rest of my lunch and spread the paper bag on my lap like a napkin and began eating, unaware whether my sandwich was chicken or turkey or salmon, chewing and swallowing out of habit rather than hunger.

I watched several pigeons, the same color as the footpath. They had taken on the same sooty coloration as the city, without any of the protective benefits such camouflage would have served them in the wild. Instead, it had made them objects of either scorn or indifference, feathered panhandlers pecking at bits of gum and scraps of god-knows-what among the candy wrappers and butts of cigarettes. Even in a park, they seemed inured to nature, preferring the pitted cinder walkways to the grass, the beneath-the-bench-seats shadows to the sun.

They took even the pretense of my appetite away, and I tucked Nina's sandwich back into the bag and set it beside me on the bench. If I had been a smoker, I would have smoked a cigarette, or if I had been younger I would have plugged in my headphones, but being neither, I found myself drifting into a daydream as a patient in the waiting room of a doctor's office might absentmindedly flip through a magazine.

In the daydream, I go from the park straight home where Nina is waiting for me there, even though she is at work now and is often never home before I am. Even so, when I arrive, she is standing in the kitchen stirring something in a heavy pot on the stove with her back to me so that she does not hear me when I come in. In my daydream, she has nothing on but an apron, which is tied with a big bow. I don't think she even has an apron. But in my daydream she does.

I don't say anything. I just stand in the entrance to the kitchen watching her like I do sometimes when I come back to bed in the middle of the night and she is still asleep. However, in the daydream, I have on a hat and am carrying a briefcase, and I am dressed like Gregory Peck in the movie *The Man in the Gray Flannel Suit*. I want to go over to her and wrap my arms around her and ask her *what's for dinner?* But then, as if she senses I'm there behind her, she turns around with this other face, a face I don't recognize but in a voice that's still familiar, and answers, "I'm cooking up our baby, silly."

I looked over and a little bird had hopped upon the edge of my bench. He was no bigger than a tennis ball, and he eyed me in that suspicious way birds have of doing, by turning their heads to the side and looking at you with one eye, like someone peering through the peephole of a door. So I watched him, too, looking through one eye while I pretended to look straight ahead at the people and pigeons in the park.

He hopped up on the back of the bench, perching for no more than a few seconds and then hopped back onto the seat, turning first one way and then the other, always keeping an eye on me. Several times he went to the edge of the bench like a diver contemplating a leap from the high board, but each time he just looked at the pigeons milling underneath, pecking the ground for specks of waste, and reconsidered, hopping back away from the edge before beginning all over again.

He was getting used to me, I think, and I to him, for I could now shift my weight, even recross my legs without causing him to fly off, although the first time I shifted positions, he flew almost straight up, helicopter-style, to a low branch just above where I was sitting, low enough that I could have reached it if I had been standing up. When he saw that I was harmless, he dropped back down on the top slat of the bench and began pecking between his toes, as if grooming himself, then began pecking under his wings, first one and then the other, executing a 180 degree hop-turn so that he could keep one eye on me at all times.

These ablutions turned into a search for parasites. When he found something, his head went back, his neck jutted out, and his beak snapped. This was followed by puffing his breast out into a fluffy ball of pillow feathers like a baby chick. Upon finishing, he gave his wings several flaps, but did not take off; it was more like a dog shaking water off after having been given a bath or come in from the rain. A cottony feather wafted into the air, drifted to the ground and was immediately set upon by the pigeons.

My friend (I had inexplicably developed an attachment to him)—I will call him Harry—watched for a moment then hopped back from the brink of the bench and began cooing with such a throaty vibrato and surprising bravado that at its conclusion (It could not have lasted more than ten or twelve seconds.) I wanted to applaud. Instead, we both just sat there, or rather I sat there, and he stood, slightly off to the end of the bench, occasionally flapping up onto the backrest, and then a few seconds later descending back down onto the seat, hop-scotching between the end and the middle, between the edge and the end.

Taking care not to move too suddenly, I reopened my lunch and retrieved a partially-eaten half-sandwich and very carefully broke off a piece of crust and set it on the bench beside me. Harry looked at me then at the bread then back at me in that one-eye jerky way that reminded me of the toy wind-up dolls they used to sell on street corners.

For perhaps thirty seconds there was a kind of face-off, me not moving (not even blinking), Harry not moving (not even ratcheting his head), and the tiny crust of bread just laying on the green slatted seat of the bench not more than an inch from my thigh between us.

I gave in first. Very slowly, I picked the bread back up and put it into my mouth, but instead of eating it, I rolled it into a ball with my saliva and then very slowly opened my mouth and carefully stuck out my tongue (Nina calls my tongue her little mouse), the ball of bread resting on it, I imagine, as a tiny pearl on a little pink pillow.

Harry cocked his head to one side, his little black eye like a bead from one of the brightly-colored, leather-craft belts I used to make at summer camp.

It was my move again, and I took the tiny ball of bread (it was now more like a piece of dough) and set it down on the bench between us. Harry's head ratcheted down to the ball and then back up to me. I just looked at Harry. Then, drawing back my forefinger to form an "OK" with my thumb, I gently flicked the ball (that was not a true ball at all, but egg-shaped) in Harry's direction. Like a miniature football, it wobble-rolled six inches and fell between the wooden slats.

Harry cocked his head again. We both could see the ball of bread beneath the bench. So too could several pigeons that raced over, flapping their wings, not to fly but to beat back their rivals. Watching them this way through the bench was like being a Greek or Roman god who had set things into motion and then stood back and watched the outcome.

After perhaps a minute of their thrashing about under the bench, a greater god appeared along the path wearing a closet of coats and sweaters, and rolling a two-wheeled laundry cart in front of her stuffed with blankets and pillows. The pigeons flocked to her, some waddling about her ankles, some roosting on her cart, some perching on her sleeves and shoulders, but all of them gathering to her as children to Mother Goose.

I followed her, too—with my eyes. But when I turned back, Harry was watching me.

I thought for a moment of the way I silently watched Nina.

I tore off another piece of bread. And then another and another until there were perhaps ten small pieces of bread along with the rest of the half-eaten sandwich lying in my lap. I'm not sure if it was a conscious decision on my part, but I did not tear completely through the bread, as if trying to avoid taking any bread that might have been pressed against the chicken—

if that is what I had in fact been eating. I did not know if Harry would know the difference or not, but it did not, since *I* knew the difference, seem right.

All the while I did this, Harry did not take his eye off the bread, and I did not take my eye off Harry.

When I had finished pinching each piece off, I moistened it with the tip of my tongue, rolled it into a little ball, and carefully lined each one up along the bench, one in front of the other and an inch apart in what amounted to an elongated ellipsis extending in a straight line toward Harry.

Harry looked at the little balls of bread. I had not thought of it before, but they must have looked like little eggs to him.

What if someone had lined up one, two, three, four, five . . . ten infants in front of me? Would I have eaten them?

Was Nina's miscarriage punishment for the abortion? Her doctor had said there was no *physical* connection.

You can't help thinking, however. Blaming.

Harry looked from the bread to me several times, hopped back keeping his eye on me, switching off, first the left eye and then the right.

I had simply sat beside the bed, watching Nina sleeping. They had given her something to help her rest. She just looked at me before closing her eyes. I was still holding her hand, squeezing it. I wished there were some way to darken the room, make it seem that she was really sleeping in our own bed and not simply in some hospital room sedated. I wanted to climb onto the bed alongside her and wrap myself around her like a cover, resting my head against her neck and my hand just underneath the rise of her stomach, rubbing it slowly and telling her it was all right, all right, as if I could somehow will it so, as if saying it enough times would make it true. As if I had any influence at all. Any role to play other than to stand in the corner of the room while the doctor and nurses did all that they could do to save the only thing I was capable of giving to her worth saving.

Suddenly I felt myself in spasm as when almost asleep you feel your entire body jerk, and I found myself holding Harry so tightly that I could feel his heart knocking in my hand.

Before anything but surprise could register in his eyes, before anything more than a reflexive peck could draw blood between my thumb and forefinger, my hand had tightened so quickly around his slender body (his feathers were little more than sham armor) that I could feel his skeleton snapping like a handful of tiny twigs.

It all happened so quickly that I'm certain Harry didn't feel any pain. He never even knew I called him Harry. Yet I continued to squeeze his body until my fingernails were digging into my own flesh.

Nina and I had talked about names. If it was a boy we had thought about naming him after my father. If she was a girl, there were several names we liked. But nothing was etched in stone. Nina had not even wanted the doctor to tell us after she had taken the sonogram. She said she wanted to be surprised.

"She doesn't even like me to give her hints about Christmas presents," I told the doctor.

Afterward, however, she asked one of the nurses what it was, and she told her it was a girl.

I was angry at her for asking and angry at the nurse for telling, and I remained angry at Nina for days after that—even when she was still recovering in the hospital, even after I had taken her back home. For the first few weeks, I would go into our half-painted baby's room and stand looking out the window or just sit on the floor staring at the wall. It took almost seven months before we were up to finishing the room, and after we did there was a faint line where we had ended the first time and started up the second, but there was not enough paint to go back over the whole wall, so we just left it.

My hand was cramping, my fingers so stiff and slow when I tried opening them that it would not have surprised me if, like in the movies, it had sounded like the prying open of a coffin's lid.

What I saw in my hand was no longer a bird, no longer Harry, but a tiny fetus, weightless and feathery, like a little soul. Like an angel.

And I ate it.

Trying to Know You

Jennifer Bryan

My mother is going to die. On Monday, she tells me she wants to be buried in her pink suit and pink high heels. I'm not to forget the high heels. She makes me promise to check her feet when she's inside the coffin. I agree because that's what oldest daughters do, and I sit next to her bed while she eats malted milk balls and drinks Tab. I ask her why she doesn't just drink Diet Coke. She cocks her head to the side like Caesar, her white poodle, and says it's because her mother drank Tab and her mother's mother drank Tab. It's just what they do. I don't think Tab has been around that long.

My mother is young. She'll be sixty next Wednesday. If she makes it to next Wednesday. She's been sent home to die, which means she could have a couple of hours or a couple of days. It depends. She practices being dead when I've left the room, and I tell her it isn't funny, but she laughs on the good days, and she cries on the bad days, and I try not to leave the room because it might happen, and then I'll miss it.

We watch Dr. Phil and Oprah.

"It's good that Oprah didn't go off the air and that I'll never know what it's like not to have Oprah," she says.

Three months ago when my mother began dying, she asked me to move into the large house with her on Beach Street, next to the library in Carnegie, a small borough outside of Pittsburgh, a place I always identified as home but never lived until now. My father belonged there, and his father belonged there.

When my parents bought the house ten years ago, they were still married, and it was three apartments. My father worked to turn it back into a house, but he was tired before it was done. Not just of renovating the house but of my mother too. My father sends me postcards from places in Pennsylvania I've never heard of, and he signs them, Tim. Which I started to be more okay with until my mother started dying.

The hospital bed takes up most of the small living room on the bottom floor of the house. I moved into the bedroom on the second floor, across from a tiny kitchen with no appliances. The lonely linoleum cracks and bends in the corners. My mother has put all of the plants in that room to have the company of each other. A spitting, ceramic fish gurgles loudly at night coughing up my mother's secrets while we sleep. I couldn't find the switch to turn it off, and I stopped closing my door so the secrets didn't have to bang against the doorframe, wedging themselves under the door where they got stuck and howled before dislodging and finding their way into my room.

At first, the secrets are small. Slips of paper, like fortunes from hard and stale cookies. Smudged black ink on rice paper, the secret moved across the floor sounding like nails on a chalkboard. It made me jump out of bed and snatch it from the floor before it could go any further. I looked at the rice paper and then the spitting fish across the hall. The fish turned and smiled at me. I put the paper to my lips, the secret's breath hot against my tongue. *When Edith was ten, she stole a box of Thin Mint Girl Scout cookies from her sister's room and ate the whole box crouched in the corner of her closet.* Thin Mints are my favorite Girl Scout cookies.

~

My mother makes me promise that I will visit Paris. It is an empty promise, one I feel 50/50 about making to a dying woman, especially my mother. But I don't like airplanes or pilled navy blue blankets and paper pillows. I don't like airplane bathrooms or terminal bathrooms with automatic flushing systems that flush whenever I'm not ready for them to flush and won't flush when I need them to. I don't like being kicked by children who can't keep their feet to themselves. I don't like feeling that I can't order the Bloody Mary spicy tomato juice without the vodka because they only have so many cans of Mrs. Ts.

A postcard arrives from Tim. It's the Alamo, but the postmark is Mifflintown. Tim doesn't leave the state of Pennsylvania. I think it's because he feels guilty he left my mother, and now she's dying, except it's unnecessary because he had no way of knowing my mother would die at sixty. If he were here, I would pat his shoulder and tell him it was okay. He could leave the state, but he should resume signing his postcards, Dad. Just because my brother Frank had disowned him—or renounced him—I wasn't sure which, didn't mean I had. He was my father.

"When you go to Paris," my mother says. "I want you to stay at this little apartment two blocks from Napoleon's Tomb. You can't miss the golden dome." She describes the one room apartment, IKEA loft bed, small kitchen with a washing machine under the counter.

"It sounds like fun," I say. And I'm not lying.

When I packed my apartment in Virginia to move in with my mother, I called my sister.

"I'd like to move to Alaska," she said.

I'm not sure why I called Allison. Sometimes I get nostalgic for the way our family was pre-divorce. People think that it shouldn't be a problem if your parents get divorced when you're an adult, but it is a problem. There is a particular ritual for all events, even minor ones like how we watch Sunday football (only the Steelers), or play Monopoly (my mother is always the shoe), or how we remember all of the animals we had (28, which included mice, fish, and birds). Allison remembers more than I do even though she's two years younger than me.

"She's going to drive you crazy," Allison said. Her two kids screamed in the background, so she took a minute to scream back at them to tell them to stop screaming.

Again, I'm not sure why I called Allison.

"Well someone has to go," I said.

"Hold on."

The phone sounded like someone crumpling and uncrumpling tissue paper for longer than seemed necessary. I hung up. I thought Allison would call back, but she didn't.

Even though I packed my apartment, I still took a leave of absence from my job at the state university because it seemed like the more responsible thing to do. My department ran programs like a film festival and a summer camp for kids. I got twelve weeks of FMLA. But it wouldn't matter for two reasons: I wasn't going back, and it wouldn't take Edith twelve weeks to die.

Today is a bad day. After my mother reminds me about the apartment in Paris, she asks for something to help with the pain. There are six prescription bottles, and when I finally find the one she wants, she needs help going to the bathroom.

After she falls asleep, I go through the photo albums. Gone are any pictures where my mother couldn't simply cut out my father. In 1988, when he stood in the middle between my brother and I, in front of the Christmas tree. I wore a green velvet dress and we all held hands—gone. But if he stood on the end, like in 1992 for my sister's high school graduation, then the picture is just a smaller version of its original self. His fingers touching my arm are all that's left.

Edith wakes up in the middle of the night because she thinks it's time to dress for the Air Force Ball. While I was sleeping, another secret hurrying and out of breath, its paper bending like a kite flying on a spring day, scurried across the hardwood floor from the spitting fish. It climbed up the leg of the wrought iron bedframe my parents bought at an antique store, dove under the covers, and crawled up my left side before nestling into my open palm. The words wet my skin. *Last year Edith scraped a car in the supermarket parking lot and didn't leave a note.*

"Do you think Tim will bring me a corsage with red roses or white lilies?" Edith asks. Caesar, snorting through his flattened face, curls into her side. Sometimes when she aches, she can't bear the little dog to touch her.

"Lilies," I say. They are her favorite flower.

My father was in the Air Force when they first met, and he took her to a dance. She wore a red dress with spaghetti straps that slipped down her thin arms. She took off her high heels and walked barefoot down the gravel road to sneak back into her parents' house. Edith was nineteen. They eloped four months after meeting. They had me a year later. My father sang "Only Fools Rush In" the night he proposed.

~

"I've been making plans," my mother says.

On Wednesday, we're watching Ellen. I feel like I'm cheating on Oprah.

Caesar is licking melted chocolate from my mother's finger. I think about telling her the chocolate isn't good for him when she says a small lick of chocolate won't kill him. We both pause a little at that word *kill*. In that space, I think about how it took me two batches of chocolate chip cookies before I got them right. She likes them soft and chewy. The gas oven made them crisp at the edges. That's what I tell myself.

"I know," I say about her plans.

Edith has two life insurance policies and a retirement account. She wants me to split the money with Allison and my brother Frank, who barely speaks to her. He's angry about something, but we don't know what. Allison and I speculate sometimes. It's like a game. We both think it's Frank's wife because she's never liked us. Sometimes I press Allison about living with our parents when I had already moved out. She says she doesn't know. We come back to the divorce. It's the only thing that makes some sense when it makes no sense. Our mother forgives him though. He is her only son.

"Frank gets part," she says. "Make sure he gets his part."

I agree Frank will get his part even though it makes me angry like I haven't been before today, and I'm not exactly sure what I'm specifically angry about. Maybe I'm angry because Allison and Frank expect that as the oldest I'll watch our mother die so they don't have to. Maybe I'm angry because Frank isn't speaking to his dying mother, and hasn't for awhile, and she still wants to give him a third of the insurance money. I'm angry because I know I'll have to box up all of her belongings, and I'll have to call Allison and see if she'll want anything, and she'll say she wants the diamond earrings our father gave our mother the Christmas he left her, and Allison will want the grandfather clock in the hallway, but she won't know how to get it from Carnegie to Columbus. I'll have to call Frank and tell him that our mother died, and if he answers the phone, because often he isn't talking to me either, he'll say that it's too bad, and he doesn't want anything from her. And I'll try and be practical about what I should keep and what I shouldn't and whether I should let Tim know and how I'd let him know if I wanted to.

~

It's Thursday when the doctor comes by to check on my mother. He listens to her heart and her lungs. He thumps on her stomach and makes her wiggle her toes. I think he's surprised she's still here. I want to tell him that I thought she had died last night when there were no secrets. I woke to the sound of emergency sirens and ran across the floor so quickly it didn't have time to creak. Downstairs, I put my ear to my mother's open mouth while watching her chest rise and fall. Caesar whined and rolled over inviting me to scratch his belly.

"Hey boy," I whispered. "You want to come upstairs?"

He didn't.

~

My mother eats the blueberry pancakes I've made her. She eats her two links of sausage and eats mine too. She wants me to make more, but then she throws up. I have to change the sheets and her nightgown, and she doesn't register self-consciousness of how her body looks. Her breasts sag, and her belly wrinkles and gathers like the empty muscle under her arms. My mother looks like Caesar. Her hair white with soft curls close to her head. I talk to her the way I think she might have talked to me as a baby, telling her not to worry, not to cry. It isn't a big deal, I say. When I get the sheets changed and her cleaned and settled into the bed, she throws up again.

"I liked the pancakes," she says. "I think they're the second best I've ever had."

The best pancakes are the ones my father made on Sunday mornings. There were only three times he didn't make blueberry pancakes: when Frank was nine and in the hospital for his appendix, when the dog was hit by a car, and when Allison was seventeen and didn't come home from a date. There was a fourth time he didn't make blueberry pancakes, but I don't know about that time until later that night when the fish spat out the third secret. This slip of paper crawled along the walls and up near the ceiling stopping to swing on the curtain shears before scuttling over the shelf above the bed to drop on my head. It nestled and tangled in the hair strands like a tick. *When Edith miscarried her fourth child, she was happy. When she cried that Sunday morning, Tim thought it was because she was disappointed.*

That evening, my mother wants to go to the drive-in. She thinks she can be demanding because she's dying.

"I'll just rent a movie," I say. "We can eat popcorn or anything else you want."

"Drive-in movie theaters are great on Friday nights," she says.

I don't think drive-ins are great. We went to the drive-in when I was eight to see *E.T.* I don't remember anything about the movie. My mother says it isn't because I saw it at the drive-in. It was because I fought with Allison in the backseat about the box of Sugar Daddies, and then I spilled my soda, so we had to sit on the hood of the car, and I couldn't hear the speaker.

In the kitchen, I make popcorn. On Sunday nights when I was a child, my father made popcorn in an old green pot with burnt on the bottom. Then we dug out our popcorn before he could cover it with lemon pepper. Allison and I shook Parmesan cheese on top of ours. Frank ate his plain. My mother never much liked the popcorn at home, preferring it in the theater on Christmas Day.

My mother and I watch an old black and white movie on cable. She in her big hospital bed with Caesar, and me in the recliner. When I pass her the bottle of root beer I cross my fingers that she won't throw up.

The last postcard I got from Tim was three days ago. While Edith sleeps, I dig out the Alamo postcard and call information for Mifflintown. My father doesn't have a listing there. I call three hotels, but he isn't registered. I tear the postcard into tiny pieces before throwing them away.

I call Allison. She thinks I'm calling to tell her our mother died.

"Not yet," I say.

I tell her it's only 177 miles from Columbus to Carnegie. She could come early.

She coughs, and we're silent for a while. So silent I think she's hung up.

"She wants me to go to Paris," I finally say.

"You hate airplanes."

And then it's okay that Allison doesn't want to come because she remembered that I hate planes.

~

Edith's last secret didn't come while I slept.

"I can't sleep," my mother says. "Go get the champagne."

Edith has kept a bottle of champagne. She bought it after they told her she was dying. She was going to drink it when she wasn't dying anymore.

I climb onto the counter just like when I was a kid to get the good glasses down from the top cupboard. I take a deep breath and count to ten in French, but I only get to *deux*.

On her second glass, Edith tells me she stopped being in love with Tim in 1995. This is ten years before he left her. I pour another glass of champagne and turn on the radio. When I was little, before Allison was born, my parents went driving on Sunday afternoons. They were too poor to do anything else. I stood in the front seat between them, my arm wrapped around my father's neck and we sang, driving down the roads unrestrained. Edith's hair was long and straight, and Tim was young and skinny. I needed them to still love each other. After ten years and my mother dying, I needed to think that even though my father had left, they never stopped loving each other.

I put a finger to my mother's dry lips. She puts her finger to mine. We have the same fingers. They are also my grandmother's fingers and my great-grandmother's fingers. I tell myself to look at Allison's fingers at the funeral.

It's after two a.m. when my mother wants to take a walk. I tug sweatpants on under her nightgown and find an old sweatshirt of my father's with Pitt in peeling, cracked letters. The sweatshirt hangs slack on her angular frame. Days ago she might have resisted his sweatshirt, but tonight she doesn't. I put on a hat and offer her one too. She declines saying she wants to feel the wind in her hair. I half smile at the wispy white curls, not much hair for the wind to blow.

Outside, Caesar walks beside us. His white silky fur sweeps the street picking up bits of dirt, a stubbed-out cigarette butt. The streets are empty and leaves collect in the gutters, on cars, and in windblown patches on the grass. A streetlamp flickers and sputters never able to catch light and shine. My mother has always been a small woman, but now I keep her off the sewage grates for fear she'll slip through the bars. She hooks her arm through mine, but I don't feel it. She only has the energy to walk down to the corner and back. Later that night when I crawl into bed with my mother, upstairs, the fish quits spitting.

Bozicka

Michelle Donahue

We're barreling down a dark mountain road. The engine of our dust-painted Dodge is smoking and leaking gas. At any minute we could explode.

"I fixed it," Manos says as he takes his hands off the wheel to adjust his cap. "This time, I fixed it." He's been saying this about the Dodge for days. He's less than four decades old and Greece hasn't stolen his optimism yet.

We're driving from his small farm and I'm inside, pushed against the car's right door, which sometimes doesn't lock, but seems to be hanging in there tonight. We're all hanging in there. Me: just barely. Jael is sandwiched between Manos and me. She's Danish and like me, is also stuck in her mid twenties, also trying to eke out an existence as an adult. We are the only farm help here. It's strange how I've found myself covered in Greek farm dirt and so far from home, so far from my plans I once made with my now ex-boyfriend Alex. I'd been dreaming of croissants in the shadow of the Eiffel tower, and instead I'm here, squeezed in this rickety Dodge. There really are only two seats in Manos' truck and the back is full of farm equipment: dented shovels, a rusted hoe, splintered plastic crates, a watering can with a hole.

"You all right, Jael and . . ." Manos pauses. I had hoped after last night he would remember my name. "Eleanor?" he says, finally. He taps the tune to "Eleanor Rigby" against the wheel, its beat an echo that blends with the rattling door and tires as they skid down the mountain.

Without Alex and the prospect of seeing him, my future has become unknown. And the smallness of this, my life and my sadness, makes me feel all the emptier. All the more shallow to feel so broken.

"We're good, Man," I say. Manos goes by Man because he says it's *real cool.*

"Bravo, bravo." He claps his hands together, letting the wheel roam free. The nonchalant arc of his tender smile mirrors the lower curve of the steering wheel.

The sun is setting and it's almost dark. It gets a dark I've only seen here in Bozika. It's as if the one hundred residents have made darkness their secret and stored it here in these mountains in the Peloponnese. The only light comes from past the sea, from Corinth, which looks farther than the stars tonight. I can't even see the lights of Kiato, the closest city, though they must be looming somewhere below us, out of sight. I wonder what else lies beneath us, this village and the sea.

It's already too black for me to see where the narrow dirt road ends and the mountain cliff begins. We stayed at the farm too late. It's too easy to let time loose because the farm doesn't belong to the world I know. Among the overgrown tomato plants is a metal face, almost five feet long. It lays flat on the ground, one of Manos' discarded artworks. Weedy flowers grow into the open mouth and empty eye sockets, as if the face were possessed by wildflowers. There's an abandoned jeep, painted lime green with thick pumpkin vines creeping up the sides, and there's a breaking metal shed with handmade metal chairs inside. There's more discarded items than crops at Manos' farm, as if the ground were growing deserted art. I first fell in love with Alex because he was a British businessman who loved art. He was a photographer by hobby only. I loved that contradiction, the practical and the creative.

We stayed too long on Manos' farm because we were feeding the three wild pigs, their hair turning blue in the setting light. We stayed too long because the water was off and it took Manos ages to figure out how to turn it back on. He doesn't know how to work the system because he steals or, as he says, *borrows* water from the large farms encircling his. The farms with acres of chalky grapes ready to be dried for raisins or pressed for wine. Manos borrows the grapes too. He always says, "The fruits are for the people." He frequently stops on the side of the road and scoops grapes into his large hands. He believes in the earth and its unwillingness to be owned.

Manos rolls down the window and it yells in protest. He whips out a cigarette and smokes. Everyone here is a proud chain smoker. I don't like smoke, but while traveling I can tolerate it. Today, I crave it. Manos turns off the headlights.

"I like to drive in the dark," he says. "It's good practice."

Practice for what, I don't know. Practice how to live on the edge. How to almost fly off it.

~

Most nights, after we return from the farm, Jael and I help with Manos' *taverna*. Bozika is small, but people come. Usually, the same people. An old man with wrinkles gullied into his skin and his granddaughter in pink. The daughter always asks for Alethea, Manos' daughter, but she's no longer here. Two young men always come. They escaped from Bulgaria, I think, though they speak no English, only Greek. I communicate with them through smiles and broad gesticulations. I know one Greek word: *yamas*. Cheers.

"Yamas," Jael and I say as we toast to each other, late at night, after the *taverna* customers leave. Manos squeezes fresh orange juice for us and we pour in the vodka, or if we're feeling authentic, ouzo. If Jael and I were real Greeks we'd drink ouzo straight, or else with cold water that turns it cloudy. Sometimes Jael does this, but I don't like that anise taste. Manos drinks cloudy ouzo and orange-vodka, one in each hand.

In the dark, we trade secrets.

Manos says, "My wife left because her mother hated me. Because we never had money. Because I was too lazy." He smokes, shoots some ouzo, takes a sip of his orange juice, those rough, tender hands twisting a paper napkin to shreds. "I don't know." His strong jaw quivers.

"I left Copenhagen because it was just too clean," Jael says. She says Copenhagen like the word is a cannon; she spits out the syllables with her tough, Danish accent. She is a grad-student in Thessaloniki and studies modern Macedonian history. The Greeks call Macedonia FYROM, said like fear-um, which stands for Former Yugoslavia Republic of Macedonia. Jael has told me why countless times, but I can't remember the specifics. It's a debate of ancient blood and history, I think. I'm not used to living in countries with such long pasts. My mind can't understand them. My own past is enough to worry about.

"Why did you leave?" Jael asks.

There are easy answers to this question. I had a job teaching English in Istanbul. I studied in England and fell in love with Europe and wished to return. Other answers are more difficult. I fell in love with Alex in England. I thought he'd be here but we both keep getting stuck in the wrong places. We both need to move, but can't seem to move together.

"Los Angeles got boring," I say.

~

I roll down my window and stick my head out. The darkness is thick now and Manos still hasn't flipped on the car lights. I know it should be fear I feel. But I think this country doesn't abide by the same rules. Instead, I feel excitement. I feel excited to feel something other than sadness.

Jael leans toward me, maybe because she wants some fresh air or maybe Manos smells bad. We're all covered in dirt and pig food. There's rabbit crap and tomato dust under my nails. I've grown accustomed to the smell now.

"You two are way close," Manos says. He puts a lot of emphasis on the "way" as if suggesting something a little less innocent. And it's true, Jael and I are close. We sleep in the same bed because that's all Manos has. And we sleep in very little because of the summer heat. And before sleep every night, we sift through Manos' old magazines from when he used to work for Greek *Playboy*. Before he was a farmer, he was a metallurgist in Athens and built kinky sets for the photo shoots. He always calls himself the "Iron Man" and then winks.

Manos would like it if Jael and I were more than just friends. And though she's attractive and maybe if we were both drunk and desperate enough we might make out, nothing serious will ever happen. Not even when we're bent over a *Playboy magazine.* It's too cliché. Though we don't want to look at *Playboy*, we can't stop staring. The hard breasts are horrifying but also alluring, like a car crash on the side of a freeway.

"The car is just small, Man," Jael says.

He laughs. "This car is a fucking piece of shit." He laughs again. "But we love her!" He kisses the steering wheel several times. His eyes stare at anything but the road. Trees darken off the mountain edge.

"Driving with no lights is good practice," he says again.

Jael and I stare out the window and we try to remember the last bits of Bozika's beauty before the dark steals it. The olive trees bend into shadows and a goat bleats somewhere in that crying darkness.

Manos says, "It's so stupid. Driving with no lights." He taps his fingers on the dashboard. "If another car going the other way is stupid too and has no lights then-" He smacks his hands together. "Boom, nothing." He takes a sharp left and then looks for his pack of cigarettes. "Stupid, so stupid." He holds out his cigarette and Jael flicks the lighter for him. He inhales and looks at us. "Good practice though."

Jael and I share a look. Put like this, we can't deny the danger here, and yet, we still can't gather the required fear. I inhale the secondhand smoke. One night, Jael told me she left Copenhagen because she felt no one there would break the rules with her.

"I jaywalked and people looked at me like a murderer," she said. "I can't live like that."

I understand. I think we travel because we can no longer live at home. We can no longer convince our bodies to be still, to exist within that routine.

Jael lights her cigarette and takes a drag.

"Bravo, bravo," Manos slurs. He slides a look at me and cocks his eyebrow. He's got beautiful, dark eyes.

"Okay?" His mind searches. "Eleanor Rigby?"

I say, "Okay, Man."

It's fully dark now and I can't tell how close we are to the *taverna*. It isn't far from his farm, but the roads are so narrow that Manos is always stopping, backing up side roads and shooting forward another direction so he can take the correct turns. I have no idea where we are.

Jael leans into me and says, in a whisper, "How'd things go last night?" She means with Alex. I have no phone here, but Manos let me use his computer to talk to Alex. I've been avoiding this question all day, but now that I'm stuck here, with half my body pressed against Jael, there's no avoiding it. I have nowhere to go. I've known her for only three weeks, but I'm closer to her than to anyone.

"We broke up," I say, though I feel she's already sensed this. Three years and we break up digitally, his voice a chasm of static. The split happened gradually and all at once like the darkness that has now fully settled upon us.

"Sorry," she says.

And there's nothing to say to this. I could say nothing to Alex. I sat in front of the blank computer screen repeating, "I love you," until even that became meaningless.

Last night, after I finished talking to Alex, I wandered through Manos' house, while I tried to find the bathroom in the dark. I kept running into all of his twisted steel chairs and metal art. I couldn't really concentrate because I was crying too hard. A sharp metal edge snagged my bare leg and the blood dripped warmth onto my skin.

Then I ran into Manos, literally ran into him, and though I couldn't really see him through the Bozika darkness, I could tell he was crying too. Crying has a sound to it, even when it's silent. Like the sound of bone marrow. I thought of Manos' wife, who left him six months ago. She took his kids too: a daughter and a son, both younger than five. I began to understand how something like that could linger. I imagined Manos alone, feeding the chickens and wild turkeys, chalking the tomatoes with volcanic dust, preparing *moussaka* and *souvlaki*. When Jael and I leave and there are no volunteers, I imagined him craving conversation.

"Okay?" Manos paused, his voice soft in the dark. "Eleanor Rigby?"

"No."

"No."

We listened to each other's breaths. I imagined his chest rising and falling. I saw him more vividly than I would if there had been light, as if suddenly he had been presented to me, human and solid. He flipped on the small bathroom light, so the darkness flickered enough to cast heavy shadows on us. My lungs expanding upon my inhale. I felt as if the air should lift me up. I could become a balloon, untethered to this ground. I exhale, a rough collapse.

We stood, both crying in the half-darkness. He was too close to me, wearing nothing but boxers, his dick hanging half out because it really was that enormous. And then, it was even larger.

~

It was good practice, I think. How to live on the edge, how to fly off it. I look out the car window and over the cliff's rim. Everything is black.

"I can't see. I'm lost," Manos says.

I think he's joking, but then who knows. I certainly don't know where I am anymore.

Manos says, "I need drinks to see!" He pulls out a double bottle of Alfa beer from underneath his seat.

"Man." Jael says. For a second, there might be real concern in her voice.

"It's good practice," he says, as he pops the top with his teeth and takes a swig. He passes it to Jael and she drinks. She passes it to me and I down a third in one gulp.

"Bravo, bravo!" Manos says. He pulls out another beer.

He's driving faster now. The left tires skid on the dirt road.

"Jael, Eleanor Rigby, are you scared?" He's smiling with his soggy cigarette in his lips. "I can slow down." His hands grip the steering wheel, his foot remains firm-pressed on the gas. He pops open the second beer.

Jael takes a sip of beer and is still and silent for a moment. Then, she looks at me. It isn't alarm I see in her eyes. Maybe this is what she lives on, the adventure and adrenaline. Maybe we both crave to break the rules. To toe the edge if only so we can see what's past it.

"Should I go slower?" Manos asks.

I look outside the car, at the sky, at the secret darkness and imagine careening off the edge. I close my eyes and smell the sugar of grapes and the salt of the ocean so far below.

"Yamas," I say. *Cheers*. "Go faster."

American as Berbere

Jacob Weber

For Meb, and everyone I know like him

When he was twelve, Tesfay came to the conclusion that all Habesha music had a drumbeat that sounded like somebody had chucked two shoes into a Laundromat dryer, and soon thereafter developed a contempt for Ethiopian music—and perhaps Ethiopia in general—that stuck with him. There had been a few years, soon after he came to the United States at eight, a fugitive of famine and the Derg's policies he knew nothing about, when he would listen with admiration to the beat of the *kebero*, as the horns and *krar* and flute-like thing with the name he couldn't pronounce all worked around it, like pilgrims weaving their strands around a Maypole. But over time, it became harder for the Greater D.C. Tigrayan People's Cultural Center to find anyone who knew how to play the *krar*, so they settled for a competent drum player and a synthesizer. In this arrangement, Tesfay heard only the drum's repetitious "ba-bump, ba-bump" drubbing away at the same speed. It filled him with a sense of futility, that no matter how many times someone hit the drum, the cycle would just keep going around, until someone finally yelled *"d'rub!"* and the drummer sped up to reach the merciful death of the song.

When he first came to the U.S. in 1984, he was a minor celebrity, having appeared as one of the crying children in a rock music benefit for Africa video, his distended abdomen hanging from him like an empty *taff* sack. A philanthropic organization sponsored his mother, younger brother Tsegaye and his sisters Meheret and Azeb to come as refugees. Their three bedroom apartment on the west side of Baltimore had been handed over to the family with some fanfare, newspapers snapping pictures of him and one of the lesser-known stars from the chorus of the rock anthem to end poverty. A councilwoman had even handed his mother the key to the front door. After the crammed-in shanties they had shared with dozens of others at the refugee camps in Ethiopia's Tigray region and later Sudan, having an entire room to just himself and his brother gave him a nauseating sense of agoraphobia. He felt abandoned, and had to keep looking across the room to Tsegaye and watch his younger brother make up stories to accompany the comic books they had been given but couldn't read. Tesfay's first winter in America, he believed his new country was cold because there weren't enough people in it to keep it warm. He came down with pneumonia that kept him out of school for weeks.

A year later, their grant ran out. His mother, who, in one year of attending English classes twice a week had learned nothing but "hello" and "nice to meet you," took a job cleaning bathrooms in office buildings with another Habesha woman who had started her own business. She didn't earn enough to put food in the mouths of her children, let alone pay rent and utilities, so the family had to move in with Aunt Sophia in Silver Spring, near D.C. There were no cameras that came to record the day the family moved out, one garbage bag per person.

Aunt Sophia was a legend in the D.C. Habesha community. She was the sister of Tesfay's late father, who had been killed (martyred, Tesfay would later learn to say) in the struggle against the Derg. Aunt Sophia's own husband had also gone out a martyr. Aunt Sophia made her money selling home mortgages to Habesha families who would not take a loan from anyone who couldn't tell them their interest rate in Tigrinya or Amharic. She must have made a lot of money that way, because she supported half the TPLA back in Ethiopia with what she sent them, along with a large number of destitute souls in America. She had enough left over for a four bedroom with a loft into which her sister-in-law's family could squeeze without too much trouble, although Tesfay and Tsegaye had to share a room with her only son, Robel.

When Tesfay entered the house for the first time, the first thing he noticed was a trophy almost as high as the ceiling. It had four pillars on the bottom, then two more pillars on a second level, and finally a golden man on top holding a stick and twisting his torso with the stick in his hand. Tesfay thought it was made entirely of gold, and believed his aunt must be the richest woman in the world. When he later learned that it was Robel's, he thought Robel must be the luckiest child alive. When he later learned that it was made of plastic with gold paint and worthless, he wondered why his aunt had such a large thing in her living room. When he learned that

Robel had won it for being the best baseball player in his Hot Stove league, Tesfay stopped asking questions.

Tesfay's introduction to baseball came five seconds after he noticed Robel's trophy. He heard his cousin yell "Heads up!" and saw a blur out of his left eye before he felt a crushing blow blind that same eye. He vaguely remembered lying, face up, trying to focus on the stalactites of paint from the ceiling while his aunt screamed in English at her son.

Later, as he was lying on the couch, his cousin was sitting on the floor next to him, holding a Ziploc bag full of ice cubes on his eye. *He-Man* was playing on the television. Tsegaye had already taken Tesfay's bag to their new room. Robel brought Tesfay sodas and held on to the ice for hours, in spite of the awkward crouch he had to maintain on the floor. He looked so uncomfortable, but was so happily optimistic through it, Tesfay started to feel sorry for him. Aunt Sophia seemed to have been won over by his vigilance. She kissed him on the top of his head, called him "Robeley," and sent him to set the table for dinner. Tesfay's mother made injerra and shiro with *berbere* pepper, and Aunt Sophia praised Robel for knowing how to open the prayer with the correct Orthodox incantation.

His mother insisted that both Tesfay and Tsegaye learn to play baseball. Tesfay thought that perhaps his mother mistook "baseball" for the English word "soccer," the only game she had ever heard of. Or maybe baseball was to be part of their education in becoming Americanized, and Robel, holder of the glittering trophy, was to be their mentor.

That spring, Tesfay went to school during the day, where he slowly learned to say he was *confused* rather than *confusing*, to hear the difference between *live* and *leave*, and to contract all sorts of things into shorter things that meant the same thing. He was in the same class as Robel, and sensed his cousin was the sort of student who did not often know the answers, but hid it through a sleight of hand that allowed him to change the conversation at the crucial moment. An ample supply of friends who knew the answers didn't hurt.

Once home from school, Tesfay, Tsegaye and Robel always went straight to the playground to play baseball. Robel was patient in trying to explain how to swing, throw or catch, but when he threw batting practice to Tesfay, Robel would not hold back, and fired one pitch after another as hard as he could past Tesfay, who could scarcely get the bat started before the ball was already past him. Sometimes, Robel hit Tesfay, and they would retreat to the couch in the living room and repeat the scene from Tesfay's first day in the house.

"You have to be careful with your cousin, Robeley," his mother would say in between calls to clients seeking loans. "He's not as good as you."

"I have to throw hard at him, *adey*. The kids in the league are going to throw hard at him."

"Just be careful, Robeley."

Tesfay played on the same team as his cousin. Robel hit third in the lineup, the spot reserved for the best hitter. Tesfay played two innings a game, the minimum each player was required to be in the game, always in left field. While Robel pitched and batted his team to most of the wins they managed that year, Tesfay did not manage once to even put the bat on the ball, or even to walk his way on base. In truth, he was terrified of the ball as a result of being hit so many times, and just hoped to survive his few trips to the plate.

He only ran the bases once. It was the last inning of a game his team was losing by one run, and one of the good hitters at the top of the order managed a double, but hurt himself sliding into second. Robel told his coach that Tesfay was fast, and would be a good pinch runner.

Tesfay was fast. He took a runner's stance at second base, like he had seen others do all season long, and waited while Robel stood in the batter's box. On the second pitch, Robel sent a screaming line drive into centerfield. Tesfay did not wait. He tore off toward third base and rounded third toward home. He was a little awkward as he took the turn, but he was more than fast enough to make up for it. He heard the cries from his bench and the parents of his teammates, and it spurred him on to run even faster. He crossed home plate, and waited for the kids from his team to come running out to congratulate him. It took him some effort to realize that the center fielder had caught Robel's line drive, and thrown Tesfay out at second base, where he had failed to tag up, for the last out of the game. He had been called out at second while he was halfway from third to home. The shouts from his team had been to go back to second. The other team had been laughing at him as he streaked for what he'd thought was the tying run.

Tesfay sat with his head down in the dugout and refused to line up to shake the other team's hands. He did not huddle with his team to hear the coach tell them to shake it off and get the next one, nor did he take a juice box and a bag of chips someone had brought for the after-game snack. He waited until his family was loaded up in the van, then dragged himself to the back seat, not looking at anyone from the dugout to the parking lot. As he sat, his arms crossed and his cap pulled down over his eyes in the van, his mother continually turned around to congratulate him for his performance. He had run so fast, she said. She could not understand that running fast was not the whole point of the game.

Tesfay tried to hide in his room that evening, but Robel and Tsegaye were there. He tried the basement, but Robel followed him there. For the first time, he began to feel that the house he was living in was too small. He eventually opted for the living room, where at least the television was a distraction for others, and he could rely on being ignored. But after *Family Ties* ended, Robel got up and changed the channel to the Orioles game.

"We need to watch so Tesfay knows the rules," he said.

Tesfay did not move quickly, or with any hint of the briskness anger brings, but he stood up from the couch, stepped deliberately to Robel's trophy, and tipped it over with no more effort than he would have used to turn on a light switch. The swinging man on the top of the trophy hit the floor, broke off and ricocheted toward the television, barely missing hitting the screen.

His sisters, aunt, mother and Robel turned to him, as if waiting for an explanation, some improbable excuse about how he had just been admiring it and not meant to smash it. Instead, Tesfay stood, his arms pushed straight down at his sides and ending in two fists balled up like burnt bread.

"You never told me the rules, Robel."

Aunt Sophia started after him first, but when his mother realized what was happening, she quickly jumped up and won the race to Tesfay, pummeling him on the ears with slaps and pulling him by the hair. Robel came to his aid, and tried to get his mother off of him.

"It's okay, Aunt Feven. It's okay! He's right. I didn't tell him the rules."

But he couldn't speak any language Tesfay's mother could understand, and the only words of his language she knew meant nothing right now. She beat Tesfay until he forgot that he was angry, and was only aware that she was hurting him. He tried to ask for mercy, but his throat was so sore from holding back his tears, he could get out nothing except a slight, croaking "*bejahi, adey.*"

~

Tesfay held his balance for ten seconds, twenty, thirty, his left hand holding his left foot aloft behind him. His knee formed an upside-down goose neck while he stretched his quadriceps. He was wearing the headphones his mother had bought him when she took over her boss's cleaning business. They were the best, and he could scarcely hear a thing outside of Brahms' violin concerto. He had loved Brahms since joining the orchestra in seventh grade, because of the way his teacher overpronounced the German: "Bwghaaahms." Tesfay had tried his best to reproduce it at home in front of Robel. Robel, instead of a violin, had a large drum set that he tinkered with sometimes. He tried to introduce Tesfay to Stevie Ray Vaughan, but Tesfay assumed that if Robel liked it, it was probably a bad influence. That was what Aunt Sophia called everything and everyone Robel liked then: a bad influence.

Tesfay never played baseball after that year when he broke Robel's trophy. Robel played through high school, and was good, but not good enough to earn a look from any scouts. Some said he had been too lazy, and relied too much on his talent. Others said he was distracted by tinkering around with music and smoking pot and the girls who had taught him how to groove to both.

So Tesfay became a violin-playing non-athlete, and had the social status to match. Robel once tried to convince some of the school's jocks not to pick on him by telling them that Tesfay had grown up during the famine in Ethiopia. When the school got a hold of a video from the library of him at six, naked with his stomach protruding beyond his infant penis, things took a dangerous turn. Phys Ed was the worst. Anytime he wasn't looking during volleyball or football, a ball somehow found its way to his head. Someone would then come running over to offer profuse apologies and explanations about how the ball had just gotten away from him. The only bright spot was that it was the last period of the day, and Tesfay was spared from showers with his tormentors.

Eventually, Tesfay offered his P.E. teacher a deal. If Tesfay ran the whole time during gym, he would not have to take part in any of the sports being played. Tesfay hoped that if he could turn himself into a moving target, he'd be harder to hit. His teacher never believed that Tesfay could keep moving for 52 minutes, so he took the bargain. Three months later, his gym teacher brought someone to meet Tesfay while he was running his laps.

"This is Coach Vetter. He's the cross-country coach."

Tesfay stopped to say hello, but felt uncomfortable not running. "You mean you travel a lot?" he asked.

Soon, Tesfay had as many trophies in the living room as Robel. Then he had more. His senior year, Coach Vetter stopped Tesfay during a practice to introduce him to someone. It was the largest man Tesfay had ever seen, both in height and width.

"This is Coach De Sapio, Tesfay," he said. "He's the track coach at University of Maryland."

Tesfay shook his hand. Coach De Sapio's eyes were hidden by small, round sunglasses perched on top of his puffy cheeks.

"We've been getting our asses kicked lately by schools with all the best Kenyan runners," the coach said. "We were hoping you could change that."

"Well, I'm from Ethiopia, not Kenya," Tesfay said.

"Well, I won't tell anyone. As long as you can run like a Kenyan."

Tesfay won his first ACC title two years later in the 10,000 meters. He won his second a year after that, a day before he found out Robel had been killed, shot in the head and the forearm. The police did not know who had shot him, but they figured he had been shot in the forearm when someone pointed at his head and he had instinctively put his arm up to shield his face. When Tesfay wanted to withdraw from the nationals, his Aunt Sophia would not let him.

"If I can lose a husband and come to America and start a business, and your mother can lose a husband and come to America and run a business, you can lose a cousin and run around in circles a few times."

He relaxed his hold on his foot, and the final strains of the concerto faded away in his ears. Rather than start a new piece of music so close to the race, he removed his headphones and looked up into the stands. Usually, it was easy to find his mother and sister Azeb. Meheret was off at college herself, as was Tsegaye, although they had sent their love and best wishes. Today, it was impossible to find his family in the crowd, because they were surrounded by a sea of Habesha faces, already bursting at the seams to cheer for him, waving the green, yellow and red flag of Ethiopia. Some wore their traditional white clothing. The heads of a few women were covered by *netsella*. They erupted into cheers when Tesfay looked up at them, and the flags circled happily like the vultures he had once seen descend upon a dead calf in Tigray. Tesfay laughed and waved, but ended his wave with a slight swipe of the hand that hinted at rejection. He wondered if they understood he was trying to qualify for the *American* Olympic team.

Some of the other runners were jogging back and forth along the straightaway, trying to get warm. Tesfay had never understood running as a way to get ready to run some more. He was always ready to run, could wake up in the middle of the night to find Robel was in trouble somewhere and run halfway around the Beltway to get him. At times like that, he would ignore his mother's disapproving looks, the questions about whether it was worth it that even Aunt Sophia began to ask after a while. Tesfay never questioned it when Robel needed help. Even Robel understood that for Habesha people, "family" was the end of an argument.

He had asked his mother once why, if Aunt Sophia was family and so well off, they had not moved in with her at once, or been rescued from the famine earlier by her money. His mother told him that Tesfay's father had wanted it that way. As a comrade of the struggle, he could not allow his family to escape the fate others were facing because they were fortunate enough to have a wealthy relative. He wanted them to fight to live, and through fighting to learn to love what they were fighting for.

The signal came for the runners to approach the starting line. Tesfay felt no nerves at all. To win or lose was in God's hands, just as to live or die was in God's hands. To be rich or poor. To choose a violin and become an Olympic hopeful, or to choose dirty blues and end up dead. All God, God, God. He had heard it so many times it didn't matter if he believed it in his mind. His body believed it.

The gun sounded and Tesfay shot out ahead. He could always tell within twenty strides what kind of a day he would have. Today was a good day, and he wanted to bury the field early, to leave them wondering for so long when he would drop off that eventually the question would slip from their minds, and they would view the race as a race for second.

As he rounded the first turn, he felt a familiar thrum vibrate through him. Someone in the Habesha crowd had brought a *kebero*, and was beating it to spur Tesfay on. It was the wrong tempo for him, though. It was impossible to match up with it, because its two beats landed too close together for him to land left-right in time to the two thumps. He tried to just land on the left foot on the first beat, but that was too slow. He tried to land once between the downbeat and once on it, but that was too fast. He tried to ignore the drum altogether, to recall Brahms or Stevie Ray Vaughn or the silence of slow death, but the *kebero* oscillated though him, blocking other music from his mind. He could not keep his pace, and he slipped from first to second, then to third, then to somewhere in the middle of the pack where he did not know what place he was in.

For lap after lap, he struggled to find his own rhythm again and to break out of the pack. He hated being in the middle of a sea of legs, where one misstep could end in tangled limbs and twisted ankles. Twice, he tried to move to the outside for a push, but each time, the *kebero* would increase the volume, and he would lose his pace and fall back into the pack.

That goddamned drum, that cycle that never stopped, never changed. Birth to famine to death, leaving your children behind to grow to famine and death. Running in a circle, hoping to get somewhere, ending up where you came from. Ba-bump.

He got nowhere through the fourth kilometer, or the fifth, sixth or seventh. He had never liked trying to come from behind in a race. He was either a frontrunner from the gate or that was that. Why couldn't that drum stop? He tried to remember Robel's playing in the basement, when, without ever having had a lesson, he did his best to keep up with *Pride and Joy*. Tesfay had wrinkled his nose at the looseness of the piece, and asked why Robel didn't learn to play decent music.

"Man, don't you know that Ethiopia is the home of the best jazz music in the world? This stuff is your culture."

"That's blues, not jazz."

"Whatever. Same thing."

Whatever. Blues. Jazz. Kenya. Ethiopia. Eight kilometers. Two to go.

Some of the field had fallen off, and he was somewhere around sixth place, in a group with several others competing for second. First place was a Kenyan who went to Stanford Tesfay knew from nationals. Nobody was catching him today.

Tesfay wished he could have grown up longer in the mountains of Tigray, so he could have built his lungs up in the altitude. He tried to recall those highlands. Right before they had left, running in the mountains was the furthest thing from his mind. He had been too tired from hunger to run. But earlier, he remembered—perhaps his earliest memory—running with Azeb and his father and mother. It seemed like the happiest game they were playing, something they were making up on the spot. Tesfay had to tag Azeb, who then had to tag their father, who then would tag their mother. Their father teased their mother as he chased her, flipping her *netsella* down over her eyes as he ran past her. The game went on and on for hours, and they wandered deep into the wild. It wasn't until they returned to the village that night that Tesfay realized that they had actually been running from the Derg, who had come to look for TPLA soldiers. The game was meant to keep the children from being frightened. Tesfay wondered what it would look like if he went back now, where the TPLA--now the EPRDF and in charge of the country--was said to be building all over Tigray.

There were 500 meters to go when Tesfay heard the shrill, banshee-like ululation from the Habesha women. The drum increased its pace. Tesfay realized that this was the *d'rub*, the final part of the song. They were trying to send him down the homestretch with everything they had left. Without needing to think about it, Tesfay fell in step with the faster rhythm. First place was out of the question, but he only needed to finish third to qualify for the Olympics. And he had never saved this much for the end of a race before.

He pushed harder. The trilling of the women's voices became louder. It was a funny custom, Tesfay had always thought. It sounded like ghosts coming from out of the grave, but it was meant as a welcome. Women generally made that noise when a loved one returned after a long time. Life is short, and we love you. We are glad you made it back. He careened around the turn toward the corner of the stands where his people were gathered. The flags bounced along with the white clothes, and the colors bled together into all the colors in the world.

He ran for Ethiopia. He ran for America. For Robel, for his father. For whatever. He ran for the finish, for home.

Picking Raspberries

Tamie Parker Song

There has been a blow and the waves keep coming, radiating against the beach—and I do mean against—and we just have to take it. The men enter it but I don't, at first. I've had too many weeks, too many years, fear-sickened by the wave of each wave above our rolling boats, again and again and again. I've done this my whole life, commercial setnetting for salmon off a small island in the Gulf of Alaska, but somehow today I just can't.

I stay on shore for the first net-pick, but my stomach heaves anyway because people I love are out in that blow, so on the second pick I go out, and no sooner have I reached the net than the ocean goes calm, as if to my touch.

On the break between the second and third picks, my cousins invite me to pick wild raspberries with them in the inner lagoon. The sea is hot blue now, flat-calm as they say. And we are picking raspberries. We came straight from fishing so we've all worn boots, arms spread with fish scales and traces of jellyfish. What is a wild raspberry if not the sun's blood as known by faith and rain and dirt? The raspberries are wild, as wild as you can get and still be on Earth. We are picking wilderness in thickets higher than our heads, tangled with the nettles and rose thorns and stinging pushki.

We all get stung, my cousins and me, by the nettles, the pushki, the thorns, and the stinging is indistinguishable from jellyfish, sunburn, sweat. The hurting slant of hillside, the startling slash of ocean open-palmed in bounty, drawing blood with the same hand. We're used to it. We take it with salt. We take it, but that does not mean we are resigned. We'll pick these raspberries, we *will* take these raspberries: fuck the bears, the nettles, the pushki, falling tide, sunburn, the muddy ground sucking at our boots, our hunger from fishing all day. Raspberries reddening our fingers, raspberries sweet as grief.

The raspberries are growing all around the cabin that my parents lived in during their honeymoon summer forty years ago. No one has lived in that cabin since, but we still call it Honeymoon Lagoon. The windows are long gone, floor risen toward roof—Earth coming to gather herself—but the linoleum still shines and a blue-painted cupboard still opens when I pull. We walk inside, look around, touch a copper tea kettle tipped on the floor. I can imagine a bed, I can imagine my mother, young and wholly ready to try something lonely and wild for love. I can imagine my father, sincere, truly believing he is able to hammer up a shelter against weather and wilderness, against his own need. Out the pane-less window, I see the view my mother must have seen every day that summer—the inner lagoon, the Alaskan Peninsula. I see the way everything has grown up now, how all that is done, has been over a long time.

We half-fill our buckets with soft raspberries, talking so the bears will know we are here, pushing against stalks and vines with our booted shins, making way for ourselves. And that is how it is in the third generation of this family: the nettles grow up together with the raspberries, so close you can't pick a berry without being nettled. But we're used to being stung, and we so want those berries. Even in half-filled buckets the berries at the bottom get crushed. I hardly eat any, as I pick. Later, once I'm home, I eat none, nor share any. Instead, I freeze mine, knowing I will want these berries more in winter than I want them now.

Then we go out for our last net pick of the day, hauling in the blue-bodied, red-fleshed salmon. The sun is on the rim-edge of the horizon. The sea is a haunted child, safe now.

Mourning with Strangers

Maggie Nye

On our second trip to New Orleans, my mother and I sat with a stranger at the covered bus stop on St. Claude at Poland Avenue. She was an older black woman, worn-out looking but tidy in her appearance. A dark floor-length skirt and her grey-streaked hair pulled tight and tucked away. My mother later called her dress conservative. *It was her teeth,* she said, *that made her look old. Her mouth was caved-in. I don't remember her mouth particularly, but my mother is careful always to note the qualities that make a woman look old. I do remember thinking I ought to give the woman my seat and that she accepted it. My mother and I were riding a bus to the streetcar that would take us to the Garden District and Lafayette Cemetery No. 1 and we were mourning. When we are together, no matter what we are doing, we are mourning, always and evenly as breathing.*

~

Without knowing it, we picked New Orleans to be the center of our mourning. Historical places are good for that—they let you nestle your small sadness inside their larger sadness, grief consecrated with plaques and statues. How many times did we say *He would have loved it here*?

Altogether, the city and Orleans Parish are 380 square miles, only 180 square miles of which is land—the rest is water, bayous and the Mississippi. And dispersed along the 180 square miles of land are 40 cemeteries, a cemetery every four and a half miles.

I am from an affluent suburb in Maryland where death is unsightly and grief, like shame, is a private affair marked only by the delivery of white lilies on a doorstep. Far enough North to have inherited Puritanical sensibilities, modesty in all things. There, we keep ourselves so far away from death that as children, when we passed graveyards, we held our breath so that no molecule of death could enter into us.

In New Orleans, I seek a new culture, whatever isn't native, not to wring out but to filter myself into. I cannot say why it is I am compelled to

217

graft my loss onto a city that owes me nothing, to inscribe my tribute of mourning in the margins of necropolis marble.

Every walking tour there wanders through one of the cities of the dead—the name the living city gives its counterpart, as prominent as an afternoon shadow. Indeed, many of these graveyards resemble a city in miniature. The gated crypts in their rows like streets, sturdy and ornate, all have front doors. And the walls of vaulted graves, stacked neatly, each with its own entrance, appear like marble motels. You can imagine a mailman in funeral black navigating the overgrown alleys between the cryptic houses, delivering dead letters—offers for credit cards with no spending ceilings.

On such a tour, we paused in queue as our guide explained how the city's high water table necessitates above-ground burials so that the dead do not float out of their coffins after the first posthumous rain. To prepare for the homecoming of a new body, space must be created. *As for the old corpse*, said our guide and demonstrated a two-handed plunging gesture, which meant down they go.

~

Corpse is a cruel word when applied to any body with whom you've shared a bath.

~

The word corpse, from the Latin *corpus* referred, in Middle English to the living body. I do not know how we, the speakers of modern English constructed such grim associations, but I hate the word. Now, only the pronunciation of the letter 'p' distinguishes our verbal understanding from the word 'corps,' a group of people united by a common purpose, or, in French, as in Middle English, simply a body.

~

We suffer from the plosive sound of 'p', that necrofying consonant.

~

In the weeks following my brother's death, my mind played tricks on me: I heard him sing down the sidewalk outside of my mother's house in goofy falsetto, I smelled him everywhere: a combination of old man undershirt and sweet sausage. And, of course, I saw him. At a crosswalk, at the grocery store, in the parking lot, I would stop and stare into the faces of young men I did not know, dissecting their features with scientific concentration to disprove the impossible. In these moments, the resurrecting silence of 'p' and he became corps, living briefly in the bodies of strangers, glancing at me through strange eyes.

I still experience these illusions sometimes, even after twenty months. Recently, I stole a long look at one of my students while he was occupied by a quiz for which he had not studied. He had the same over-stuffed cheeks and rounded chin and the same pointed nose. He lacked, however, the look of perpetual inquiry my brother had when he wasn't too stoned to focus. These days though, I'm more interested in the similarities—in trying to reconstruct his face from the collected features of passers-by.

~

The correct procedure for making space is as follows: the remains of any body entombed for over two years may be removed from its casket and stored in a burial bag, which is transported to the back of the crypt to make space for the new body. In four more months, when my grief will have shrunken and softened, I should be ready to accept new grief, to advertise the coming vacancy.

~

We fussed over who would pay and the woman watched us.

Four dollars for an all-day and you can ride the rails until 3 am, *she said, nodding at us,* but don't give them a twenty and expect change. They won't give you any.

We fingered through the bills in our wallets. Neither of us had singles. Hurry over and buy something at the Dollar General, *said the woman,* while the bridge is up.

Run, *said my mother and I did, right across the traffic of Poland Avenue.*

~

My brother was a voracious and unbiased listener. He listened to smooth jazz radio personalities, documentary film makers, idiot friends, conspiracy theorists, pseudo-scientists, and YouTube spiritual gurus and rejected nothing. It was even possible for him to embrace contradictory beliefs, accepting the logic of both as unequivocally valid.

So unlike me, he was a generous vessel. Bodily too, only an inch taller and over a hundred pounds heavier, accepting into his mouth whatever was accessible regardless of nutrition or taste. Where I reject whatever is beyond satiation—selfishly I cherish the limits of my container, admit only what satisfies, he had no limits but stretched always, widened as he grew older to make room for more.

~

Therein lies the danger of being over-filled. The elasticity of his belly skin bearing the purple-white scar bolts.

~

To a lesser extent, my mother also possesses this ability to accept and to hold. She is a woman with an alarming ability to unbody secrets from strangers. As Epsom salt can painlessly bring a splinter to the surface of skin, so too can she. It makes sense that such a gift should be passed matrilineally as women, I believe, are both better witnesses and have a deeper reservoir for the storing of sadness. Though truly, I am not her inheritor.

When she calls, the secrets of strangers slide down the East coast and empty themselves into my room. A shin-deep flood. The other day, she told me a neighbor woman whom she had met only twice revealed to her that she had caught her husband grinding himself against a younger lover as she was bent over and illuminated in the midnight light of the open refrigerator. Some of these strangers are victims of infidelity, some of loss. All of them grieve.

~

What else but grief is a secret?

~

Above all things, my brother listened most hungrily to jazz, that arterial music that conveys its blood so generously. Miles Davis, John Coltrane, Pat Metheny, Wes Montgomery, Herbie Hancock, Victor Wooten, Theolonius Monk.

I confess I have never understood jazz in all of its nuances, even finding it boring at times, like a long story that refuses conclusion.

Down the street, the Saint Claude Avenue Bridge, a bascule bridge, which connects (or separates) the Upper Ninth Ward to the lower was drawn over the industrial canal below. I read that in the days following the aftermath of Katrina, people took refuge from the flood atop the bridge. I can't find any pictures to corroborate this report and I think about the article writer, shivering alone, on top of the bridge, nestled in a soggy sleeping bag,

looking down into the fast brown water before he sleeps and wondering what
unseeing eyes might be looking up.

It was a windy day in late March and the sun, still a little feeble at mid-
morning, couldn't dry up the fine gray mist that lingered on from winter, a
saturating lens on the grime layered over this part of the city. I was happy for
the errand, the urgency of this race against the bus. I like to be in motion and
I preferred to be dodging traffic, unresting, than to be sitting at the stop,
talking with a woman I didn't know.

~

On the last night of my brother's life, a rumba played on the car radio.
I wanted to change the station. For me, the music was excessive in its
happiness. He swatted my hand from the dial and said there was *no such
thing.*

~

There is no too much. To distinguish what is desirable from what is
excessive: this is a fiction of privilege.

~

Jazz, which thrives on improvisation does not adhere to the meter of
desirability in the way that classical music does, for example, executed with
fine muscular control. Instead, it is porous and flexible, temperamental
even, absorbing atmosphere, bending time and space to express all
impulses from the nearly silent to the utterly explosive. Buddy Bolden and
blue note.

Behind a chain-link fence in Mid-City, a chipping white wooden sign
announced HOLT CEMETERY in blue letters punctuated by cartoony red
asterisks like a sign for a pop-up Christmas shop. My mother and I went
there, behind the parking lot of Delgado Community College on a
recommendation from Bywater minor celebrity and self-proclaimed folk
artist, Dr. Bob, whose day-glo *Be Nice or Leave* signs, with their bottle-cap
frames hang on the walls of nearly every restaurant in the city. *It's all
Spanish moss and shit,* he told us. *You'll love it—or your camera will.* And he
was right.

I took dozens of pictures of the potter's field cemetery where the Live
Oaks gave shade to graves like sandboxes, small squares of land framed
simply with wooden beams, some of them littered with dead children's
toys: molding stuffed dogs and dark-skinned dolls, their plastic faces fading

221

pale. The uncelebrated cemetery with its underground burials and makeshift headstones on painted pedestrian street signs and wooden paddles. I read that shallowly buried bones sometimes burst through the soft ground, companions, in spring, for the yellow dock and clover. A cemetery with no regard for permanence, like the dead buried there, the city's poor, for whom the tides of storms change all histories rooted to the ground.

Holt, in German, means to fetch or take away. Even the cemetery's most famous resident, the enigmatic jazz cornet player, is absent from his body. Only his name, Charles Joseph "Buddy Bolden" is contained in his memorial, which, unlike the handmade others, mimics the look of expensive graves in other parts of the city. Bolden's body, separate from his stone-carved name, lies in an unmarked grave nearby. In memorial, in absentia, after 83 years, whatever remains of him there has given itself over to the cemetery's other dead. What goes on there underground, in those unlined graves, how the bones trade places and how they embrace.

~

There was a worm-holed chicken crate in the basement of my childhood home, which my brother and I would lock ourselves into, wound around each other, indistinguishable. Though we would fast outgrow the space, I'm sure we fell asleep like that.

~

In his 1976 novel *Coming Through Slaughter*, Michael Ondaatje imagines the disparate pieces of Bolden's mythos into a man fighting to keep himself together. Ondaatje imagines him a communal repository in life, permeable and limitless: *His mind was the streets* and now, here in Holt, slums of the dead, so his body is the city. And the music that rises is unbridled, uncontainable. On Bolden's gravestone: *THE BLOWINGEST MAN SINCE GABRIEL.*

~

The bridge was still up when I exited the dollar store. My mother, I knew from across the street by the way her hands moved so excitedly, was deep in conversation with the woman. And because my mother inspires such candor in strangers, I returned to hear the woman's account of the personal devastation she had suffered. I lost three, *she told us, though mostly she told my mother.*

Her dad, her nephew, and her daughter, also named Katrina. Ain't that funny? *She lived in the Upper Ninth Ward and the three she lost, just across the bridge. There was a mandatory evacuation and she went to Houston but her dad, she said,* didn't want to come. *He had lived through Betsy in 1965 and* he just didn't want to come.

~

Tennessee Williams writes of *blue piano* in his famous New Orleans-based play *A Streetcar Named Desire.* There are seven mentions of *blue piano* in the play, though one feels, reading the script that in fact, the *tinny piano being played with the infatuated fluency of brown fingers* never stops, nor never truly begins, but exists in perpetuity, organically as birdsong or the noise of traffic.

I do not know if Williams' insistence on the brownness of the fingers is a visual contribution to his focus on colors, if he intended to exoticize the sultry atmosphere of the Marigny neighborhood for his all-white audiences or if he meant to suggest that such blueness could not be achieved by white fingers. Of the *blue piano*, Williams says only that *it expresses the spirit of the life that goes on here.*

Blue piano is Williams' invention. The blue note, however, or worried note, as it is sometimes called, is a common jazz device, though to call it a device suggests an artifice that does not exist in jazz in the same way sonic devices exist in strictly scripted music where a composer's *cresc.* denotes an increase in volume on the part of the musician and, as it is conventionally understood by an audience, emotion. The blue note is played or sung at a pitch just below the major scale, typically a semitone or less. A spasm of unconscious chill deforms the thin skin of the neck and next to the mouth until the muscles find ease again.

I understand the measured temperament of the aria, the comfort in the possibility of precise duplicability, pure, arithmetical beauty that vibrates in the cavities of the face. In high school chamber chorus, my best friend and I would play a game where she would sing a sustained note and I would sing an overlapping note a half-step below her and we would slide our voices, as slowly as one breath would allow, toward one another, willfully resisting unison. This dissonance requires force of will. Our classically trained ears were desperate for harmony and could not maintain contradictory truths. Our voices collapsed to vocal embrace. We could sustain our breath for 20 seconds before our voices began to waver. We had to focus so intently on the space between our individual pitches that I wondered, even when I knew we had resolved, if our voices could ever meet, if we could ever really shudder off our blueness.

~

I sometimes found my brother's blue notes around the house. Written on car dealership envelopes, smeared in the clumsy left-handed graphite smudge of a child: *Because my mind was off the bad part for a while, when I came back to it I got scared and thought that feeling good had brought some feeling bad when really it was there the whole time.*

~

The woman's eyes welled up and the tears that passed over her cheeks did not make her lip tremble, did not make her raise a compulsory finger to dab at her eyes, did not make her turn her face away. They were matter-of-fact tears and they belonged to her story.

The hurricane hit at three, four in the morning when you're getting that real good sleep.

I asked my mother later what the woman's name was and she said it had seemed too personal a question to ask.

~

On the car ride back to my new home in Tuscaloosa, I listened to an interview with New Orleans neo-soul singer Ledisi. The interviewer, pleased with Ledisi's adherence to melody over flourish, asked her about the intentionality of her music. To which Ledisi replied, *I always focus on if you can whistle it. Like if you're on a bus ... I want to be with you everywhere.* This desire for omnipresence, I found so striking. The album's titular song, *The Truth*, opens with the lyric *Like a hurricane, without warning.* The confrontation of a relationship's end—the transition from love-death to the unnamable aftermath, which she describes as a kind of joyful release. Her melodic company imparts her personal loss on her listener, not as a burden, but a generosity.

~

To lose together with a stranger is a gift of love.

What We Say

Paul Crenshaw

It's the 4th of July and we're sitting in our uniforms, hot and sweating and half-drunk in the last sunlight, when the reporter asks to interview us about the war.

This is 1991 and the troops have just returned home. There are parades in every city, the entire country rejoicing over the victory in the Gulf, which is, we have been told, a victory for democracy and the forces of good in the world.

Now the fireworks have started, unfurling overhead, concussions echoing off the sides of the buildings, fire mirrored in the glass towers of downtown Columbia, South Carolina, not far from Fort Jackson, where we are in the second half of our military training. A few hours earlier we had assembled near the mirrored buildings, then marched through streets packed with thousands of people waving little flags, the air so hot it was sucked from our lungs, the asphalt burning beneath our boots while a military band played "Off We Go Into the Wild Blue Yonder" and "The Army Goes Rolling Along" and "The Star-Spangled Banner." People cheered from every street corner. They hung from the windows of the buildings as fighter jets flew overhead and helicopters landed in parking lots so people could crawl inside them and imagine engaging the enemy.

After the parade there was a huge celebration in the city, streets blocked off by policemen with mirrored eyes. Loudspeakers played music and food trucks sold hot dogs and hamburgers and a general sense of revelry hung in the hot air. Freed from parade duty, my friends and I wandered the vendor stalls, all of us eighteen or nineteen years old, just out of high school or just starting college. Several times we were stopped by civilians who thanked us for our service, but when we explained that we had been stateside for the war and had not fought, we received strange looks, some of them angry, as if we had set out to deliberately deceive the entire gathering and perhaps the entire United States, so we began to accept the thanks, nodding our heads and taking on pensive looks, saying, "Well, it was about what you'd imagine," and "Of course you got scared at times," when asked what the war had been like.

As the afternoon lengthened into evening the beer trucks rolled in, and the celebration continued. The loudspeakers played "God Bless the USA" a dozen times, then two dozen. They played "Born in the USA" and "The Times They Are A-Changin'" and everywhere we went men shook our hands and women hugged us. People stood in groups, arms around each other, swaying back and forth to the music, loudly proclaiming how proud they were to be Americans.

A year earlier, in August of 1990, we'd been in Basic Training when Saddam Hussein invaded Kuwait, and every morning we received updates on the battle groups slipping through the Suez Canal, the Airborne divisions activated, the numbers of troops massing in the Middle East. We heard about Hussein's chemical weapons, his Republican Guard, his SCUD Missiles, and we practiced every day for chemical and biological and nuclear attacks.

By the time the war started, I was in college. I spent most nights in my dorm room, reading newspapers I stole from the library or watching live coverage on CNN. My step-father and step-brother were fighting in the war, and my roommate and I got swimming drunk every night in our room watching the bombs fall on Baghdad, ghostly images of explosions lighting the city, anti-aircraft fire streaking skyward. When my step-father returned he told me of the artillery battles, of the jets thundering past, of night turned the color of hell. The oil wells always burning on the horizon, the black haze of hovering smoke, the air shimmering from the heat. The way the light bends in the shockwaves of bombs. The constant rumbling of engines, the ground shaking beneath his feet, a pit of fear always forming in his gut that they would be gassed.

Now, as night falls, we lie back on the grass as fireworks begin to light up the city and a chant rises from the gathered crowd. We drink until the world spins around us. Sweat tracks like tears down our faces. We are hot and tired from marching, from standing in the sun all day, from the constant noise. All around us people watch the fireworks hitting high above the buildings, their faces lit in the brief white flashes, the reports echoing sharply from the glass and steel.

When the reporter comes we look at one another, smiling a little, drunk with heat and alcohol and what passes for pride. We stand and wipe the sweat from our eyes, then give answers just as stupid as the ones we gave before, saying, "We only did what we had to do," and "We're just happy it's all over with."

By the time the interview ends and the cameraman snaps our picture a crowd has gathered behind us. In the picture there is no war. No visions of destruction like we had seen on TV or heard about from those who experienced it firsthand. No bombs exploding overhead. No vehicles bullet-riddled along the sides of the road, no empty streets where people huddle in fear. Just fireworks lighting the night sky, a drunk crowd chanting "USA USA," as if the war had been a football game and the outcome only as important, and when I try to remember that moment now, I see faces red from the day's lingering heat, eyes squinted in the light of what looks like exploding bombs, none of us with any idea what we are saying.

Winter 2015

It's Summer This Dream

Mitchell Untch

Wind circles. Apricots fall.
Noises from the highway drift upward.
Like water from streams that splinter
against rocks, a car horn becomes a splash,
an arrival that moves toward then
away from me, the only thing that opens
the day's stillness, stirs nests.
Early, I feed the horses, fill troughs,
ice I break with warmer water.
In the afternoon I stalk crows, hunt lizards.
I pitch stones across the surface of pond.
Each one flies further than the last,
each one, a note that rings.
I count the circles of sunlight.
I run through sheets my grandmother
pins on the clothesline, wrap myself
up like a ghost, turn my face into a mask.
I live inside the laughter I become.
Where my voice takes shape,
my arms fly open, wide as barn doors.
Let's say it is fearlessness.
Let's say it is the completeness of love.
Let's say it is being for all the right reasons,
here, where my grandmother sits
in her lawn chair, quiet as silk, here,
where the brim of her hat scoops upward,
a veil of shade I sail past as she watches me
squirt the wind with the garden hose,
shake the water from my hair,

my laughter as loose as I will ever know it,
all these years gone, like the ringing
on the pond, where a breeze shuffles
through me, thick with love.
It's summer this dream.
And she is the breeze. She is the pond.

If Mourning

Jane O. Wayne

then the waves swooning
      at the foot of the beach
and the letting-go that lets
a body float when nothing's left
         but surrender,
    world without gravity,
grief, the sea's crescendo
      that drowns out everything—
it could happen again.
      I could be standing on the dock,
    waving to an ocean-liner,
farewell streamers still in the air—
      and all around, the vacancies
and dislocations—solids turning
into liquids.
I might open my mouth
to call, and my voice fail,
      instead a shrill would start,
a thread tearing
between my teeth no one else
       can hear,
some terrible high A—tinny
and relentless.
      Come night I'll dream past
the bridge where
the figure stands in the painting—
and keep walking, hands
      clasped to my ears.

Foreign Hand

Mark Mitchell

He ties fresh knots in old silk. He spells names
in an alphabet he can't remember.
This awkward business matters to someone
whose face is out of reach of the mirror.
His fingers work. They think he plays a game,
these commuters. They will never get where
they mean to go. The silent train just runs
through each dull stop. Nothing's close, nothing's near.
He mutters words that aren't even plain
to him, but hold their dusty power.
Each knot, each fragile slip of silk becomes
something he fears—a pure, perfect cipher
his mother would decode, except the grave's
her home. He can't pull an answer from there.
He's alone on a train. His work isn't done.
He'll never make this language go clear.

Ritual with Fish Water

Jennifer Givhan

When the doorbell rang this time, she knew
      it would be different. The driftwood
of his shoulders knocked his rigid chest

like hooves. Her floating man. "This
      rotten world," he said almost before she could
react, "it's half-gutted, isn't it?" Did

she nod? She opened the door wider, allowed
      him in—dragging his fish, his strings of light,
his wounds—from the rain. She didn't feel hope,

exactly, nor dread. "A drink?" she asked.
      "Scotch," he said, folding
to unfold as an origami lantern on her couch,

muddying her pillowslips. She said nothing.
      She'd gone on living without
his good nights beating against her

like a broken radio signal. "I've missed you—"
      She watched him hold his glass restlessly,
a bit of brine pooling at his pant legs, his loafers.

"There's albondigas on the stove." Out of habit,
      "Will you stay? Can you eat?" He set down
his empty glass, picked up some walnut husks

from their little basket on the table
　　　and began cracking them on his knees,
her prince of gnats and ache, her shining

mollusk king, debuting from death in
　　　minor latch and key. "Hey, look. Dorothea—"
But she lurched toward him anyway. There'd be no

confetti tonight. No clean pears on the windowsill.
　　　"You need to know what I'm here for," he tried
again, not quite pushing her back, not quite

accepting her embrace. "Never mind that,"
　　　she said, her neck growing scaly, salt
spindling her hair. She waited for the drowning—

Remake: The Kiss

Colleen Abel

Again, we fuck
to a soundtrack:
Baby Einstein's Classic

Lullabies. The plink
and wretched plonk
of toy piano,

tinny synthed cello
buzzing *Die Moldau*
or Pachelbel's syrupy

trill. The baby
won't sleep deeply
without it, wakes

in the silence
at the slightest
sound: a moan

or gasp, inane
words we murmur
to each other.

So we go
soundless. After, we
exhaust, the blear

of not-quite-
Mozart casting us
toward sleep, bodies

fused in this:
something close, though
not-quite-bliss.

The Take This Job and Shove It Ode

Stephanie Lenox

Soon the children will come home having learned
new obscenities to hurl at each other
across the cul-de-sac, meaning "end of the road,
bottom of the sack that is your body."
Division and subdivision, each weekend
there is a new fence hewn from raw wood
that draws more hornets, too many wind-chimes
at the mercy of weather. Your son has a puzzle
in a frame with one piece missing
that he pushes around and around
trying to make a picture. Your dog lacks control
and greets you so ferociously you fear
one day he will turn on you and eat your face.
What other life did you think was possible?
Sit down, you're having spaghetti again, and yes,
you must finish it. There are days when you are the best human
humanly possible. And then there are all the others.
Failure, you will say in your next interview,
is an opportunity. Like the open window a bird flew in
was an opportunity for the lazy housecat.
You want to scream, *Because of you I'm ruined!*
You have not slept well this past decade.
At the office, there is a cake that says *Farewell.*
It is loaded with frosted roses
and it would be a shame not to partake.
A co-worker confides: *It's only the first and last*
weeks that they even take note of you.
They, meaning management, handing you a balloon
and an engraved pen, smiling.
You are closer to the last week of your life

than the first, so squalling naked in a crowded room
would be hardly appropriate now.
Your boss once said, *Don't you ever think?*
And you thought, I will have my revenge,
not like the others. I will take retirement
from these sons and daughters of bitches and never
look back. There is no sense explaining
to a beetle what it means to be you,
to get your kind of mail, to feel the electricity
up-surging through joints every time you rise from bed.
The sun goes down and everyone heads into
separate living rooms to watch different shows.
With such flickering, you might think
we have something in common. Oh, but we do.
The boss is the same everywhere and for everyone,
an asshole in a black suit holding a flaming cake,
coming closer and closer, and beyond that, the door.

R is for Rhoda Consumed by a Fire

J.R. Tappenden

from Edward Gorey's Gashlycrumb Tinies

She burns as only little girls can,
her whole body turned to heat
and light, arms and legs mere arcs
of dark ink against the white
space of her hatred, her ire. The drapery,
the carpet can only hope she'll
allow their embrace against the flames
before it's too late.
                    But the wall
has seen this all before and recedes.
He could feel her heart begin to brew
while she hid behind the couch, knew she'd soon
be desert dry and ripe for the lightning
of her mother's voice, calling her to come out
and say she's sorry, when Rhoda,
very definitely, is Not.

The Pleasure Dome

William Black

Our father came home grumbling and smelling of motor oil, axle grease, and beer. He pushed past my brother and me as we tried to fit our fingers through his belt loops and wrap ourselves around his legs. We followed him to the bedroom, where he fell back onto the bed like a timber, and we each took a boot, unlaced it, and struggled to pull it off, our father saying, "Come on now, boys. Come on and pull like a couple of mules." When we finally yanked them off, stumbling backward from the sudden release, there were his toes, dirty and unclipped, peeking through the holes in his socks, and we jumped on him, crashing down on his arms and chest, pinning him with everything we had, only to find ourselves somehow aloft, balanced in his huge hands, and then brought down on our backs, forefingers pressed fast to our sternums, both of us immobilized at once, held helpless and ticklish beyond belief. We half-laughed and half-screamed for our lives.

"So," he said, his beery breath warm and close. "Have I earned a moment's peace and quiet?"

"Yes yes yes!" Though we would have said anything to win our release.

He let us go and we stood. Our clothes, the bedspread, all smeared with his sweat and black grease, and our mother appeared in the doorway to usher us out, redirecting our attention to our chores.

I took the meat scraps our mother had set aside and fed the hound dogs in their chain-linked pen. My brother laid out clean clothes for our father when he was finished with his shower. Together we set the table and then took our seats to wait quietly, as we had been taught, for supper to be served.

When our father reappeared, he was clean-shaven and changed into the t-shirt and shorts my brother had laid out for him. His hair was wet and combed back off his face. He looked relaxed and restless at once, inspecting the table. When he saw no beer by his plate, he got one from the fridge. Our mother said she could not stop him from drinking, but she would not serve him either.

After supper, when our plates had been scraped clean and set in the dishwasher, our father poured bourbon over ice, and we were sent to our room. There, we could do anything we wanted until lights out. Mostly, we turned on the TV and waited for dark, and as it came, we leaned on our windowsill, looking out on the backyard, where our father sat in his folding chair, parked in the middle of the lawn, with a long view across the wooded valley and distant hills. Our father surveying the land. What would have been his land. Once his grandfather's land, bought because someone someday would want the anthracite still buried under the valley floor. Then his father's land, parceled out and sold before he left our father's mother, cash being easier to hide from her lawyers.

Darkfall obliterated the view, and the lights of the Pleasure Dome came up. From the deepest spot in the valley, a pastel glow that lit the hazy air, coral pink, aquamarine, otherworldly colors hanging like aurora borealis above the black trees. Spotlights cut through the colors, sending white beams into the sky, illuminating the undersides of clouds, swiveling, crossing each other, separating again.

"The fall of man," our father had told us about the Pleasure Dome, because he knew how we loved the lights. "The beginning of the end of things," he said. Or in a different kind of mood, "The end of the end of things," and the hound dogs started up, like warning sirens. Sending their mournful sounds across the nighttime valley to come back as echoes. Soon it would be lights out.

Once, our father took us there. "Want to see what those lights are all about?" he asked. We were all three crammed across the bench seat of his truck, and my brother and I bounced up and down with joy. Our father nodded and turned off the road home. He drove down the steep hills, along narrow two-lane roads we'd never seen before, all of it crowded by tall trees. The air smelled of the paper mill nearby. The river came into view, and along it, a stretch of three or four abandoned houses. Then woods again.

When we got there, the building was cinderblock, painted midnight blue and speckled with glittery stars. Across the front wall, *THE PLEASURE DOME* was written at an upward angle; behind the words, a comet-like tail stretching away into the cosmos. The door was huge and metal and red. And then we were inside. Five or six men sitting alone at their tables, wet-looking bottles of beer before them. Cigarette smoke hanging in the air. We knew what kind of men these were. Men who used to work in the mines, now men without jobs. We saw them everywhere in those days. Their hands were hard and heavy as stones and useless. They watched the woman doing her slow, sad dance. Above and below her, colored lights pulsed. Red, yellow, blue. Until someone told my father we weren't allowed.

We waited outside, stretching ourselves to make human rocket ships that launched along the trajectory of THE PLEASURE DOME, traveling among the painted stars, making the sonic noises of spaceflight. Then growing bored and throwing pebbles from the driveway at the parking lot lights. Then throwing them at each other. Until our father appeared, ruddy-faced and a little unsteady.

We climbed into his truck. He asked, "Are you happy you saw it?"

"Yes!" we said, with enthusiasm, as though we hadn't seen what we'd seen.

Back up the switchbacking roads, watching for glimpses of The Pleasure Dome through the trees, until we couldn't see it anymore, and then it was dark and the lights came on. From here, they were even more awe-inspiring than from our bedroom window, the fuzzy pastel glow reaching through trees, until we were above it looking down, a spaceship landed in our valley. The spotlights like laser beams piercing the sky. We leaned our heads all the way back to see how high they went.

We pulled in the driveway at home, and the dogs went crazy with barking, their sounds urgent rather than mournful. *Watch out, watch out!* they cried. *Danger is near!*

Our mother was furious. She had fixed supper but had no one to feed the dogs or set the table or eat what she had made, and now it was ruined.

"Where have you been?" she wanted to know. "Where the hell have you been?"

We told her what our father had instructed us to tell her. "We have been to the end of the universe," we said. "We have seen the end of everything."

Heart of Glass

Daniel Enjay Wong

Mrs. Walker sat alone. I recognized her immediately. I thought it was funny because a Blondie song was playing, and she kind of looked like Blondie from the comic strip. She still had that big yellow nest of hair.

Until then, I'd really only known her as the astronaut's wife. Rich Walker was the most famous person in our town. When he and Mrs. Walker came to our school's Space Adventure Day last year, he introduced her only as "my love." I remembered her smiling the way a lot of my friends' moms smiled. Like it stung.

I wandered between empty chairs to the back of the room where Mrs. Walker was sitting. Earlier in the afternoon, the second space shuttle ever built had launched Rich Walker and his team into orbit. For five days, they would circle our heads. Mrs. Walker had rented out the community center for the after party and invited everyone I'd ever known. We re-watched the launch on a TV. There were moon pies, star-shaped Jell-O molds, and even cupcakes topped with edible miniature spacecraft.

Now, everything swam in our bellies. The party had fallen into a lull, and Mrs. Walker and I were the only ones in the back of the room. The other kids watched cartoons on the TV while the adults smoked outside.

I'd never seen Mrs. Walker without her husband. It was like approaching a wild animal. As I came closer I saw that someone had left crayons out, and Mrs. Walker was doodling on the butcher paper that covered her table. I always wondered what adults drew when they were bored.

"What are you drawing?" I asked. I'd never spoken to her before.

Mrs. Walker looked at me. She might have been surprised to see me there, but her expression looked like she was watching me through a thick pane of glass. "Just my name, darling," she said. "Do you ever practice your own signature?"

I looked down at the repeated pattern of curls she'd drawn. "Your name is Arlene," I said.

Then I looked back up and the glass was gone. Arlene was there, in the room, staring at me. Her face gathered together in places, like she was going to cry or laugh or sneeze. She leaned in so close that I could see light yellow hairs on her cheeks. I was sure the miniature space shuttle in my stomach was going to blast itself out of my throat. Then Arlene gazed up to the high ceiling, and I knew she wasn't thinking of Rich in space because she didn't have the look of love. She bobbed her skyward head to Blondie for a bit. Then she picked up her crayon and put it to the paper again: "You are my heart." She didn't actually write "heart," she drew it.

For me. The heart was for me. My body filled with lightning, and the electricity jumped down my arms and into my hands. I grabbed a crayon and wrote, "I love you." I knew I was doing something wrong because Arlene wasn't family, and kids weren't supposed to love adults, but I couldn't let her disappear behind that glass again. Arlene read my message. She rested her chin on her fist and asked, "Really? Are you sure?" She seemed to regard the issue seriously, which I liked. Most adults talked to children the way they talked to dogs. "People say 'love' a lot when they don't actually mean it." She brought her hands together like a tent on the table. "I need to be sure. Do you love me?"

The space shuttle inside my body had now become a tractor, pushing its way out. She wanted me to say yes, I was certain. If I didn't obey, I foresaw disaster. Either she would tell my mom what I'd said, or the party would end, or Rich Walker's space shuttle would collide with an asteroid.

"Yes," I said. "I love you."

Arlene blinked a few times. Then she dropped her head and nodded, like I had delivered bad news. "Thank you." She got up, slipped her purse off the back of her chair, and left.

Rich Walker touched down to Earth five days later, his mission complete, and a month after that, he and Arlene filed for divorce. Both of them moved out of town. I don't think they would have survived the gossip anyway. Neighbors said that it was because space had changed Rich. Arlene realized she was sleeping with a stranger. At least that's what they'd heard.

"It's a sad thing," said my mom the day someone bought the Walkers' house. We were cleaning up the dinner table. "But it's true. Astronauts get this disease. The doctors can't figure out what it is. They go to space, they come back, and it's all they talk about. They can't stop thinking about space."

I set a plate down in the sink and rubbed my face. My eyes felt like balls of yarn. I'd spent the entire day at the arcade, playing Space Invaders until everything I looked at appeared to be growing endlessly.

"Are you alright, honey? Take a shower, you'll feel better. I'll finish the rest."

As soon as the hot water hit me, I could barely stay awake. I wanted to curl up on the floor of the shower and sleep, but I was afraid of drowning. I got out and went straight to bed without drying my hair. That night, I dreamed that Arlene's hairstyle was contagious. Looking someone in the eye was enough to transmit the disease. Soon, the whole town had hair like birds' nests.

I woke up to a dark blue sky outside. I went to my mom's bedroom and tapped her shoulder. "Mom. Mom. Rich Walker got divorced because I told his wife that I loved her."

My mom wasn't sleeping. She spoke with her eyes still closed. "Mmm. It's so funny, I had a dream about space, too." She opened her eyes, and they were puffy like she'd been crying. "You didn't do that to them, baby. They were having trouble. That's what adults do." She sat up and scooted over. "You want to come into bed with me?"

I nodded. I climbed up and curled against my mom's back. I felt safe. I pretended that she was an astronaut on the moon, and I was her tank of oxygen. She needed me to breathe. She couldn't live without me. The longer I thought about this, the more I relaxed. I could tell whenever I was falling asleep because I started to think crazy thoughts, or things that didn't really make sense. The last idea I remember having was that I really hoped that Arlene did love me back, wherever she was. I wished for her and Rich to have a fight about me, Rich's face hard with rage upon discovering a love letter. He would see the heart. They would scream at one another. They would throw things, because that's how adults demonstrated passion. I fell asleep to picture frames rotating in emptiness, plates breaking apart in zero gravity. Everything looked better in space.

Hate It Here

Kate Wheeler

Alison, Lisen and me on Highway 54, driving west out of town. Alison drives with one hand on the wheel, leaning back in her seat. Lisen rides shotgun, and she and Alison balance their wrists on the edges of the open windows and smoke. When a song we all know comes on the stereo, Alison and Lisen make their thumbs and their first two fingers, cigarettes in between, into guns and pump them out the windows in time with the chorus: *puh puh puh –chk CHING- take your money.*

It is fall. The highway is empty. We pass the flat brown fields, the tall silent trees. In the car it feels like something is happening. It feels like solitude and company at the same time. James has been gone for six months, and lately I cannot stand to be with people. I cannot stand to be alone.

We are looking for pumpkins to carve and have glowing about the house we live in together. We have been meaning to make this trip for weeks, but things come up. We have work. We have papers due. We are tired. There is some party.

When Lisen and Alison are getting ready to go out at night they take ages in the bathroom, changing sweaters, curling hair or straightening, adding eyeliner. I sit on the floor in the hallway. We can all see each other in the mirror. We talk. When we are hours late, Lisen says, "Let's go, let's go, it's dark at the bar," and we collect our bags and leave the house.

We are never on time. The longer we stay in this town, the worse it gets. Lisen and Alison have been here for five years. I have been here all my life.

Now, in the car, we pass a sort of shack, brown and set back from the road, a white sign: BOBS TUESDAY BINGO NIGHT BUDWEISER 50¢.

"I've always wanted to go there," Lisen says. "I've always wanted to go there for bingo night."

Lisen is tall. Her hair is brown and golden. She has a mild voice and a mild expression, and when she speaks you listen.

"Let's do it," Alison says. "Let's go on Tuesday."

"Well," Lisen says. "You want to?"

We shoot down the road. The bar is behind us.

"It's all the way out here," Lisen says. "How would we get home?"

"I'd drive home," I say.

I drive when no one else can, when they've all been drinking for hours. Once suddenly at midnight we were hungry, and I drove Alison and Lisen through town to the dumpster behind the Harris Teeter. Lisen rode shotgun.

"Left lane," she told me. "Stoplight."

"You drive better than I can," I said. "Even drunk."

We returned to the house with three trash bags full of pastries and bread, poptarts, ritz crackers, frozen pierogies. We stood on the front porch and passed around one cherry danish, left the rest sitting out there for the raccoons.

"We should go to that bar right now," I say. "Let's go right now."

Alison slows and makes a U-turn. We head back to the brown shack of a bar. She pulls over onto the highway's grassy shoulder and shuts off the engine. We look out.

In the gravel parking lot are three pick-up trucks, shining and silent.

"I don't know," says Lisen. "I don't really want to go in there without a man."

"What?" I say. "What could happen? It's four o'clock in the afternoon."

"Yeah," says Lisen, still looking.

"We could call Andrew," says Alison. "He would come out here with us."

I call Andrew. No answer. I leave a message. We sit in the car and look out.

"It's just that it's out here in the middle of nowhere," Lisen says.

When Lisen is bored or tired and ready to leave a place, some party or bar where we are, she says, "I hate it here," and we know it is time to move on.

Alison turns her key and the engine makes its low noises. "We'll find pumpkins," she says. "And if Andrew calls he can meet us at the bar on our way back."

We slide out onto the gray road again and drive for miles, quiet. Andrew does not call us back. Not a pumpkin in the North Carolina countryside, for some reason. The car's stream comes in the front windows and blows over my face and through my hair. I think how we could keep driving and get to the ocean, stand on the edge of the earth looking out over everything.

"I'm turning around at the next intersection," says Alison. She does, and the golden sun is behind us.

"I'll try Andrew again," I say. I do, but he does not answer.

We pass the brown shack bar.

In a few weeks, at some party at our house, when I leave the crowded kitchen early to sit alone in the living room, Alison and Lisen will come and find me there. Lisen will take whatever record it is off the turntable and put on Stevie Wonder, and Alison will take my hands and pull me off the couch. We will dance around the room together, the three of us, our own party. When it starts to rain, sudden and rumbling outside the open door, we will run out into the yard and up the gravel drive and down the hill on the other side, to the creek. Lisen will climb right into the shallow, rushing water and lie down.

"Lisen!" I'll shout, because the water will be surprisingly rough, but Lisen will laugh, grab onto the stones of the creek bed, and let her legs bob behind her. Alison and I will stand, soaked past help or caring in our clothes, laughing too, and the water will flow over Lisen's face and her forehead as if it is baptizing her, new, into this world.

Today, in the car, we drive back into town and buy three bright pumpkins from cardboard bins in the parking lot outside the Harris Teeter. We take them home and dig our hands into their cold, clean-smelling guts, put the oven on, toast seeds, spend the evening in the kitchen, carving.

(dis) Connect

Dani Sandal

Teacher Thompson was without Habit. City smart with coiffed do and starched collar, we thought she had that Unknown, Life's coveted Mysteries, all jacked up like Houdini in her ironclad briefcase. She was so slick in her optimism. We almost believed it.

She came to us just before summer break. Another replacement for old Mr. Jenkins who lost his wife to The Cancer and his mind to The Loss. Something about poison in the well, from where we wetted our youthful calves on a mountain spring we believed still ran pure. No matter. Our parents knew him when they wore nickers and now he was gone gone to that place where the old teachers go. When they've nothing more to teach, and have learned too much.

Teacher Thompson was no mistress to Jesus or slave to history, like the others. But, we learned, a soldier to grander illusions. For, there was no real war. Not out here, she said. She'd escaped it. Found solace in those tilled fields of our fathers and jars of gin, stilled by our mothers. The only smell of Death, horsehair and vegetables beginning their rot under ground in fall. Her first summer assignment: *Examine the Birds. Connect Nature to Human Existence. Enlighten me, Rural Child. Well?*

Well, we'd spent that summer burying boys who drove 8 cylinders of steel into familiar trees like folding into the fat arms of big breasted waitresses going nowhere soon. We buried sisters, brothers, would-be lovers. Unraveled bones from grain threshers. Swamped stalls and popped cherry in river banks where we rose like angels stinking of earth and sweet cum. Now, school had begun and we waited for someone to rise to the occasion.

We sat there sweating in our follies, in our ignorance of her failed quest that returning fall. Teacher's blackboard, a benign battle zone of blankness set against her will.

What birds?

Then the school bell tolled. And Jimmy Bowden suddenly took a stand in back. That fall, he'd shed his Pendleton for black trench and surely carried a piece in his brown sack lunch, snuggled to peanut butter and jam. He blew us away. Claimed he got a sad box of crap in the mail, instead of his brother. Lost to some war no one whispers about anymore. Not out here. Where is Fallujah   anyway?

Thompson could take that whip of a ruler and point across the map like a magician. But wouldn't. *What of birds? Of seasons? Of life?*

Jimmy fired on, boasting that his older sister went out the third story high on meth, their brother's tags wrapped tight round her neck like some junkyard dog. She didn't jump. Hell no. For a second, she flew. Jimmy knew. He'd been sitting in his underwear, notepad and pencil in hand, as requested. He'd observed the old oak outside their brother's bedroom window, its dark wetted knot, home to baby swallows.

A vision that should have horrified us. But didn't. He was gunning for It, man. He didn't spare one detail. He unchained all Life's Mystery: He didn't give a shit anymore. For, Sister found It. Birthed Enlightenment. He witnessed her wings taunt in denial. Noticed how they seemed unearthed, those little swallows. Untouched by The Madness. Disconnected.

Thompson dropped her chalk, motioned with fluttering hand for him to *Ssshhh, please.* But who was she now? Some page turner, projector flipper, quoter of things already quoted. Giver of lessons already learned. Her iron-clad case melting down, smoking from within. Toxic from the trash of hearsay and reality. From news reports and edited Truths.

She just needed a little bump.

Well, hear this Thompson: Sister just missed it. The oak. On the way down, a wicked limb tore her satin drawers. They swung soft in breeze like tattered flag. An offering to fledgling nests, Mothers carefully gathered it as twig from wind-blown willow. And the chicks, they never skipped a beat, chirping for worm when her head hit earth, cracking

like egg to spoon.

Vickie Fang

I sat on that cold front stoop, and I knew he was coming, but I didn't think about that. I looked at the birds, and I watched how they fell out of the sky. The sky was very blue, and the clouds were big and white, and the birds fell out of the sky over and over again because they were hungry and they wanted to eat the garbage that was in the streets.

I knew he was coming for me, but I didn't think about that. I sat, and I watched the birds, and they jerked back up, and they went down again very fast like they were toys on God's string, and maybe that's why He made them be so hungry. Because He wanted to keep them there. And I knew my brother would be here soon, and he had never come for me before, and the birds were white birds, and I kept thinking about them because I didn't want to think about what my brother would do.

Anyway, it was better to think about the birds, because they came from the other end of Pratt Street where the bay is, and I heard them call out sometimes like they were birds flying over a beach, and before Tony came I wondered if they called like that because they were remembering the ocean and the sand.

But I didn't think about the birds anymore when I saw Tony pull up because just when he did, I thought of the perfect words to say to him.

"How do you like it?" I asked, getting up slowly because he didn't get out for me. He didn't even open the door, just lowered the window and stared with his lips pressed hard together so none of the Baltimore air could get in. "How do you like it out here in God's country?"

And when I got in the car, all he said was what he would have said anyway. "Look at yourself, Mary Ann." And then he said, "You don't care about anything, do you?"

"You know me," I told him back. "Don't care, don't scare."

But all he said was, "This is a respectful occasion," and his voice stayed heavy, and quiet, and slow. "So you will show some respect. You will remember that my mother is dead, and my father is a widower now, and there are certain things you will not do."

And I heard him take a breath, and I waited, and then he made a list that I knew he must have practiced with his wife. "You will not steal anything. You will not use your drugs in the house. You will not have sex with anyone in the house—not for money or for otherwise. You are being given one last chance here. Do you understand me? One last chance."

My brother never hit me, not in a long time anyway, but I looked at the floor when he talked. I don't like to look at any of their faces when they get like that. Not when I can already feel the explosion coming—the ground slamming against me and my arms and legs and my chest all trembling like water that's about to spill out of a cup. I don't like to look at their faces, and sometimes they only pretend to hit you with a fist or something else, but they don't really do it, and then they like to laugh.

"I'm not starting this car until we have an understanding, Mary Ann."

And I was still looking at the floor, but I said it anyway. "They're my mother and my father too," I told him. "You don't have to say it like they're only yours." And then I told him fast before he could say anything that I would respect my mother and father, and not act ghetto like I did at the funeral, and in the silence after that I was still looking at the floor.

"This is against my better judgment," is what he finally said, and then he started the car. And we rode all the way to Laurel without saying anything after that, but while we were still in the city I looked out the window at the birds, and they were so many, and they are what I thought about because it is better not to remember things. And they were turning and falling and going up again, and sometimes their wings were all white, and sometimes they had a big band of black on each end. And the black was like the darkness that comes from under a door, a bedroom door, when the light is turned off.

And all the way to Laurel I could still see them in my head, their wings all white one minute, and then they turned, and the tips were black. Dirty birds. Shit birds. Rats with wings. Bad ju ju.

And I felt like nothing then because now I knew my brother might cut me off again, and I would probably do something stupid, and he would be through with me, and I had been cut off for so long before, and I hadn't really been back on. Not really.

Not for seven years because I got in a fight with his wife when they came back from their honeymoon. And I don't even know what we were fighting about, but I remember she said she wasn't married to anybody like me, and nobody she knew even smelled like me, and her voice got bad, and I saw her face, and I knew right then it would be a long time before I saw Tony again.

And I didn't see anyone else in the family either, except T.T., and when he came back from visiting them on Christmas, he showed me what presents he got, but there was never anything for me. He said nobody even asked about me, but I asked about them. I kept asking, and when he told me Mommy was sick I made two cards at the Sisters of Mercy Drop-in art program, and I sent them with T.T., but nobody said whether she looked at them or not. And I thought I would never see her again, but then Mommy came to visit me, and the seven years were broken, and I thought I had my family back again.

And when I saw the house I asked the question that had worried me the most; I asked was Jean there, and Tony answered me, "You're on thin ice, Mary Ann." And I knew his wife was inside, and I felt sick in my stomach, but there she was at the door already.

And she hurried over to the car, so as soon as I got out she was explaining how it would be, and she said Daddy wasn't there; maybe he would come back in time to say goodbye to me and maybe he wouldn't. And she was telling me something about how she got everything all set up, and I knew I needed to listen to what she was telling me, but when I saw her I started thinking about the funeral instead because I was afraid she wouldn't let me come in the house. And Jean was the one told me I couldn't come into the funeral because I wasn't appropriate. And I was afraid when I saw her because I had relapsed at the funeral, and everybody saw it.

They wouldn't let me come inside because I was falling down, and the church walls were so white on the outside where they left me. They were so white, and my eyes were opening and closing. And when my eyes were closed there was a soft, dark spell on the world.

And when I opened my eyes again, my whole family was going to their cars, but not with me because I was no one they wanted to know. I saw them walking away together, and I tried to catch up with them, but it was no use because Tony came back and said I couldn't go to the grave either.

But I had loved my mother, and love made me strong, and I stood in the church parking lot, and I closed my eyes until I could see her again. I saw her the way she was when I was eight years old, and my parents were having a party and she sang *Fly Me to the Moon*. I could see her the way she was, and I could hear her voice, sweet and slow, and she still had one hand on her heart and one in the air the way I remembered her, but there were no drunk friends laughing this time.

But I couldn't sit there remembering something like that because I knew I had to be appropriate this time, and I told Jean as soon as she stopped talking that I wouldn't be like I was at the funeral. And she said, "Well I should hope not!" And she got a big smile on her face like a jack o' lantern when she said it, and I didn't tell her I thought she was a bitch. And when she said she was making nice fresh scones for everybody, I thought she said stones, but I didn't tell her what I thought about that either. And besides, the next thing she said was let's go see what my mother left for me.

She had it upstairs for me, and I got nervous then because that sounded like it wasn't money. And T.T. got a thousand dollars; he already showed me, and I wanted a thousand dollars too. But then I thought it must be Mommy's diamond rings because she had three sons, but I was the only daughter, and she had two rings, and they might be worth more.

So Tony said, "All right, let's get down to business," and we went upstairs with no more talking except Tony told me twice that Jean did a lot of work getting everything ready.

"I don't mind!" is what Jean said when we got in my parents' bedroom, and there were paper bags of my mother's clothes all over the floor, and Jean had washed and sorted them so that I could pick what I wanted. And that was all I was getting.

And I said Uncle T.T. got money, and Jean said she was sure he would share with me in his good judgment and in his own good time, but I couldn't share lady's clothes with T.T., now could I? And she laughed at that, and I could have cut them both then, right in their laughing faces if I had a knife or a good piece of glass, but I tried to smile instead. And I did smile, but I felt sick all over again because there were eight bags, and I could see one of them was full of wire hangers, and another one had a bathmat and some worn-out slippers. And I wasn't getting diamond rings or money, and T.T. got a thousand dollars, and if he wants a cigarette, he buys a pack, and most of the time I pick the butts off the sidewalk to smoke, and he laughs at me too and calls me "butt mouth."

But I am smart, and I didn't think about that, and I didn't look at Jean's hands either because I didn't want to find out what she was wearing on them. And nobody said anything. They were waiting for me to look at the clothes, and finally I started reaching all through one of the bags the way they wanted me to. And most of the things in there I didn't even recognize. I wondered if they really were my mother's clothes, but then I saw her Christmas sweater at the bottom of the second bag.

And I looked at it, and it was soft with white angels and a gold star, and for a minute I forgot all about what I could get for it because I remembered her giving me soup when it was cold. She wore the Christmas sweater, and I think she put her hand on my head too. I think I remember that. The boys hit me with a hard snowball in the face, and I came inside then, and she put her hand on my head. I think that happened to me.

And Jean and Tony were looking at me, and I couldn't say anything. Because after I saw that soft sweater, I started to feel what I usually feel when it comes to my mother, and it is worse than being dope sick. The sweat goes down on the inside of me instead of up on my skin, and it is like water dripping down slowly the hollow part of a pipe or the walls of a house nobody lives in anymore. And I looked at the bags, and I said, "O.K., I'll take it," because I wasn't getting anything else anyway. So I said "O.K."

And when Jean said, "Which one?" I told her all of them, but I was still holding the sweater in my hands.

And Jean said didn't I want to pick the things I really wanted? And when I said no, she wanted to know was I sure Uncle T.T. would let me bring so many bags back to his apartment. She said she didn't think so. She didn't think that would work, and besides she already made plans to donate most of it to the church yard sale.

That's when Tony said, "She's going to sell it, for Christ's sake."

And Jean looked right at me and said, "Sell it?"

And I didn't know what to say, and Jean said, "Is that right? Would you really sell these nice things not even a month after the funeral?"

And I knew I was in a trap right then because I wanted to say I would never sell it, but I saw Tony starting to snicker, and I knew he would call me a liar if I said that. And if I told the truth, Jean would say I didn't deserve

256

those nice things, and I didn't want to be greedy and lose my last chance. And they were both looking at me, and Tony was already starting to smile out one side of his mouth like little boys do when they smell a fart or somebody's b.o. And I knew he was going to make fun of me in front of Jean, and I tried to say something to make him stop.

I tried to tell them both that I respected Mommy's sweater. I hugged it to my chest, and I said I remembered Mommy wearing it. And I tried to tell them that I remembered how my mother looked right at me when I came into the house with my lips hurt from the snowball. She didn't look mad. She gave me soup, and I remember her hands didn't hurt me, not that time. And she was wearing the sweater with the angels on it. And I was tasting blood with my soup because my lip was cut on the inside, and I remember I was happy because she was smiling at me. That was another time I saw her smile, and she had her sweater on that had the angels.

And I could see what their faces were doing while I was trying to explain, and after the first few words I knew I should have told them to fuck themselves, but I kept telling them about my mother instead. And all that time, I wanted to cut my own face and not theirs because you are less than nothing if you let people shit on you like that, but maybe this was my last chance to make them see how much I respected my mother. So I told them everything I could, and when I finished, Jean said, "Well, I'm sure I didn't understand any of that!" And I knew she was sure she didn't want to understand it either, and they were both going to make fun of me after I was gone.

And all I said was, "How much should I take?" And my own voice sounded very bad to me, like there was a trembling wind behind it, and soon I would fall to pieces, but maybe it really didn't sound so bad because Jean smiled. It was a little smile, and this time I noticed that her face was very still, but her eyes made movements like she was looking for a way to run, and I wondered if she always looked at me like that and if she could have been afraid of me the whole time.

Or maybe she liked to hear me sound bad, because she said, "You just have to know how to manage things" to Tony and not to me, and her voice had little bells in it. And she told me I could have two bags full and held up two fingers I guess so I would know how many "two" was.

And when they were on the stairs, I heard him say, "Great management, Jean. Leaving a crack whore alone with everything in the house," but they were already on the stairs when he said that. He didn't want to stay up there with me And I still had her sweater in my hands, and when I was in the darkness with Uncle T.T., sometimes it was my mother I would think about. And sometimes I would think about her with one hand on her heart and the other one in the air singing about going to the moon, and that's when I found out I was hollow inside because of the sweat that rolled down the inside of me, down to where there was nothing left anymore because sometimes Uncle T.T. and I made noise in there, and I even screamed the first time, and still she never came into the bedroom.

That was the year I failed the 5th grade, and then Uncle T.T. and the boys liked to knock on my head and say "Nobody home!" so I guess I was hollow there too. That's the other thing I remember.

And I took my jacket off and put Mommy's Christmas sweater on instead. And I could feel how soft it was, and I was wearing my mother's white angels. And I hoped I would find something else like it, but I had never seen most of her other clothes. I don't know if she really wore them. And there was one bag full of her underpants that Jean thought I could have, and there was a scarf and a couple of bras in it, and I looked through them again and again, and I wished I could find the white scarf that she had with pink flowers, little pink flowers. I kept looking because the scarf with the flowers was what my mother was wearing the last time I saw her. And that was a great day in my life. She came all the way up to Baltimore to see me, and Uncle T.T. didn't tell me, but that was how the seven years ended.

He waited till he looked out the window and saw her coming, and I ran down the street looking for her and ran beside the car too when they drove up. And I yelled, "Mommy! My mommy is here!"

She had cancer, stage 4, and under the scarf she was bald as the moon, but my mother came to see me. She came to see me, and she stood in the shadows behind where me and T.T. lived because she was afraid to go inside; she never wanted to see what we had in there. And she said she was worried about me. She said maybe I'd like to live different and get out of the ghetto? And I said, not yet, I wasn't ready yet.

And she said, "You're forty years old almost. When are you going to get ready?"

And I said for her not to worry about it, but she did worry. All of a sudden I could see how much she was worried. That's when I knew my mother was really dying. She was old and dying, and old people are like children, especially if they are going to die. They get to be afraid. They are children, and you have to protect them, and you have to protect your mother most of all. You always have to protect your mother.

And when she said she was afraid she wasn't a good mother, that was the saddest thing she could have said. And I told her I was the bad one all along. I told her everything she did was perfect.

And she looked up where me and T.T. lived, up into the shadows, and she said she was afraid. She said she was afraid she'd been the one to put me on the road I was on, and I knew what she was thinking. She was thinking about when I was fourteen and she gave me to T.T. because I was so much trouble. I'd been caught stealing so many times, and I'd been to reform school already, and the whole family had a meeting, and they were all fed up with me. She and Daddy drove me over, and she stayed outside while Daddy took me in, but first she leaned over and slapped my leg and told me to stop that crying. And we never talked about that day. And that was twenty-five years ago, and she had never yet come into any bedroom I had with T.T. And I didn't want her to have to. I didn't want her to think about that. She wasn't the kind of person who should have to think about that.

"I'm afraid I might have done something to get you started on this life," my mother said.

And I said, "No, no, no," all in a rush. I told her not even to think that, not even for a minute, and she looked so small and afraid. "You're my mommy!" I told her, and I took that scarf off and kissed her head. I felt so good kissing my mother. And I wasn't hollow then; no I wasn't. A whole ocean of warm water ran through me, and lifted me up under the sun, and I covered every naked inch with lipstick kisses, until her head wasn't white anymore. And when I stopped the kissing I told her I was where I wanted to be, and I was doing what I wanted to do, and I would run wild until I was ready to settle down, and there was nothing anybody in the world could have done about that.

And she said she felt better then. She was happy my life was not her fault. And I was so glad, and I kissed her some more until she told me to get off I was too big.

I stood in her old bedroom remembering, and holding her underpants instead of the scarf, and wondered when I would be sick like her. People with the HIV get cancer or something else, and it would be my turn soon. And I had never been a beautiful mother; I had just run wild with my life.

And downstairs Jean was cooking her scones, and I could smell them. I could smell apples warming up and lots of cinnamon, and I was glad she was Tony's wife because I could tell she would take Mommy's place, and he would be safe and not turn ghetto. She would be his protection against someone like me. And as for me, I think I knew that nobody but Uncle T.T. wanted me around anymore.

They must have just promised Mommy to let me come back and take some of her things, and then I think they told me I had a last chance so I would behave. And I wondered if maybe Daddy would come back and see me one last time. Maybe he would do that, I thought. Maybe he would do that at least, but I didn't really think so because he didn't see me for seven years, and he didn't speak to me at the funeral, and I had been dead to him for a long, long time.

But if I was dead to him and everyone else, I still wasn't dead to myself. I could still remember that there had been a time before I was stupid and failed 5th grade and started running wild with T.T. Back then, when I lived in the county, in Laurel, I played in my own yard in the summertime, and those were the days when everything I dreamed of could come true. And it still could.

All I have to do is think about it, and it's like I'm a little girl again. I'm standing barefoot in the grass when it gets dark in the summer. And the lightning bugs rise up into the air and fall back down again, and rise up again, and still they are always in the same place. And they are my own stars—more than I can count, and so close I can catch them in my hand.

Eating Together

Michelle Bracken

August, 2005

I am a vegetarian now, have been one for two years. My mother asked me, the last time I saw her, a month ago, if I found that my diet causes me to be depressed. I shrugged this off, said no, not at all.

If my diet were hurting me, I told her, I'd be real thin by now. I'm healthy. I then proceeded to dig my fork into a veggie burrito, the tortilla covered in cheese and red sauce.

~

I can go back, year before year, and recall the feeling of starvation. Though I do not live with my family, have not lived with them for years, whenever I feel closest to them, whenever I feel that even though I am away, I am really there, I have not eaten for hours, sometimes days.

I starve.

But before that, before anything, there is the time that I binged.

I am eight years old. I live in San Leandro, California, in a two-story apartment, with my mother, my five-year-old brother, my four-year-old sister and my two-year-old brother. We do not have a father, but fathers. My father lives in Nevada and sees me once a year, if I do not beg too much to stay with my mother. Their father, my siblings' father, is gone, in the Navy, overseas. Though my mother says he will be coming back for Easter, I know that is not true and that she is just saying this for our sake.

My mother works for the San Francisco Chronicle; she is awake at one in the morning, in jacket and jeans, and leaves for her job, delivering the daily paper. I used to go with her, used to sit in the bed of her truck and toss and toss and sometimes run for my life from barking dogs.

But I must stay with the kids now, especially with the two-year-old, while my mother goes to work.

And so I am awake at one and two and three and four in the morning. And to stay awake, I take a gallon of Mint n' Chip ice cream from the freezer, sit on the stairs, and binge. I am half done when my stomach boils over, when my mind is swollen. I hide the ice cream behind frozen vegetables, hoping that no one remembers it. And I sit on the stairs, in the dark, crying and bloated.

I do this for two years.

~

I think back now and remember that when I was eight, my mother made lots of money. Perhaps the most money she ever made at any job. The kitchen was always stocked, my closet full of dolls and I even had a thirteen-inch, white television that sat on my dresser. That time would not last, though.

I would gain, in those two years, enough weight to haunt me for the rest of my life. Chubby, I was called. Chipmunk cheeks. I hid behind men's shirts and baggy jeans, wore shorts and sometimes shirts over my bathing suit, constantly assessed my appearance in the mirror. I was, even at the age of eight, a dedicated participant in Richard Simmon's *Sweatin' to the Oldies*.

~

I am ten now, almost eleven. We no longer live up north, but down south in Hemet, California. Our apartment lacks furniture; we sleep on the floor, covered in blankets my mother bought from the thrift store. Sometimes, in the morning, when she can afford it, my mother makes rice and raisins for breakfast. This slides sweetly down my throat and I tell my mother that if she needs it, I can stay home, do not really need to go to school.

Sometimes she says no, sometimes she gives in with a sad smile, and sometimes she says nothing at all. When we are hungry, when my siblings cannot take it anymore, the free lunch of school long gone from their stomachs, my mother and I make Rice Krispi treats. I slice the squares for my brothers and sister and watch my mother on the carpet, belly bulging with another baby, eyes hungry.

~

We live in Modesto when I am twelve, in a gated community. We live with a man named Joe, the father of my baby sister. I have a room to myself, a bed to lie in, and a dog that shits all over my new thrift store clothes on the first day of school.

I don't eat much of anything. My Halloween candy sits in the freezer and when my mother is crying in her room, when the house is silent except for that crying, when my eight year-old brother is slapped and forced to stand in the corner, I reach for that candy. I swallow the Snickers and the Milky Ways, chew and chew until I am swollen again. And after that, I eat nothing for days.

~

I am still twelve but no longer live in Modesto. We are in the desert now, in Twentynine Palms. We live with my mother's sister, in her house, with her four boys. Space is cramped and food is tight. My mother fries potatoes and I smother them in barbecue sauce. My mother makes macaroni and cheese and I also smother this in barbecue sauce.

When I can afford it, when my grades are high and the teacher allows us to buy candy with our fake money, I purchase five Fireballs, red jawbreakers that explode in my mouth. I lick them, in the kitchen, and when they get too hot, when I feel my tongue squirming, I place them in the freezer, saving them for later.

~

Months later and we are living in a trailer. My mother cannot afford groceries and on occasion, my uncle, her sister's husband, comes by with bags of food. My mother tells him to take it away. Her face is tanned and beautiful and she is ashamed.

I sit on the floor and watch her push the food away.

Please don't, I say.

My uncle sets the bags on the table, and touches my mother's arm.

When he leaves, she bakes a frozen pizza.

~

There are those who will say my mother is an awful mother; lazy, stupid, ignorant. There is birth control, people have said to me. My father, my uncle, my aunts, my teachers, even certain friends, have all told me when I was eight, when I was ten, eleven, twelve, every year of my life, how worthless my mother is. Doesn't she know, they say, doesn't she know that kids come from sex? Doesn't she care that you go hungry? Doesn't she know what she is doing? Yes, we were hungry, yes we were poor, and no my mother was never lazy. At every point in my life, at every empty house, at every overdue electric bill, my mother was out there, in the day and in the night, working. She cleaned houses, fed and bathed the elderly, cut hair, sold burial plots, delivered papers, printed business cards. And there are those who will wonder, why then, why were you hungry? And I will say to them: one woman, seven kids. You figure it out.

~

I am thirteen. We are on welfare, food stamps. This allows us to eat just fine. We live in a house now, with another man. In a few months my mother will bear him a son. He does not like me, thinks I am rude, fat, and trouble. He does not like my mother talking to me, is jealous of our relationship. When he is at work, on the Marine Base, and when I stay home on days I am too sad for fractions and the War of 1812, my mother and I sit outside and watch the quails run. At noon, his lunch break, I hide in my closet while he eats in the kitchen.

"Why'd you make so much?" he asks, his voice booming. My stomach moans and my body aches. "Is she home again?" He is angry.

When he leaves, my mother feeds me steak fajitas.

~

When I'm in seventh grade, I am thin. I spend the previous summer starving off the weight, wanting to make a new me for a new beginning. But by eighth grade, the weight is back. I have, over the course of the year, discovered the snack bar. Chocolate chip cookies are thirty cents. I buy three. There are ice cream bars and nachos and turkey sandwiches and cheese popcorn. I try my best. I eat the free lunch. But then I think of after school, when I will be home and sad and afraid. When I will hear my mother's boyfriend beat my brothers and scold my mother. And so, before catching the bus home, I stop at the snack bar and buy as many chocolate chip cookies as my change will afford.

~

I knew girls who purged, who took their toothbrushes with them to the bathroom and vomited up everything they had just eaten. And I wished it could have been that easy for me. I did try, once, purging cookies and Coke. But I thought it too disgusting and instead opted for suppressing my hunger with cherry cough drops.

~

Fifteen is good for me. My mother's boyfriend is gone and in his place are a new brother and a new sister. I am their other mother, and raise them while our mother works. We live in a big house out in the desert, far from town. During the summer, during the heat, while my mother is scrubbing floors and scrubbing ovens, my brothers and sisters and I dance in the living room. We play on the stereo a CD that my mother received free in the mail. It is by a group named Cake, and every afternoon we dance to their music. For lunch I pour honey in the middle of a tortilla, and fold it over. We eat this for days. Usually my mother brings dinner home, but her paycheck is always late and so everything is stretched.

She meets a man who owns an auto shop in town, and because my mother is beautiful and because my mother sometimes goes out at night to play pool with him, he stops by while she is at work and unloads boxes of beef sandwiches wrapped in aluminum foil. We are hesitant at first, open the fridge day after day to see them staring back at us. With no choices, we eat these beef sandwiches. We eat them cold, the gravy sliming over the bread, warming our mouths.

~

My mother once told me that she never loved the men she was with, only the children she had. My mother was abandoned by her mother when she was eleven, and left alone with an alcoholic father. And when she was nineteen, she had me. I can only speculate that having children somehow filled her emptiness.

~

I am twenty-two now.

My mother calls me every other week and gives me updates of her daily life.

I listen and I give advice and I laugh and tell her that things will be better. They must get better. And when her voice is gone, when the phone is on the hook and I am left with a tight throat and wet eyes, I never feel more alone.

I've not eaten much over the past two days: two slices of bread, a graham cracker. This is the feeling I've been longing for. My arms quiver, typing this. They are hungry. I am hungry. It is like waiting, this feeling. By eating what little I did, I am back to long ago. I am back beside my mother. I can feel the sun on my face through the window, can hear the desert wind howl. I am back to my sisters and to my brothers and to the comforting feeling of knowing that sometime soon my mother will be home with dinner.

I am back to the comforting silence of poverty.

~

Last month, I was home. And I sat on my mother's couch, in the stench of dog, and watched my mother race home from barbering to shower, and then leave again for a seven o'clock night class.

"Oh, you're home," she had said, smiling, exhausted. There was no time for a hug, for a touch, for a word. When she left, when my nine-year-old brother and eight-year-old sister trudged into the kitchen, staring at the fridge, looking for dinner, I stood. They wanted pizza, hot dogs, bread, soda. And my nine-year-old brother asked about tofu.

"I want to be a vegetarian," he said, staring up at me.

And I said that was great.

"But my dad," he murmured, looking down, "my dad said no."

And I thought of his father. I thought of him and of steak fajitas and of my brothers crying and of myself crying in a closet over his insult to me: fat cow.

I opened the kitchen cupboards and scanned. Black beans, scalloped potatoes, rice, canned corn, green beans. "You'll eat vegetarian with me," I said.

For seven days I cooked. I boiled, fried, chopped, sliced. My other brothers and sisters turned up their noses at my food, said there was nothing to eat.

"But look," I told them. "Look at how much there is."

We sat together on that couch, and ate. The emptiness was there in my stomach, pulling me back, saying, *aren't you glad to be home?*

And I was.

The Cooldown

Paige Towers

It's a glorious ritual, the cooldown.

The run is over. I pull my headphones off, grip my hipbones with my hands and reflexively tilt my head back, struggling to get more oxygen. Central Park is swarming with tourists on rented bikes, kids in strollers, dogs on extendable leashes, runners who are finishing or starting, stretching and shaking out their legs. Sweat gets in my eyes and everything goes blurry. My muscles burn. I feel powerful.

As I slowly walk the three blocks home from the park, my endorphins continue to pulse, and I'm not thinking, not worrying, not aware that others are aware of me. My self-consciousness has been transported elsewhere. As a young woman in a city full of gazes, these moments of ownership are so good.

I own this sidewalk. I own my footsteps, my body, this space, the droplets of sweat on my neck that are being soaked up by the ends of my hair dangling from my ponytail—all mine.

But then, I'm walking through a tunnel of men.

They're standing across from each other on the sidewalk, claiming more than half a block, which leaves me with a narrow runway. There are maybe fifteen of them, speckled in dust and white paint, leaning against scaffolding. I could have crossed the street, I should have crossed the street, but when you start to feel like you *own*, you start to feel like you can do this. It will be different this time.

Yet, the first inner, tiny fight for freedom is the first prick of awareness. The shift is so natural, so ingrained, like putting your hands out if an object is flying at your face. As soon as they look at me, I am also looking at me.

My arms cross in front of my chest. My gaze tilts down. I'm studying boots, studying cement. Two men to the left look me up and down. A man to the right smirks and makes a clicking sound with his tongue. That guy, the stereotypical man who always leans against something is leaning against the back of the truck with arms spread out behind him, and he signals his friend with a hand gesture. He smiles in a way that suggests he knows something about me, that I have something to offer him, or if I'm not careful, he could just take it. I have to be careful.

The image of myself is back, so I adjust it. Put your head up higher—no—you overcompensated. Lower it, then relax your expression—eyebrows too furrowed and they'll take it as a challenge. Tug your tank top down. No, this is my stomach, it's a stomach, don't cover it and show them that you're embarrassed. That makes you weak. Pretend like you're not even aware of it. Walk faster. Not too quick—they'll laugh and make kissing sounds. Don't smile, but make it obvious that you're not thinking, "Don't smile."

Sometimes, I think about how fantastic it must be to spend every second owning space, and to not even know that there is another way. Imagine: to stretch your arms out on the backs of chairs, or to splay your legs open wide on a packed subway train, to move freely without being commented on or watched. In fact, you get to be the watcher. You get to be the subject and thus create a verb—an action, whichever you choose, that you can enact on an object, whichever you choose. You would forever feel like that moment when you've pushed your body to the point of exhaustion, when you are pulsing red hot and pumping a weird mix of pain and good feelings and that self-awareness is lost, or at least buried deep down, for a short time. You are powerful.

But walking down this block of construction, I'm lowered right back into my reality. The awareness is so heavy, so stifling. At the end of the tunnel, a taxi makes a last second stop at a red light, and the sounds of the brakes jar me at the same time that I turn my head away from a pile of rancid-smelling garbage bags. I am back in the real New York City. Then I'm at the door to my building, first glancing in the large antique mirror that's hung in the foyer because I'm so conditioned to this action that I swear the frame is magnetized and my head is attracted to it. It's not vanity; it's just so I can know what everyone else is seeing.

I climb the stairs to my apartment and cringe at the tightness in my hamstrings, but when I look down, I notice that there's an expanding space there between my thighs. I've lost weight. Good. As I turn the key, I notice that my biceps seem more toned and my abs feel tighter. Good. I don't feel hungry. Good.

When I undress, I'm aware of my nudity. I'm aware of the body parts being revealed with each thing I take off. In my mind, I watch myself bend over, pick up the soggy clothes I've dropped on the floor, open the closet, throw them in the hamper. I simultaneously hobble to the bathroom on tender feet and *imagine* what me hobbling to the bathroom on tender feet would look like to an observer. It's here again: me, but me from the perspective of a man's gaze—a weird, mostly inescapable double image.

But the image of myself won't be here forever, because tomorrow evening I will run up and down hills, cough for air, make my muscles burn and my shins pound with pain, fight myself mentally not to stop until it becomes animalistic. I will sprint to my self-appointed finish line—the entrance to Central Park—and then stagger through the crowds as my chest heaves.

And with all of this, it's back: freedom from my reflection. For those sweet, cool moments, I've earned my body back as my own. I'm nobody's object; I'm only subject and verb, subject and verb. I'll walk forward and will simply only be a person walking forward. I'll reach down to touch my toes and it won't occur to me for a second what me touching my toes might look like. I'll just float amongst the masses, rising up like my evaporating sweat. I'll just walk and stretch and breathe.

And be.

The Stone Masons

Joanne M. Clarkson

Not out of faith, but stone. Two men,
atheists both, built the town's
church. Rock rivered
to the smoothness of loaves. Heft
and sweat. The mortar.

       This was no
cathedral. No tower for bells. No crimson
or indigo windows. In those hard times
they toiled for food alone and a place
to sleep where silence breathed
its deep calm. They seldom spoke,
yet there was always communion
between them. July sun
called the house of god upwards
though neither of them believed; the war
had been too hard.

       They married
sisters. Lived in the city. And after
one of them lost his mind, the other
sat daily at the bedside, accepting,
while the women prayed. He recalled
then some remnant of Bible lore
from childhood when Christ, fasting,
was tempted by the Devil
to turn rocks into bread.
And he had refused. *Let stones*

be stones, indifferent to weather,
worship, what breaks a man and what
builds him.

"Work" Theme Contest Winner – 1st Place

Beep

Bill Snyder

Two class hours of Diamant and Danticat—their
tents and bones—then seventy thistly
minutes of fledgling poems—the intro class—
and I'm feeling hollowed out, like
a conch might, by current and sand. By centuries.
Now three o'clock, and a stack yet to grade,
but by my office, a woman. Not
a student here, her eyes say as much,
and her body, harnessed and slack.
Who are you looking for? I ask, recalling our
homecoming day. *Professor*, she says,
you remember me. I took poetry.
I say, *oh, yes, I remember.* She says
her name, says it's been five years, and
I ask what she does these days. *I'm a cashier,*
she says, *at Wal-Mart,* and I say, *oh, good for
you, but, sorry, got to run—a meeting, you know.*
She walks down the hall, and on to dinner,
the concert tonight, lunch and game tomorrow.
Then back to work on Monday—the buttons
and screens, the swiping beeps, the spinning
stands of plastic bags, prayer wheels
of America. Don't judge, I think. Arrest your
disappointment. But it's more than that. It's
the helplessness. And fear—that
I'm a kind of machine myself—kinetic,
perpetual—another rotary-something,
beeping as I spin—turbine, flywheel,
windmill—that I'm spinning around

and all the kids are hanging on, or I'm
hanging on to them—whichever—who knows
the physics of it. But they all let go eventually—
they want to, or have to. Or I let go. And what?

"Work" Theme Contest Winner – 2nd Place

Bullet in the Back

Mark Pritchard

There's a man up and pacing in the aisle of this plane. Up and down he walks, looking suspiciously at everyone. He looks into the face of the young man with long straight blond hair, he looks at the light-skinned woman and her dark-skinned companion, at the athletic-looking woman seated in front of them, at a little girl sitting by the window, and at the businessman seated in front of her. He walks slowly up and down, watching us, and we all watch him. He is holding a gun.

He paces up and down the aisle, looking suspiciously at everyone. Any one of us might be of a mind to, as they say in the bank heist movies, "do something stupid"—to stand up and try to tackle him, or to throw something, or even to speak. We are not to speak and not to move—so he says.

He has asked, demanded, that we keep our hands in the air, and we have complied. Whatever we were doing to keep our hands busy until now, we have stopped it and raised our hands. We hold our hands at a height just above our heads, not obscuring our faces, the better for the man with the gun to peer into them, as he goes up and down the aisle.

He holds the gun in one hand and steadies it with the other. The gun is pointed in no particular direction. Sometimes, briefly, it is pointed at a person; most of the time it is pointed down the aisle, or at an inclined angle, so that if it goes off, the bullet will hit the ceiling.

He passes me by, and turns and looks over his shoulder, right into my eyes, with a fierce expression. I am scared, or I try to be. I'm having a strange daydream about him firing a bullet that strikes the latch of a luggage bin, and the door of the bin flies open, a heavy laptop hits his gun hand, and the gun goes off again. The bullet hits another luggage bin, causing another avalanche of luggage and another inadvertent discharge. I can't keep myself from smiling.

The man, a craggy Shakespearean actor whose role in "Star Wars" movies made him world-famous, now turns to me fully. He points the gun casually toward the floor. "You think this is funny?" he asks, in his familiar Irish brogue.

I let my mouth flop open, and then before I can think, I respond, "No way."

He looks a little surprised, but without shooting me or saying anything else, he continues up the aisle toward the front of the plane, still peering into everyone's faces.

The director yells "Cut!" and a bell rings. We all gratefully put our hands down. My seatmate on the aisle, a slender teenager in a dark green Oregon hoodie, fishes out a cell phone. The woman in the window seat takes out a small mirror and looks into it intently. Someone behind me calls out, "Hey, is this a non-smoking flight?"

The gunman goes to consult with the director. I can't hear what they say, but I'm hoping they are discussing whether to keep the improvised dialogue. It means a close-up for me and a speaking role. Instead of getting paid an extra's wages, I'll get SAG scale for a day and a credit in the movie—Plane Passenger #1. Maybe I'll appear in later scenes, at least long enough to get killed.

But what I'm really wondering is whether the gunman—that is, the film's lead actor—remembers me. We worked together three years ago. The context was different; it was not an action scene. I played a hotel clerk and my line, as he approached the front desk, was: "Yes sir?" and he responded, "Reservation for Wickman, Martin Wickman." The rest of the scene between him and his co-star, a Spanish brunette with a beguiling accent, was done in close-up; only my hands were occasionally visible, doing desk clerk movements. But we made seven takes of that simple interaction, and I'm thinking that the reason he stopped and peered into my face during the shot just now, is that he recognized me.

"I worked with him before," I say to the woman with the mirror. She glances up, over the rows of seats, to the crew surrounding the director and the star, then looks back into her mirror. "Look," she says, pointing to a blemish beneath her eye. "Does this look malignant?"

The blemish looks like a blemish. "There might be a dermatologist on board," I say, "but probably in first class."

She acknowledges my joke with the smallest smile possible, more like a tensing of the lips.

The teenager pipes up and recommends a blemish cream, and he and the woman proceed to have a conversation about skin issues. Like all teenagers he's a know-it-all, and he's relishing his chance to show off his skin-care knowledge in front of someone who actually cares. I don't care about skin issues.

The director emerges from the scrum at the front of the plane and addresses the passengers. "We're going to do a few more takes, and then we'll shoot the next page, which has some action," he says. "Then we'll break." Someone asks him how long. "If I told you, and then it was longer than that, you'd be disappointed," he says. "Just hang in there. I know it's tough to sit there for hours. Just think of it as the longest transoceanic flight on record."

"Can we get miles?" someone jokes. "Of course," the director says, "Aqua-Oceanic Airlines will give you all double miles." We laugh as he retreats behind the camera. Aqua-Oceanic is the name of our fictional airline; it says so on the bulkhead.

A production assistant tells us to be quiet. We put away our phones and mirrors. "Hands up!" the man with the gun calls out, a smile in his voice. We groan and raise our hands to the correct height. The next take begins.

The man inches up and down the aisle again, his gun raised. This time the gun is pointed more consistently at people, a detail the director must have suggested: keep the gun higher. I can hear his footsteps in the aisle. Unlike a real flight, no droning engine noise obscures subtle sounds. I can hear the breathing of the woman next to me. Like all actresses, she is probably older than she looks, and she looks young middle-age, which means she is probably 50 or so. Keeping her hands in the air isn't as easy for her as for the teenager: her audible breathing means exertion. Even so, when he passes by, the man motions with the gun and gives her a hard look. She immediately raises her hands higher.

Then music begins playing. It's the phone in the pocket of the teenager's hoodie. The man with the gun gives the kid a playful cuff on the ear, and the director yells "Cut." A production assistant takes the phone away from the kid, who protests, "Oh man!"

"A lot of troublemakers in this row," jokes the gunman. He glances at me without recognition. Before I can remind him of the scene we did together years before, he smiles at my seatmate. "Susan, isn't it?" he says. "How are you?"

"We did '12 Angry Men,'" she says, relieving him of the burden of remembering when they worked together. "'You're alone. What do you think you're gonna accomplish?'"

"Ah, yes. You know, that's a wonderful line. What can the lone man accomplish? The question Goliath asks David, the question Grendel asks Beowulf: 'What can *you* accomplish?' Even this script," he adds, referring to the movie we're shooting. "One man, alone, on a plane. He doesn't know who the murderer is, no one does. Or indeed if there is only one."

"Maybe it's me," I put in.

He turns his head slightly to look at me and smiles. Before I can remind him that I too once worked with him, the director calls that the crew is ready. The gunman goes back to his starting place. "Dude is, like, already practicing for his Cannes interview," mutters the teenager.

"You did '12 Angry Men' with him?" I ask the woman.

"Off Broadway. I was Juror 7."

"Oh, me too. I'm mean, I've done the show. I was Juror 2." Not off Broadway, though. Not even in New York.

"Oh yes," she says in a polite but knowing tone. Almost every actor has done "12 Angry Men" at some point in their career—either that or "Our Town"—and Juror 2 is, famously, the worst part. Juror 2 is a nebbish, easily swayed.

The teenager is less diplomatic. "Juror 2," he scoffs. "Loser."

The gunman calls out "Hands up!" We raise our hands and the shot begins. Who is his character supposed to be, a cop or a hijacker? I think it's supposed to be unclear to the plane's passengers; that's why they didn't tell us. But he said something about how any of us could be a murderer. So he must be a good guy, a cop. I'm not supposed to know this, though, so I frame my facial expression with pronounced uncertainty.

Then it occurs to me that if this really is the plot of the movie, that a murderer—which is to say, an actor with a featured role—is hidden among us extras, then who could it be? I'd like to do as the gunman is doing, scan every face. If I recognize any of them, it would be because I'd seen them in movies before, and therefore they are likely to be more successful than the rest of us. That would be the murderer's face—the one that's familiar, yet still the face of a stranger.

The gunman creeps past our row. This time he doesn't even look our way. I guess I don't get to say my line, or what I started thinking of as my line. What was it? "No way."

The director calls "Cut." The woman next to me—Susan, isn't it?—takes out her mirror again and studies her face. "I don't like the looks of this. It has this subcutaneous wincy pain, an almost stabbing pain. Not like something's wrong with the skin. Under the skin."

"It's probably nothing," I say.

"Oh, it's something," she retorts. She hasn't taken her eyes off the suspicious spot. "But we all have to go sometime. I die on page 63."

She has a death scene? She has a copy of the script? "What happens?"

"I get shot. But like I say, almost everyone dies." I ask if the plane crashes. "No, they manage to land it, but meanwhile they blow a hole in the fuselage, and a lot of people get sucked out. Probably our whole row, but I don't care, I'll be dead by then. They'll have a dummy do the stunt. I have a 'Law and Order' to do in August anyway."

"Do we get to do anything like charge the cockpit?"

"It's not a hijacking story. It's a murder story. The plane just gives it a container."

"High concept," says the teenager. I want to elbow him in the face.

We all raise our hands. It occurs to me to wonder how much time I'll spend in the next month—the time they said we extras would be needed—with my hands in the air. It's not as bad for me as for my seatmate. When the director calls "Cut" again, she lets down her arms with a groan.

After two more takes of the gunman stalking up and down the aisle, the shot seems to have been completed successfully. The director says they're going to reset the camera positions—"Everybody stay put."

I'm thinking that this could be one of those legendary jobs extras talk about. Once I met one of the bus passenger extras from "Speed." That was a great gig, because even though she didn't have any lines, she got to do a lot of physical acting, jumping from one side of the bus to the other and so on. This is similar, except that I'm belted into a middle seat. Maybe there'll be more physical movement for me later.

"So we all die?" I ask.

"Pretty much," the woman says, taking out her mirror again. "Some of us sooner than others."

"I survive," the teenager says confidently. I ask him what makes him think so. "I just do."

"I doubt it," the woman says, gazing at her reflection. "I hate to tell you this: you're not special. Now that girl on the window," she says, indicating the little girl a few rows ahead, "she's special. She gets two pages of dialogue at the beginning, and a whole scene toward the end. She did a project with the Muppets last year. She survives. You, on the other hand, get sucked into the void at 35,000 feet."

"Suck on this," the teenager says.

"Maybe you just need a better agent," says the woman.

They move the camera behind us to set up a new shot. And now a secondary cameraman takes a passenger seat a few rows ahead and aims right at us. I envy the extra whom he displaced, somebody probably off taking a leisurely pee. The whole time, there's also been a guy with a steadi-cam stalking up and down on a platform outside the plane's fuselage, in tandem with the gunman. Now that they shoot in video and not on film, they can have as many cameras as they want. Those guys must be getting some pretty good union scale, several times an extra's pay. Hmm.

The director comes down the aisle and stops at our row. He looks at each of us: The teenager, me, the woman in the window seat. He looks fore, he looks aft, he walks down the aisle behind us. I crane my neck and look around. There's another hand-held cameraman back there.

"I've got a bad feeling about this," the teenager says, in his best Han Solo voice.

The director returns, stops and leans over us. "I've got good news and bad news." He points at me. "You're going to die."

"What's the bad news?"

He laughs, claps me on the shoulder. "Here's the thing. I'm going to have an A.D. yell your name. What's your name?"

"Alex."

"That's too long. He'll yell 'Two.' That's your cue. You stand up and start to turn around this way. Yes, to your right. You're panicking because you hear a shot. One beat later you get shot in the back. You go straight down against the seats in front of you, wham—no, harder. You're getting hit with a big bullet from thirty feet away, you go down hard. Got it? You hear your name, you stand up and turn slightly. You hear 'bang,' you're dead. What's your name?"

"'Two.'"

"Right." The director departs, and I take my seat again.

"Very good, Number Two," the teenager says in his best Doctor Evil voice.

"Pretty hard to shake that Juror 2 tag," says the woman in the window seat.

"I'm sure it's just coincidence."

"What was your big line?" she asks.

Despite myself I find myself repeating it, as I did every night for weeks during the rehearsals and performances, and, to myself, for many nights afterward. "'Anybody want a piece of gum?'"

"A job's a job," she intones—one of the verities of the actor's creed.

We rehearse the shot several times. I try to imagine what it would be like—they've left it up to me to imagine where I'm struck—to be hit by a bullet in the back. My whole life, I've had a sort of vulnerable spot, akin to a funny bone. It's in the middle of my back on the right side, where an enraged classmate struck me with a football on the playground one day in fourth grade. After he had messed up several plays that day, I called him stupid, and he got angry and threw the ball at me as hard as he could. I turned to protect myself, and it hit me in the back, right there. We had not been very good friends before that, but after that, I was his enemy. Even though I told him I was sorry, for the next three years he took every opportunity to trip, insult, undermine and upend me. It got to where I dreaded coming to school, for fear he would appear around a corner and find a new way of humiliating me. But it all started with that heavy football striking me in the back, raising a bruise that, in my imagination, has never completely healed.

They're ready. "You ready, Number Two?" calls the director. I say that I am.

My seatmate smiles up at me. It feels like the first time she's looked directly at me. "One things leads to another. Even if he didn't recognize you, maybe he'll remember killing you today." I didn't reply, but I doubted it. He must kill several people, even several dozen, in every film. How could my death be that important?

"Hands up, everyone," the gunman demands. "I don't want to have to tell you again." This time it doesn't sound like he's joking.

A bell rings. The director and crew issue their commands to each other. The scuffling begins behind me. I count seven beats. I hear the A.D. shout "Two!" I spring to my feet and begin to turn toward the noise. The last thing I hear is a loud report, and then the bullet enters my back—just in that thin, vulnerable spot—and my body recoils, pushed by a heavy blow. My ribcage pounds against the plastic seatback, my legs give out, and I slide to the floor. I find myself with my face in the woman's lap. The shouting and scuffling continue for a few long seconds, and then it's over.

The woman strokes my head. The camera can't see this gesture, and the shot is over anyway, but I don't get up. It feels comforting, so comforting. "You'll find something better," she says. "Soon."

"Work" Theme Contest Winner – 3rd Place

Spring 2015

Theology

David Hornibrook

I wonder if they taste the rot bloom in the mouth
       as a wooden ship might feel ghost life stir

when planks remember briefly how it felt to grasp the earth

I'm as far from the love of Jesus as you can make it in winter
       in this place where a bible is a nightstick

where love is a chokehold
       & mortgaged temples grow new wings each year

while snow falls so heavy over the baby in the plastic manger
       now the mother's up to her neck

but even the most trusted disciples turned like locks in their sleep
       while nearby a mountain heaved quietly into the sea

Faith means God is hiding somewhere on the rim of this disaster
       all this anger mistaken

for righteousness all this white noise

Grace means every curve of the earth will listen
       every edge fail

Heaven on Earth means
       a land where blinds can never close entirely

somewhere still subject to change

Enchantment

Jill McDonough

We're in Eberswalde, where they burned
the synagogue on Kristallnacht, where Ravensbrück
had a subcamp. After the war the East made it into
a club. A perfectly good building; why tear it down?
Before the band plays we walk through, beyond
the Christmas-lit bar, bright stage, to a dark room
of upturned leather club chairs: I think
of lampshades made of human skin.
Darker corridors and doorways, sunken
cardboard boxes, moldy overhead projector.
The doors are heavy. Concrete absorbs
all sound, though we're only rooms away
from the DJ, dancers, happy hour.
In one room we find thirteen sewing machines,
oak tables. I imagine they're the women,
under some enchantment. Freed from body,
breath, made into this, and we're come here
to save them. The music starts at ten.
Kids who come to see the show have shaved heads,
drab jackets, combat boots, tattoos. *I'm through,*
I'm thinking, want to fly home, cart off
the sewing machines. Scrub one sewing machine
with brushes, steel wool, Murphy's Oil Soap.
Rub warmed linseed oil in the table's thirsty grain,
let oak, enamel rest, soak it in on sheets of Sunday's
New York Times. The stoves are lit for hours,

but we still see our breath. The whitewash, disco
balls, and colored lights are new, but it was cold like this
for them. Our visible breath historically accurate.
We are burning all the coal we want.

Home

Matt Broaddus

I go into the mist tonight. Another black man is dead. My country is authorized. I am allowed to be angry in the mist. To get to my mist I cross the signs repeating in the important languages, *You are leaving the American zone.* It is important to know what I have given up by crossing into myself. In the mist it's misty, but I can see. Okigbo is there with the goddess. So's a knight in full armor charging thin air. There are silences where screams should be. I wanted to come here to consider the origin of heaven and earth. But today a man is dead. Today is every day of my life. No one taught me to be angry. Okigbo immerses himself in the river that is his goddess. The knight rides aimless, thrusting a lance into darkness. Riot police show up and throw tear gas. *Hey, this is my mist,* I say, and they fire.

Oracle Machine

Matt Broaddus

A blanched skull is enough
to know desert is underfoot.
I am propelled forward
with no highway, I dream
without a body. It is easy
to find answers—a tea kettle
gurgling in the sand, a fire
unattended. Across the plains,
an archive of destinations spreads.
The smell of mint, half a footprint
in the sand. Every grain yearns
for the unasked question.

September Requiem: In Which Sköll Swallows the Sun

M.K. Foster

—which is the Norse myth about the wolf-god who hunts, pursues the sun
around the earth, mouth open, lantern jaws sprung wide to consume, finally
snap down around the glowing orb: how the people of that land once described
solar eclipses to one another, believing that, breaking the neck of their only light,
the wolf-god had damned them to darkness—*the kind that only burial understands,*

I tell myself when I find you asleep in our empty bathtub and wake you from
another dream about drowning. Reaching up, you hold onto my ribcage as though
holding onto a stone in the middle of whatever river threatens to erase you in sleep.
You're grave-making, again. Through the soap, I can still smell the soil soaked into
your shoulders, feel the weight of the dirt straining across the nape of your neck as

your shape curls like a fist into my chest cavity, pulling me in with you and down—
so this is how light must feel, I think: exhausted, knowing that, once broken open,
it will never stop running, trying to escape itself. Mother, you are your mother's
daughter. People say this when they meet you. And it's not an answer, it's an
apology. I'm sorry. *Sorry she's not here,* they say. Or *sorry about her, she couldn't help*

being herself. Sorry she didn't get to see how you turned out. And you turn away. Here's
a riddle that keeps you up at night: *a man dies in a locked room with a hole in his head,*
there's water on the floor, blood in his hair, what happened? Not unlike, *a man falls asleep*
and wakes to find that he's killed 200 people, how is this possible? But more like *if your*
mother is X and your dreams Z, solve for Y—which could either be your father's memory

or a bottle or everything else you didn't want to inherit. Something is always missing. It's
noon: every window of our house is a mirror reflecting her silhouette from yours,
carving your form out of sky, and leaving a plague's worth of grackles scattered
beneath the wall-length glass outside, a constellation of wet, iridescent torsos
shivering into stillness, a cosmos you rake into piles and burn like damp leaves—

why is that? That we bury what won't stay up or go down? We were raised
to think more of our dead than as something to bury, raised to believe there's no
way forward but down, no way out but through. We pray for what destroys us.
I haven't lived enough to explain this kind of sacrifice to you with anything
that isn't my body lifting yours from the porcelain to move you to your bedroom.

The cause of death is always an icicle. The murderer is always a sleeping lightkeeper:
I'm sorry to be the one who has to tell you. I'm sorry how it's supposed to be noon,
how the days are shorter now, how the woods beyond us have become an orchestra
of abandoned trees, wild and hungry for wind, for anything that would move them
without being seen, bodies aching for touch without contact, how you shudder

in your sleep by night and shout, howl into cloud by day for anything, something
to obey you or come back to earth. Mother, the sycamores grieve for you like cellos:
how else can I convince you that this kind of safety is love? *Come out—*, they say.
You must come outside to scare the wolf away: an entire nation gathered beneath
the sky, screaming to bring back the star that sooner or later blinds us all.

Nox Manualis

M.K. Foster

A is for aperture, an opening with no guarantee of closure, a broken window dark with damp smoke. B is for your bones, exposed or otherwise. C is a crematorium, a way to leave by entering. D is for doorway, a way to enter, but not necessarily leave. E: exposure. *I tried to fall asleep in the snow on the day they burned you.* F is ninety-four degrees Fahrenheit, the beginning of hypothermia. G is glass, the condition of my skin as it froze. H is hypothermia, the outcome of trying to sleep in the snow. I is the ice in my water glass splitting the silence over our kitchen table. J: *just*— K: *know I*— L: *left an empty plate in the* M: *microwave if you're hungry, in case you come back from the dead in the middle of the* N: *night*, a nerve, exposed or otherwise. O: your oranges, forgotten gutted exposed on our kitchen table. P: the panic of cardinals collapsing on our snow-bleached yard. Q: the queries I left for God in the votive beside the cathedral reliquary. R: the roof lifting away from our house, landing like a broken bird in the yew tree across the street. S: the skin on the roof of your mouth, the shape of your body in sleep, the sleep you lost through the floorboards the season you spent wanting a way to fix things before they could break from weather or wear, the sleep you lost through yourself and you scarred with night like the sky scarred with cloud from the storm that carried you, the storm that carried you into the river, the silence your body spoke when they pulled you from the river, your body swollen into the soft slick shape of sleep— T is for *noli me tangere*, do not touch me. U is for *ego postulo ut sepeliam*, I need to bury. V: my vena cava, exposed or otherwise. W is a crematorium window filling with black smoke. X is the dark window of an x-ray of your chest cavity filled with water. Y: the lost yellow teeth collected into a cereal bowl on our kitchen table below Z: a zero, a hollow black frame hammered and hammered and nailed white-hard into the only wall that faces the sun in December.

Christina's Field

Virginia Konchan

(after Wyeth)

My only dream the dream
of becoming modern,
jilted bride crawling a
vacant field, bereft.
Host to parasites,
I, motherboard,
am the only
matrix left.
Capital's unholy,
naturalized birth
not in a roadside inn
but the grave, abloom
with the vulgar gaucherie
of clematis and snapdragons:
metaphor-on-wheels
(floating signifier,
shining signal flare)
of my avatar mind,
winged, singed body,
desperado mouth.

Composed in the Form of Falling

———————

Douglas Smith and Jen Town

Here is the farmer, turning and turning in the fields near the sea. Here is his empty house on the cliff, and the birds calling at night. Once the farmer believed in a separate god, a god who contained the sea with doors, but now he walks, without company, under a solitude of stars. *To swim in those white waves*, he thinks, but he is no diver descending through air. He is a farmer of dry earth, and the blessing of water is away.

She sleeps each night in her boat on the sea, and rows toward a distant cliff each day. Once a man said *Dawn* to her there, night a distance to travel. A bottle might contain her words, she dreams, and those words might be a field after rain, or the surface of flesh over bone, or a tongue. When she wakes at dawn, she presses her empty hands together, remembering.

Somewhere upon the sea, the farmer believes, a small boat rides. Look closer, for in that boat the body of a woman turns, alone, muttering into a bottle from the chamber of sleep.

Rowing in light, she imagines insects descending over those fields near the sea. Summer hums and churns the dangerous air, each kernel of the ripening corn a farewell. She still sees the hands of the man who held her there, the creases of dirt and halos of nails. In the stalks, where their bodies once mingled, pollen-drunk bees drone.

What else is a body, the farmer once wrote her, *if not a figure of desire?* Now he imagines, in a prayer, the curved scar on her left thigh, and the way his tongue slid down the ladder of her spine, and the unfolding of her body in joy. Each day he reads, in her absence, an unanswerable sentence composed of sea and sky and the punctuation of birds.

Here is the only world, she whispers, the lone mast a mark written against the given sky. She yearns to tell him how the arc of sea birds is the end of a story she once knew, how the lap of waves is the murmuring of a voice after love, how the night makes a consolation of stars. Each morning she rows toward his waiting figure, the hum of oars a slow song in her hands.

There, on the sea, held aloft, the cuneiform of a mast appears. Consider the farmer, his mouth open with sound, amazed on this earth by such return. Imagine the birds wheeling above her distant boat, and the light between. Now, in time, let the farmer leap with his body from the cliff, descending below the earth and the house and the unmade bed within. Let him leave the bees of the fields behind. He has become, in the abandon of his fall, an offering.

End of Evolution

───────────

Karen Skolfield

All the changing things had reached
their final forms. The lettuce: perfect and buttery.
The housecat: the correct balance of fur and aloof.

The human: if the brain case were any larger,
they'd fall over. Grassblade: every one a whistle.
The world studded by its own unchanging.

The alpha animals rested. With the pinnacle reached,
there was no reason to fight. The male wolves friendly.
The female wolves chose mates by lottery.

What was the difference? One as good as the other.
In the city, speed dating became speedier
with all choices equally compelling.

Children held the hands of the nearest adult
without ever looking up, since any random adult
made the best parent. The adults never minded.

She'd had her own children once—she vaguely
remembered this—and she had loved them,
but she would love whatever child was near her now.

She led the child to her home, or to a home
that might as well be hers, they were so similar.
She made noodles, which all children love.

She imagined that her own children must be
happily eating noodles with another adult
who was doing an equally excellent job of parenting.

There would be talk about school and soccer,
the new kids' book about magic which read just like
the old kids' book about magic. Children these days

have such great lives, she thought.
None of the cowlicks of her youth.
Later they cuddled on the couch, watched reruns.

The little boy fell asleep with his head
in her lap, the best sleeping posture of children.
The evening had been perfect. Tomorrow

would be more of the same. She wondered
at the twitch of muscles across his little face,
what he dreamed of, if he even dreamed at all.

Used Doors and Windows for Sale

David Wagoner

Here in this vacant lot
the dislocated doors
and windows have no houses
        or even walls to hold them,
        no thresholds or lintels
        to turn away from, nothing
to close for or reopen
as they lean against each other,
no longer measuring
        or defining the difference
        between inside and outside,
        but simply being themselves
as they were in the beginning,
reflecting the glancing blows
of sunlight, undersides
        of leaves, the superior
        appearances of clouds,
        the indifference of the sky.

The Song of a Dog

_____

Caroline Bruckner

It was because I had fallen out of the tree no one liked me. We were seven children on the farm. You'd think I'd find a friend between my sisters and brothers. It didn't matter. I had Rascal. Rascal wasn't allowed into the house, so I slept out in the barn with him. We lay there together, protected from the world, pressed close, body to body, for heat and comfort. I listened to the cows grunting and the soft turning of the mill by the river as the shadows came down and felt how lucky I was to have a best friend.

When I came into the kitchen, Mother was arranging the breakfast. "Trudi," she scolded as she saw me in the door. "I don't know what to do with you." She shook her head and handed me a bun. She put extra sausage on it because she knew I would give it to Rascal. "You can't live in the barn forever, girl," she continued as she poured me a glass of warm milk.

"I don't live in a barn, I live in a castle," I answered, and she smiled then, turning away so I wouldn't notice.

"Do we want our breakfast, Lord Rascal?" I asked as soon as we turned the corner behind the mill. Rascal barked and stood up on two legs until I threw him the sausage. If I had known in time how much friendlier dogs are than humans, I would have chosen to be born a dog. I liked running, and barking, and scratching myself behind my ear, so maybe there had been a mistake in the making of me. My siblings certainly thought so. And most of the other children in school agreed. We rarely had anything to do with them, Rascal and me. Our days were full with burying treasures in the woods and chasing each other and taking long naps in the sun.

The road to school was long and crooked. Winter and summer we walked for an hour. We started off before Maria and Rudi so we would be free to do as we liked without any comments from their dull hearts. Maria was vain and Rudi strict. "Don't *bark*, Trudi!" Rudi would scold and throw a stone at me. "Don't destroy your *skirt*!" Maria would cry and put her hand in front of her mouth. "You are *embarrassing* us!" they would shriek together.

Pride made me bark even louder and roll in the dirt one more time, as anyone with a noble soul would understand.

We were not afraid of anyone. We ran through the fields and stole apples from the orchards. We stuck our tongues out at the train passing and barked at Postman Fritz on his bike. There was only one person in the world we looked out for and that was Hunter Lizt. Hunter Lizt was rotting from the inside, and worms had eaten his heart. His moustache looked like a dead adder curling above his dry, thin lips. His small, black eyes were cold as bullets in a box. Every child was afraid of Hunter Lizt. "That shit-dog belongs on a chain!" he'd shout at me and rattle his shotgun. I was terrified of him. If we had to pass him on the road, I'd hide in the bushes at the side of the street. "Never ever cross Hunter Lizt, Rascal," I whispered in the dog's ear, his curly hair tickling my nose.

I could not sit quiet for long, knowing Rascal waited for me outside. Every few minutes I'd stretch my head, trying to look outside into the yard to see what Rascal was doing. It was a fine morning; the sun was shining and spring was everywhere.

"Would you continue reading, Trudi?" Fräulein Rosa's sharp voice cut through the room. I had not even opened the book. I felt my cheeks turn red as I flipped through the pages. "Page twenty-one, start at the top of the page." Fräulein Rosa half sat on her desk and looked out over the classroom. I bit my lip and tried to remember what twenty-one looked like. I used to know it, but since I fell out of the tree, all letters and numbers seemed to have fallen out of my head. I could feel them giggling behind me. "Who will help Trudi find the page?" They were quiet then. Only the sweet, freckled Anna leaned back and turned the page for me. It didn't help much, of course. I felt inside of myself for the meaning of the black pattern on the paper. I looked close, trying to understand, trying to decipher the signs. But the closer I looked, the more the page blurred, and suddenly the things that I knew must be letters started turning and flying and dancing, and after a little while all the words had danced off the page, and there was only a big, empty hole left. Just at this moment Rascal howled, feeling my distress. It came from deep inside, from that place where love lives. *Woff woooff wooooofff!* The children shrieked with laughter. Fräulein Rosa slammed the stick on her desk. "Vile child! Stop at once! At once!" Dark stains spread under her arms. The letters danced around my head and I could not stop barking.

I was sitting in the outhouse with the door open as she biked into the yard. Fräulein Rosa must have been mighty upset to come all the way from the village in the rain. I saw her face and chilled. She had been to the farm once before. My brother Erwin had forced a kid to eat a spider, and the kid had vomited on his desk in the classroom. Erwin got ten "lessons" with the belt from father. The boy could not sit for a week without pressing his lips together. I knew I only had a minute or two before my mother would see her from the kitchen window. I looked at Rascal, who sat at my feet, and I shivered. "Better run," I warned him. "I'll get you when we're safe." Rascal licked my leg before disappearing behind the outhouse.

I stepped through the door to the sitting room. It seemed unusually cold inside, even though the sun was shining straight in.

"Close the door," Mother said with her *fine* voice. I had only heard Mother use her fine voice when talking to Pater Alfons after Sunday Mass. Fräulein Rosa sat, posing as a very important lady, back straight and lips pressed together. Her pale fingers held onto the delicate teacup, the gold-rimmed ones with the violets that were only used on special occasions, in a way that made me want to scream. Both women stared down at me, frowning. One does feel guilty when people are looking at one in that way. "Gertrude, I am ashamed of you," Mother continued. "Apologize to Fräulein Rosa for your childish, vile behavior."

The grandfather clock ticked restlessly. I could not take my eyes off the heavy pendulum swaying back and forth. *Tick-tock. Tick-tock.* "Gertrude!" Mother's voice was shrill now. There was a clang as Fräulein Rosa put her teacup back on the saucer demonstratively. I wanted to say something; I searched my brain for the right words but I couldn't find anything. My mind was empty but for the tick-tock. *Tiiiick-toooock.* "It is because of the fall." Mother tried to sound rational. "She was the sweetest child before the fall."

I felt an urge pushing in on me, and then there was a kind of leap. My hands touched the floor suddenly. I realized I was on my hands and knees only after I had started barking, only after Fräulein Rosa had dropped the violet teacup, only after Mother stopped cursing.

Mother placed the two hot bricks in front of the stove. I rolled up my trouser legs above my knees.

"It is for your own good, Trudi," she sniveled.

"I don't mean to!" I shouted. "I can't help I fell out of that stupid tree!"

"Do it quick."

"Mami!" I pleaded, but I knew she was right.

I kneeled down on the hot bricks. Mother cried as I screamed. She held me then as tears streamed down my cheeks. "Promise me to never bark at people ever again."

My knees burned, my legs were shaking, my head spun.

I promised.

I was sent to bed without supper. Lying next to my sister Maria, I wished I was in the barn with Rascal. I wondered if he was missing me too, up in the hay. I was waiting for everyone to go to sleep so I could sneak out and go home. "You have to stop this nonsense, Trudi," Maria whispered suddenly. "It will all end badly."

"I already knelt on the bricks," I whispered back.

She turned to me then and looked at me in the dark. "Father will shoot Rascal."

Her words hung in the air, suspended like hot air balloons. "Father says they have been letting you run wild for too long and you need a lesson."

My heart stopped beating and I could not breathe. The air was locked.

"Trudi, can you hear me?" Maria shook my shoulders. "Trudi?"

The terrible, terrible words curled around my throat, strangling me. I lay there and I was dead. "Look, you *got* to start behaving like a normal girl!"

I thought about Rascal running around the meadow behind the farm. I felt the wet grass under my naked feet, the sun in my hair, the strength inside me as I ran after him. Breath came into me again.

"He won't really shoot Rascal, will he?"

"It will be all right if you just stop being bad," Maria said almost gently.

"I already did sit on the hot bricks! My knees are all red, Mother had to put Marigold cream on them!"

"Will you stop behaving like a *dog*? Will you?"

"Yes."

"Will you be a pretty, sweet girl like before?"

I sighed and nodded. Maria leaned on her elbow, satisfied. "Got a kiss for your big sister?"

Hating the touch of her, I withdrew my cheek quickly.

I knew better than to leave right away. A good escape needs careful planning. I had to find Rascal before Father did. I had to pick a warm sweater and a blanket. We would need food to last us a few days and a good knife for life in the woods. I would take a roll of cheese, two smoked sausages, a loaf of bread. I was waiting for Maria's breath to slow down. I saw us, me and Rascal, living in a cave overlooking the Great Alp. I saw us; I cut up a small piece of sausage and offered it to Rascal. His round dog eyes shone then, and I knew all would be well.

I poked Maria on her arm but she didn't stir. "Rascal, Rascal, Rascal," I whispered, calling him to me as I snuck to the bedroom door.

I struggled with the door for a moment before I realized. The door was locked. Mother had locked the door.

The next morning Maria insisted on combing my hair and braiding it. I had to press my legs down with my hands to force myself to sit still.

"Are you nervous?" she asked and tugged at a piece of my hair.

"I need to pee," I said but it wasn't true.

"Oh, you can sit still for another minute. Fräulein Rosa will have to forgive you with such nice braids."

She is doing it deliberately, I thought, to make me suffer, to prevent me from going to find Rascal.

"You look almost like a normal girl!" Maria exclaimed proudly. "Aren't you going to say thank you?"

I had a feeling, a feeling that something was going to happen soon. There was a heaviness waiting in the air. "Yes," I said uncertainly. "Thank you."

Rascal was chained to the wall in the courtyard. They had strapped a leather pouch over his muzzle. Someone could have chopped my right leg off, and it would not have hurt more. I kneeled down beside him, pressing his head against my heart. I looked down onto his face; he looked up at me helplessly. "I'll get you out of this!" I whispered. "I'll get you out of it."

"Your dress will get dirty!" My mother's voice like a whip behind me.

"Why is Rascal in chains?" I asked, even though of course I knew the answer.

"The dog will stay here from now on, Trudi."

"But he always walks to school with me!" I pressed back the tears.

"Hurry up, we'll come too late!" shouted Maria from the kitchen door.

I looked up at my mother.

"Where is Father?"

"That's it, Gertrude! You have worn down my patience!" She grabbed me under my arms and forced me to stand up. "It's ruined!" She pulled and tugged at my dress, her hands shivering. "What will you say to Fräulein Rosa?"

"Father won't hurt Rascal, will he?"

"You will beg her for forgiveness and you will mean it!"

"He won't hurt him? Mother?"

"He won't hurt the dog."

"Promise?"

"I promise, you stubborn child!" She slapped my behind and I knew I could trust her.

I walked next to Maria all the way to school. My legs were twitching and feet itching, but I kept on putting one foot after the other, slowly and orderly. There was a dead cat at the side of the road. I longed to get down on all fours and sniff it. I longed to tell Rascal about it. About the way it was lying there, the texture of life gone out of it. Poor Rascal, tied to the wall like a criminal. A burning flame of hate came over me. Stupid, stupid grown-ups, I thought over and over. Stupid, stupid grown-ups.

The class was sitting in neat rows, all faces in quiet anticipation. Fräulein Rosa sat with her hands carefully folded on her desk.

"I believe someone has something to say."

Everyone turned to look at me. Obediently I stood up. There was a sharp burn in my throat. "I am terribly sorry for the despicable way I behaved. There is no excuse even if I *did* fall out of a tree and hurt my head. I promise to be a nice girl from now on and never bark again."

Suppressed chuckles from the back row. Fräulein Rosa nodded vainly, her sharp, dry face grave.

"You are a selfish girl, Gertrude. From now on I want you to stop trying to be the center of attention." She unfolded her hands and tapped the tip of the desk to underline her point. "A little actress you are, quite the sly wench."

I bowed my head in shame. Fräulein Rosa went on and on but I didn't hear her. I listened for Rascal breathing outside, but of course he wasn't there. I was perfectly still and I listened. I listened all the way down the road, past the dead cat, over the old stone bridge, and back home until I finally heard him. Fräulein Rosa babbled in the background, low and steady like a river. Rascal breathed. I could feel his chest rising and falling. I bowed my head and I adjusted my breath to rise and fall like his.

"You are a very spoiled girl, Gertrude," Fräulein Rosa stated. "Spoiled girls need to learn humility."

Steps on the gravel. Then suddenly a shot.

"STOP IT," I moaned in wild panic. I could not breathe. There was no breath left. I searched for Rascal. Fräulein Rosa stood up abruptly, quiet now. She started to hum as she opened the lowest drawer on her desk. She took out the pipe she sometimes used for punishment. The class gasped in silence.

"I didn't mean for Fräulein Rosa to…"

"Quiet!" Her eyes were black as bullets.

"Please let me go home!" I pleaded with a shrieking voice I had never heard coming out of me before. "Please, Fräulein! My dog!"

Fräulein Rosa needed only to blink for me to walk up to the front of the classroom.

I held on with both hands to the desk. As the pipe hit my behind, all the bones in my body rattled and cried with icy shock. I tried to listen for Rascal, but my head was alight with electric spasms. I stared down at my hands, holding on so tight to the edge of the desk the bones shone ghostly through the skin. The boys could hardly suppress their giddiness. Sweet Anna had a tear running down her cheek. I didn't care about either. Mother promised, I thought. Mother promised he will be there waiting for me.

I hobbled straight into the main stall and climbed the ladder upstairs. My body ached, my knees burned, but my heart was full of yearning. "Rascal?" I wheezed. My eyes had not yet adjusted to the dark, but I knew this place well enough to navigate in the blackest night. I had not crawled a meter before I felt something missing in the air. "It's me," I whispered, ignoring the shivering, cold thing growing in my gut. "Where are you, boy?"

I knew he was not there, and still I searched the entire haystack and each and every corner of the barn. The panic grew thick in my throat. I closed my eyes and forced myself to become entirely still. *She promised. He will be running about, chasing mice on the field.* I pressed my face against the wall and listened to the sounds of the farm. A loose door somewhere was shutting and opening quietly in the wind. Mother, walking back from the vegetable garden, resting for a moment under the tall cedars behind the main house. A dog that was not Rascal barked in the neighboring farm.

"I am back," I shouted. "Where is he?"

Mother's face was colored a dark green as she sat under the tree. She did not look up.

"Did Fräulein Rosa forgive you?"

"He is not in the courtyard!"

"Well, he must be here somewhere," Mother said, flattening out a wrinkle on her apron. "I saw him just a minute ago."

My heart became a cup of light full of stars. How silly I had been! How silly it had been, feeling afraid when Mother had promised! I ran up to her and threw myself into her lap. She put her heavy hand on my head and sighed.

"I found some wild strawberries. You want some with cream?"

I buried my face deeper in her skirt and shook my head.

"Trudi, not wanting wild strawberries?"

"Trudi was bad," I managed to stutter. "Maybe you can beat me up tomorrow."

"Why tomorrow?"

"Fräulein Rosa already gave me the rod today."

A quiet came over her then.

"I remember now. I saw him running into the woods a while ago." Mother's hand tightened around my neck. "I hope he is careful. Hunter Lizt is in a bad mood since his front tooth had to be pulled."

Slowly I raised my head to look at Mother. In the darkness beyond the words, there was a quiver. Mother did not look at me. She swept up, brushed me aside, and collected her baskets of vegetables.

It was humiliating. Nothing was said at dinner. I was served a thick piece of rye bread with sausage and lard just like the others. My father grunted as he ate, as he always did. For a few minutes I almost believed nothing had happened. Maria passed the salt, Rudi ate all the pickles, the older ones had their beers. No one mentioned either my bad behavior earlier in the day or the disappearance of Rascal. I stared at their faces, one after the other. The features seemed to not belong to them individually but to a monstrous being with multiple eyes and many legs, like a spider. They talked about Greta, the cow that was soon to give birth, and Farmer Hannes, who had tried to cheat with the wheat again. I sat there among them and wished I had died falling out of that tree. You are murderers, I wanted to shout. You will burn in hell.

This night the door was not locked. I smiled brokenly up at the house as I crossed the yard. The moon shone on the roofs and the river and my hands when I put them up in front of me. As I had suspected, the muzzle hung orderly on a hook in the garage. My fingers worked with an intelligence of their own. The leather smelled of earth and dried meat as I strapped it over my nose and mouth. Rascal, I thought, Rascal my brother, my friend. What they did to you, they did to me.

The rain started sometime after four. One by one the stars disappeared, and the vastness of the sky was lost behind the clouds. I closed my eyes and put my ear to the ground, listening to the sounds of the earth beneath me. I could feel the buzzing of life from ants and worms and grass trying to grow. Far down I could hear the heart of the earth beating, whispering its ancient secrets to those who knew to listen. This is my place now, I thought. I will never leave. My skin seemed to welcome the wet rain in spite of the chill. I was not cold, not really, not in the place that counts.

It was when my mother propped the kitchen door open it came over me again. The warm scent of bread in the oven swept out behind her. "Trudi!" Mother shrieked, her hands moving up to cover her mouth. For a minute we stared at each other, just breathing. And then I let it loose. I barked and bellowed and howled. I yelped and wailed and growled.

"She has chained herself to the wall!" my mother cried. "Franz, come here! She is even wearing the muzzle!"

She tried to step up to me. I stood on all fours and lunged at my mother, baring teeth and shrieking. If she so much as tried to touch me, I would bite her hand off. If anyone tried to touch me, I would fight like a dog.

.

How We Live

Tally Brennan

Here she comes, the queen of Caroline Street. Watch her stalk right by us and not even look. That poor *imbecille* she's dragging behind by his wrist? Johnny, her son. A grown man, treated like a bag of trash to be hauled to the curb. And the whole time, *she's* the reason he's like that. You can ask anyone.

I'm telling you. If that woman made even one friend in the neighborhood, she wouldn't be living off junk food. Half an hour it takes her to tow Johnny as far as the convenience store when it's only around the corner on Eighth. Remember where DiCicco's pharmacy used to be? Some foreigners have the place now. Arabs, maybe? I don't go there myself. Not even for milk.

See that? It hurts me to my heart to watch her yank Johnny's arm. His shoulder jerks forward. The rest of him stays put. His joints could pull apart, like those Tinkertoys kids used to have. You think he has to fall on his face. Then his foot moves. His bones stumble into line. There he stands, with no more idea than an infant of taking the next step. *Madonn!* He's turning forty. Five months younger than Dominic, my baby. Him and Dom were so close once they could of been Siamese twins, except for Johnny's blond hair and blue eyes. His hair's still the same but his eyes are empty, empty and blue as the sky.

So. How's life in the suburbs? Makes me sad, all you young people moving out. Where are you headed? Your mother's? I'll walk with you as far as the curb market, if we stay on this side of the street. All of a sudden I'm wishing for fennel. A fennel and cucumber salad. For me, fennel is a taste of spring.

It's been thirty-five years. Can you believe it? Thirty-five years with that woman next door and her refusing to talk. That's not how we live here. You grew up in the neighborhood. You know how close row house people are. Like family. Used to be, I would hear her husband coughing at night through the party wall. We could of been in bed together. *She* never spoke, except back in the beginning when she would call on the phone for me to send Johnny home. *Sono la madre di Giancarlo.*

La madre my ass. Did she ever step outside to see him back safe? Poor baby had to stretch up on his tiptoes to reach the bell. *Her* door was always kept locked.

Know what I'm thinking now? Braised fennel. With black olives and thyme. Ever try that? Does your stomach good, like a tonic.

Listen. Hear those car horns going crazy? It takes her forever to cross. Makes drivers nuts. Once, some guy with Jersey tags yelled at her out his car window. Go back where you came from, lady. I had to laugh. He didn't live here no more, but he knew just from looking: *She* didn't belong.

She only ever had the one child, but she didn't have no time to watch him. It was all about the violin. Her playing her violin while he was out playing by himself in the street. I brought him inside. Let him watch TV with my boys. That's how he learned to talk English. He never would of learned at home. I tried to tell her. *Iddu è sularinu.* He's lonely. Know what she says? *Lui è solitario.* Like I should learn good Italian.

They came from there, her and her husband. From the North. Milan. He got hired to teach piano at the Institute of Music. Hiring her too was the price of his coming. When they practiced with their groups, neighbors sat on my steps to listen. No one got invited in. What do you expect? We all come from immigrants, but we're Sicilians. Or Calabres'. Too dark. Too ignorant. Not refined like them, with hands so delicate they couldn't pick up a broom. Us peasants cleaned their sidewalk. My Chuckie still shovels her snow, even when I tell him don't bother. Let the city give her a ticket if she can't put her head out to say thanks.

And San Rocco's parish school that was good enough for us? Not good enough for them. Johnny had to go uptown, to Wentworth Academy. After school, a cab took him for music lessons. Sight reading. Ear training. Finger exercises. Practice? Ha! He was always over to my house, while *she* was at the Institute, teaching brilliant students from around the world. He never practiced. The lessons stopped.

Just walk across to Claudio's with me while I get my olives. I'll buy you some nice cheese to take home. A couple of Dave's artichoke hearts. Make you wish you never left the neighborhood.

307

Know what Johnny missed most, not going to school at San Rocco's? He wanted to be an altar boy, like all four of my kids. They got out of class to serve funerals. But Johnny, he was dying to dress up in the cassock and surplice. Carry the incense boat. Tap that three-tiered brass gong when the priest genuflects at the consecration of the host.

I was the one begged Father Lorenzo to give him a chance, so guess who had to wash and iron the lace surplice. *She* didn't even show up to watch him, the one Sunday he got to serve.

Like a little blond angel he was, kneeling on the altar step, face lifted, eyes on the priest, holding the leather-wrapped mallet ready. With the church all hushed and waiting, Johnny tapped that gong perfect. One, two, three. But he didn't stop there. He had to go on playing a tune. "Mary Had A Little Lamb." Played it right to the end. I never had to hand-wash no more lace for him.

They started a band together, him and my two youngest boys, down in the basement where I put up tomatoes for gravy. Johnny on keyboard. Pat on drums. Dom on that electric guitar Chuckie bought him. Eighty bucks, new. Could of fell off a truck maybe. I knew not to ask.

If Johnny heard a song once, he could play it, but he wouldn't stay with the tune. He had to wrap it around, up, down and sideways, with all kind of extra notes. Dom said it wasn't rock. Johnny just laughed. The madder Dom got, the more Johnny laughed. Laughed so hard he fell on the floor. Him rolling around on my cellar floor laughing with Dominic all the while kicking him, kicking him. That *mamaluke* thought it was a joke, anyone trying to hurt him. I had to pull Dominic off by his hair. That was the end of the band.

Feel this fennel how nice. Solid. Not a spot on the bulb. When Johnny used to cook with me, he browned his fennel in butter. Liked it more than in oil.

He wasn't like other kids, Johnny. He'd sit in my kitchen and talk. Chatter, chatter, chatter. If I asked my own boys what happened at school, they'd tell me nothing. Nothing happened.

Talk, talk, talk. What a twitch he was, playing with my garlic press, my juicer. No idea what his hands was doing. All the time asking questions. Why wipe a fish before you sear it? Because oil and water don't mix. Why use only male eggplants? Less seeds, and they're sweeter. How do you tell the boys from the girls? You look at the bottom.

He choked.

I'm serious, I told him. Have some respect. Do a thing right or don't do it.

He tried not to laugh. He held his breath to keep from cracking up, like I had to be putting him on. I wasn't.

Johnny blushed when he laughed. His face turned red as boiled lobster. Eyes squeezed shut. Tears leaking out the corners. Tears so clear they looked blue. Pale blue tears.

When he handed me back my zester with the handle broke off, I said it's time you got serious. I showed him how to strip lemon peel without digging into the white. Chop with his fingers bent. He laughed. When I went to add it, the zest was red with his blood.

I tried to teach him to measure. He wanted to cook the way I do, by feel. A pinch of this. A handful of that. First follow the rules, I told him. Rules are there for a reason. He never did learn no respect.

It was all new to Johnny. They must of lived off antipast' over there because *she* never cooked. Johnny said she hated the garlic smell coming through the wall. Still, she had to live in our neighborhood. Where else could she walk two blocks and find every imported cheese? Fresh macaronis. All kind of seafood. Proscuitt'. Salami. Oil they sell by the ounce, like perfume. She wanted to live in our neighborhood, but she didn't want us to.

Know what's nice with fennel? Chopped anchovies. Four or five, if you have them. Don't make it fishy. Just add some depth to the flavor.

Johnny took his time growing up. In his teens, he was tall and thin and soft as overcooked spaghetti. My niece Gina pushed him around and she was two years younger than him. Johnny just laughed.

My boys were sneaking *Playboy* into the house. Johnny bought *Gourmet* magazine. Making fun of them. And me. Mocking what anyone thought was so all-important. If we got mad, he laughed more. But good natured, you know? Amazed and delighted, like it was some comedy routine, us taking serious what to him was a joke. He'd be wiping his eyes, waiting for us to laugh too, once we caught on that we were fooling ourselves.

See where the t-shirt place is on the corner? That was my dad's restaurant. Angie's. You can still read the sign painted up there on the stucco. It's faded now. Maybe someday I'll bring a ladder and freshen it up.

My dad ran a card game when he was younger. Behind Orsino's camera shop. Remember him? Jerry Orsino? On Sixth Street? Before your time, I guess.

Even gamblers get hungry, my dad said, so he learned to cook. Then, when the street tax doubled, he shut down the game and opened his own place. Nice, with white table cloths, candles. If he was short-handed, he put us kids in the kitchen to do the prep. It was only another neighborhood restaurant, but you don't make it here serving crap. Eating good is our tradition. People come from all over. And people like you come back.

Celebrities too. Frank Sinatra. Dean Martin, when he was in town. Nico Papelino—Papa, they called him—that was head of the mob here for twenty years. Papa loved my dad's veal rollatini. When the big boys passed though on their way down the shore, he brought them along, but he never did business there. He had respect. And he got respected.

Eighty-dollar bottles of wine Papa would order and share with the tables around him. Try a little of the white pizza. Give me your plate. Like the fresh mozzarell'? Calamari? Tonno? Don't be afraid. Taste the pepperoncini.

Papa had French cuffs with gold cufflinks. The manicured nails. A pinky ring with a ruby. Three-piece suits, all custom. But conservative, you know? Never the flashy silk those young guys liked to strut around in, trying to draw attention. You were from the neighborhood? You had a problem? If Papa could fix it, he would. He was generous with the tips. The room got brighter when he came in. That's the power he had. Like a prince.

It was my dad's place those young Turks picked to blow Papa away. Three shooters in a room of innocent people. Mirrors all smashed. Eleven bullets in him and Papa still took two nights and two days to die.

That started the war. You won't remember, but thirty people got whacked before it was over. Bodies left lying in the street. All those young guys dead or disappeared into witness protection. Too greedy to wait their turn.

Johnny read every word they wrote in the papers. Couldn't talk about nothing else. None of our business, I told him. We don't bother them. They don't bother us.

To him, the mob was a joke. Like *The Three Stooges* on cable TV. Johnny loved *The Three Stooges*. He would love those tours Marie Martello gives. A bunch of mayonnaise faces stand around staring at a patch of sidewalk while she tells them how this one and that one got hit. What the medical examiner found stuffed down their throat, up their ass. A roll of cash. A canary. The tourists laugh, but it's a nervous laugh. It should be.

Back on the bus, Marie tries to sell them her book. *Cucinare con La Nonna*. Who is she kidding? Our grandmothers never followed a recipe in their life. They couldn't read. I read fine, but I don't do real gourmet. Mostly I cook what my mother cooked. I feel more comfortable, knowing what to expect.

What do you think? Can somebody like Johnny still taste? A clear, clean taste like fennel, maybe. How hard would it be to buy extra? A couple more bulbs. Just take me a minute. Okay?

Even as a kid, Johnny had a talent for combining flavors. Said he'd go to restaurant school after graduation. That was just talk. They sent him away to college. He flunked out his first year.

No kid that age should have so much time on his hands. I said I'd find him a job bussing tables or prepping. I still had the contacts. He would of learned how professionals work. He would of had something solid. Johnny just laughed. He looked at me and he laughed, face all red, eyes floating like oysters on the half shell. I told him don't come over no more. That's how mad he made me. I got past it soon enough, but he never came back. What was I supposed to do, chase after him?

He did fill out, finally. Johnny could of been a male model, he looked that good in clothes. Maybe the Rossi girl thought she could have him on the side. She should of known that's not how it works. Some women get a thrill being close to danger.

I swear to God. Everybody knew Carla Rossi was Tommy Tassone's *comar'*. Tommy Two Toes, they called him. Toes wasn't a made man. Just an associate that still had to prove himself. He couldn't let nothing like that slide.

Everybody knew, but nobody said nothing. Not to Johnny. Not to her. They lived in their world. We lived in ours. What are you going to do?

Used to be, Wise Guys took their girlfriends out Fridays. Saturday was for wives. Rules like that would make Johnny laugh 'til he cried. If he even knew.

That Saturday, Toes took his wife to Atlantic City. He made sure plenty of people saw them. Left three of his crew waiting outside Carla Rossi's apartment.

Johnny would think it was a game, three thugs dancing around him, Larry, Curly, and Moe. He'd be laughing himself limp. Until he got beat into the ground. Left to lay in his blood until morning.

He woke up with a metal plate in his head. The piano player took off back to Milan. No music comes out of that house now. She's busy changing diapers, spooning in the convenience food. *Sono la madre di Giancarlo.* What kind of joke is that?

So. Am I kidding myself thinking a taste can reach him? Would Johnny laugh if he knew? Will she slam the door in my face?

Wait a minute. Cardamom. I forgot the cardamom. That's how long it's been. Johnny would taste the difference. At least I hope he would. Thyme I got growing in pots on my windowsill, but for cardamom pods, I go to the Vietnamese woman down the end of the block. If she's still there. The Vietnamese are moving out to the suburbs now. Mexicans moving in. Taking over the Italians' stalls. Selling mangos, papayas. Cactus. Those people eat cactus. How do they cook it? Maybe the way I cook fennel, simmered in chicken stock. Unless they use a microwave, like everybody your age does.

Seen those new houses? Used to be the market's parking lot there. Town homes, they're calling them, but you and I know they're row houses, even with roof decks and garages underneath for their cars. The rest of us fight for what street parking is left.

Did your mother tell you San Rocco's school got turned into condominiums? The candy stores are all gone now. You don't smell garlic on every block in the late afternoons. Everything's changing. Except me. And her. Me on my side of the wall. Her on hers. The two of us blaming each other, like Johnny himself didn't do nothing. He'd be laughing for sure.

Now I'm wondering. What if Johnny was right and it is all a joke? What if how we live doesn't matter? Thinking that makes me feel dizzy. Like in this dream I have where I open the door to a room with no walls, no floor. One step and I'm falling, falling through empty space with nothing solid to grab. Who can live like that? Not me.

Never mind. I'm doing fennel for Chuckie and me. How hard can it be to chop some small enough to eat with a spoon? Brown it in butter. Three cloves of garlic. Four if my garlic's not fresh. I don't skimp on garlic. If she throws it back in my face, that's on her. The wall will be there between us, like always. I can live with that. But you know what I'm missing? Music. I miss hearing the music.

All the Varieties of Hunger

Sean Prentiss

I should have grabbed the pizza, Sean thinks as he drives from his brother's Midwestern town.
   Sean thinks as he heads toward the interstate, *I should have grabbed that goddamn pizza*.
   I should have thrown it all away—the box, the slices, everything.
   Everything in a dumpster, in some alley where they would have never seen it again.

As Sean drives home, he thinks about how happy he'll be back in his mountains.
   He also thinks of how difficult his brother Jon has always been, on everyone he loves.
   Hard on Sean, hard on Jon's first wife, hard on this second wife, Annabelle.
   Straight hard, Sean mutters, *Straight hard*.
   But Sean has never seen his brother like that—never broken like that.
   Sean wonders if it's somehow this long and exposed Midwestern landscape.

Sean enters the black interstate and thinks to when he was eight and Jon was twelve.
   Back to when their father abandoned the family.
   As Sean stares at untended roadside fields, he thinks, *Gone, straight gone.*
   After their father left, Jon grew calloused, maybe believing he had to become the father.
   Maybe this taught Jon to keep those he loved at a distance.
   That way the hurting lessens when they leave you.
   As Sean drives, he thinks about how losing a thing can change you.
   Sean understands how losing something makes you never want to lose a thing again.

As Sean drives west, toward his far off state, he thinks of Jon last night.
   It was the second and final night of Sean's visit to Jon's new Midwest town.
   Jon said, *Let's get some pizza*—his voice light as a spring bird.
   Jon said, *Annabelle loves pizza* (as if he had never thought of anything but Annabelle).
   Jon paused and said, *She's had a hard time lately—this move has been hard on her.*
   Jon went on, *You know, the Midwest, the unemployment, all of it.*
   Jon almost never said these sorts of things.
   We'll get pepperoni. Her favorite.

As Sean and Jon drove to the pizza place, Sean thought of how different Jon seemed this visit.
   Gentle—that was the word Sean kept returning to.
   Almost as if Jon was trying to fix something that no one even knew was broken yet.
   Maybe this feeling of being broken was from the Midwestern distances.
   Seeing from here to forever.
   Maybe it was the town—the boarded up stores and potholed streets.
   Maybe it was the surrounding landscape—the bankrupt farms, the barns collapsing in.

Maybe Jon felt the wind blowing through the next fifty years of his and Annabelle's life.

Maybe Jon was trying to build a windbreak.

Back at the apartment, Sean and Jon brought the pizza into the kitchen.

Jon took out plates and tore paper towels for napkins.

Jon grabbed three lagers and said, *Annabelle loves lagers.*

Sean wanted to cradle his brother for this new compassion.

Jon popped opened the beers and said, *She should be home soon.*

Sean and Jon sat at the table and waited.

Ten minutes later, the apartment door opened and cold winter air thrust in.

Jon met Annabelle in the living room, kissed her on the cheek.

Sean was sure he saw Annabelle smile (absolutely positive).

I made dinner, Jon said, *Pizza.*

Annabelle said, *I need to get out of these clothes.*

Jon called toward their bedroom, *Pepperoni.*

Ten minutes later Annabelle came into the kitchen.

On the table, the pizza still hot, the bottles with dew dripping down their sides.

Jon served everyone a slice, starting with Annabelle.

As Sean took a bite, hungry from waiting, he thought, *Annabelle looks straight tired.*

Jon, waiting for Annabelle to eat, kept his hands in his lap, as if saying a silent prayer.

Annabelle took a sip from her beer as Jon asked, *Any jobs out there?*

Jon paused, knowing he had asked the wrong question by a million miles.

Sean wished there was some way he could grab Jon's words, bring them back.

Annabelle said, *Not a one*, as she stood from the table.

She took her beer and said, *I'm going for a walk.*

Jon said, *Sean's leaving in the morning and I'd love to eat as a family.*

Sean wondered, *How can anything be held together by paper towels and pizza?*

After Annabelle left, Jon said, *Let's go to the Riverside Bar.*

Jon said, *It's two-for-one night, Old Style drafts.*

Jon and Sean walked across this Midwestern town.

No one crowded the streets, the shops closed—not just for tonight.

Each store looked, to Sean, like some physical version of lost hope.

With a biting wind blowing, Jon said, *I get so sick of that apartment, sick of this town.*

Sean pulled his collar up and thought of these Midwestern landscapes.

Sean buried his hands in his pocket and thought of having no mountains to hide in.

Just rows of corn or soy during summer, dirt come winter.

Sean and Jon sat at the bar and ordered Old Style, one after the other.

Sean and Jon sat at the long oak bar and talked about high school.

They talked about this new job Jon had gotten.

They talked about Sean leaving tomorrow, heading west.
Sean ran his hands over the bar counter, scarred with etched initials of lovers.
While they drank, Sean constructed a list of everything they never spoke about.

The next morning, this morning, today, Sean wakes before dawn.
He has eighteen hours of driving to get home.
He dresses quietly, folds the blankets, straightens the sofa.
In the kitchen, Sean opens the fridge, reaches for milk to settle his hung-over stomach.
Sean sees the pizza box, Annabelle must have put it away last night.
After she had returned from her evening walk to the empty house.
Sean opens the box—a single slice gone, his.
Sean closes the box and closes the refrigerator without getting milk.
He grabs his bag and looks around the empty kitchen.
He quietly shuts the front door behind him.
He doesn't want to disturb Jon and Annabelle—they need sleep.

Sean starts the car and drives away. He thinks of Jon waking this morning, hung-over.
As Sean drives away, he thinks of Jon opening the fridge, seeing the pizza—stale slices.
He thinks of the tense air when Annabelle walks into the kitchen, still unemployed.
Still untethered to this landscape, weary and tired and exhausted from dark dreams.
Sean envisions Jon saying, *This town sucks*, while meaning nothing stops the wind here.
Or meaning, *The clouds take days and days to get from that horizon to here.*
Or meaning, *Winter lasts forever.*
Or meaning, *Nothing lasts forever.*

Staying Up All Night

Lynn Gordon

One morning Artie is late waking up Paul. He lies in his bed at Distel House with his whole body spread out, the covers soft and heavy on top of him. He wants to stay still and not ever move, but finally he goes to Paul's room and knocks and goes in. Millie is in there, handing Paul his shirt, and she says, "Artie, this was your job and you didn't do it." Artie opens his arms to hug Millie, but she's moving around and he can't hold on. "Go shave. Get dressed," she says. She flipflaps her hand. "We don't need you in here now."

Paul makes a face with his eyes wrinkled up. He says, "It's Artie's fault, Millie. Isn't it, Millie?"

At dinner that night, Paul tells in front of everybody that Artie made him late. It's Artie's best dinner, meat balls, and Paul is making them taste awful. The van came to take people to work, Paul says, but he wasn't ready and he had to leave without eating his egg. He had to run to the van with his shoe laces flinging around, while everybody waited and laughed. And then he had to fix his shoes on the way to work, and the knots came out wrong because the van was bumping up and down. Artie stops eating his meat balls and yells at Paul, "Did not!" until Millie says to be quiet.

Later, under the covers, Artie rocks from side to side and holds his big belly. He has a squeezing feeling inside his eyes, like the beginning of crying. He has done a good job waking up Paul for a long time, maybe for fifty or a thousand years, so Millie and Paul shouldn't be mad at him if he made a mistake. If he was lying in bed in the morning for once, accidentally.

The way to show them would be to stay awake the whole night. He has never done that. In the morning he would be ready to wake Paul up at the exact minute. He could even do it early if he wanted to, get Paul up early, and that would be better than good. Millie would say it was fantastic, that was her best word.

At first it's an exciting plan. He can stay in his blankets and wait for morning, and maybe think about big, exciting things while he's lying there.

Maybe practice whistling. He knows you have to open your mouth just a little and then blow the air through. He tries it for a while. He rubs at the beard hairs in his cheeks and stares up to the ceiling, only there's nothing to see, just black.

His eyelids start to close like they're melting. The pillow feels warm and squashy. For a minute he is going to just start sleeping, pull the soft covers over his head the way he likes. But then he pushes up, waving his head around. He swings an arm through the dark, then the other arm.

The best idea is to get up, that's how to stay awake. He can tell by the window that it's nice outside. All he has to do is get dressed and he can go out there. He's been out at night before, sometimes when they've had a fire with marshmallows, and once when a volunteer talked about the moon and the stars. The stars were supposed to make pictures in the sky, of people and animals. Artie couldn't see the pictures, but everything looked different and silvery at night, and when you breathed there was a smell like leaves and water.

He has his clothes folded on a chair, even the socks—that's what you do at Distel House, so in the morning you know exactly what to put on. He gets out of his pajamas, which is really a pajama bottom and a T-shirt, because the pajama top wore out and lost its buttons, and the bottoms are still all right.

Usually he's good at putting on his shirt, but this time it chokes across his neck. Backwards. He has it backwards because of the dark. The pants are easier. To save time he decides to do flip-flop sandals instead of shoes. His mother used to help with his shoes, back a long time ago.

Getting out of Distel House is easy. He opens his door and walks through the living room. By the night light from the hall, he can see Furball the cat lying by the TV, curled up quiet and tight. He turns the knob of the front door, which pops out the button thing that makes it unlock.

He's outside. Sharp leaves are all over the ground, they come down from the big oak trees. They prickle the edges of his feet. He can see the leaves because of the porch light, and then a dark edge where the light stops. He kicks some leaves into the black side, and they disappear.

His legs hurt, walking uphill to the road. At the top he sits down and rubs his knees. The tree branches squiggle over his head. Cricket sounds beep out of the dark, from little bugs that you could never see. Nobody comes. He puts his hands on the ground, on the sharp leaves, and pushes back up, even though it feels like needles. The road is on a hill, so he goes the downhill way.

The road is dark and empty. He goes down and down. There's nothing along the road, except sometimes a house. Artie sits down to rest again. The air smells like cold rocks and dust.

Then lights are up in front of him when he walks again, from a big building. He holds his belly and marches faster down the hill to get to the bright place. It has tall walls and windows, and sidewalks with lights shining down. He walks, punching his hand against the tall walls, and sings: "O Susannah, o ho Susannannah, for I come from Alabama, o Susannah."

The door opens when he pulls it. It has a square thing that you can just pull. There's a big room full of benches, with wood boards across the ceiling. It's like the church he went to one time with his mother.

She wore a grey dress that day with a belt and held Artie's hand. She held his hand all the way, walking from Distel House. It was before she died. She sat with Artie on a bench in the church— there were benches everyplace and windows that had colors. The light came through the windows and Artie's mother had green on her nose. He started to tell her— it was so funny, a green nose—and she pressed on his arm and said to behave. "Remember what I told you. We have to be quiet."

Music played and all the people stood up from their benches and sang a song. Even though they were supposed to be quiet. Artie pulled at his mother's dress. His mother looked at him with her frowning eyes and shook her head back and forth.

The music stopped. A man walked out in front wearing a long white dress, all the way to the ground. When Artie started to tell his mother about the dress, she put her finger against his mouth. "No," she said. "No. For crying out loud." The man talked and talked, getting louder and softer, up and down and up.

While the man in the dress was talking, Artie saw a book, a blue one, on a shelf to one side where nobody was sitting. He leaned far over to grab it. Books were fantastic. Millie would read them at Distel House, or sometimes volunteers did, and there would be pictures and voices and colors, and each page was a dizzy surprise. Only you could tear the paper if you didn't watch out. Paul had torn a book. So had Artie. But that was a long, long time ago. He knew how to turn the pages at the corner now; he knew how to take care of books.

After more talking and more singing, his mother stood up to leave. The man in the white dress was at the door. He shook hands with Artie and noticed that Artie had the blue book under his arm. The man said it was okay to take the book back to Distel House, and after that it was Artie's book, all his, all to himself, for a million years if he wanted. Until one day it got lost. He wanted it and it wasn't there.

In this church now, tonight, the windows are black and he is alone. Artie looks at the ceiling and listens to the quietness. Nobody comes. Then he giant-steps up to the front where the man in the white dress would stand. He is going to be that man and do the talking.

Artie stands very straight and breathes air into his throat. He pretends that everyone from Distel House is sitting in the benches, listening. He starts to talk, about how he's staying up all night, how he walked through the trees out in the night and came to this building. When he runs out of things to say, he sings some more of "O Susannah." He circles his fingers around his eyes, trying to see everybody in his life making a crowd in the benches.

He walks in a line through the whole room, up and down. Finally he sits on a bench near the middle and nods his head down and holds his belly. The light is too bright now, the bench is hard, his flip-flops too tight. He closes his eyes and thinks about sitting on a bench like this with his mother. Her grey dress and the black belt around it. Her hand moving over to touch his mouth.

A long, long time ago, he used to live in a house with her. He can hardly remember it—a staircase and a white dog named Floppy, and hamburgers once, with cheese on top. His mother whistled when she combed his hair.

Then they found Distel House for him to live at. Because children have to move away. He has been there his whole life now, all the time, and his mother would visit. Before she died. She came on Christmas sometimes; one time she brought him a flashlight.

He opens his eyes again, and right that minute he sees a blue book, like the one he had before it got lost. He opens it in the middle—lots of lines and black dots, and also he finds an *A* like in Artie. He knows how to write his name and that's how it starts, with *A*.

Holding the book makes Artie want to have it. He could take it with him to keep in his room. That would be okay, because the man said. Along the bench are more and more books, blue ones and red ones. He reaches way over and rubs one of them with his hand. It feels smooth and thick, with a little ribbon thing hanging down from the bottom.

He stands up, holding his blue book, and walks around the room again. Every bench has books on it. He picks up as many as he can hold. If it's all right to take one, then that's the rule: they are all right to take home. They don't cost money that you have to pay, like in a store.

Artie has trouble opening the door, leaning with his body and still holding on to the books. He picks up the ones that fall down. It happens and happens, that they fall. Finally he gets outside, with books in his hands and under his arms. He has to squeeze them hard as he goes along walking, away from the building and out of the light. This time he has to go the uphill way on the road. His legs are very tired now. He drops another book, a red one.

He sits at the side of the road, puts down his books and stacks them into a high stack. It's going to take a lot of work to get all the way to Distel House with the books, but he will do it, after he rests.

On the third time of resting—or fifth? —Artie spreads the books all around him. He rubs his legs and thinks to himself about Millie, how she didn't let him hug her in the morning and he really wanted to. Also she has big nice teeth, and wrinkles that spread out from her eyes that he likes to look at.

He lets his body go backwards and down to the ground. The sharp leaves stick into his back and his head, and he ruffles away the ones he can reach. A smell of worms and dirt comes into his nose. He wants to lie there, one hand touching his big pile of books. Red and blue. He shuts his eyes.

The books stay on the ground next to him. He could come back lots of times and get more of them. They could fill up a drawer in his room at Distel House, and then all the drawers, and under his bed and the whole room.

Having his eyes closed makes the ground colder and the leaves sharper. He opens them up again, stares into the black sky. Stars are all over the place up there, some big and bright and some like dust. Artie wants to find those pictures the volunteer told about. He wants to see a cat like Furball, a leaf, a clock, a man in a white dress. A belt like his mother's. Everything, everything should be up there. He looks for a long time, but the stars are too crowded. They shine down their light.

The Prisoners

Sam Katz

Ask any resident who has been here long enough and the day he looks forward to most is the annual prison rodeo. Contrary to popular belief, there are many days we anticipate. To the down man, Salisbury steak is a holiday. So is the occasion a guard falls ill. We anticipate the first morning of autumn when the heat breaks. Executions come and go, but those hold little interest to the balance of us. More than the memories of our birthdays or Christmas, even more than seeing our wives on visitation days clutching our bewildered children, it is the rodeo that sustains us. The only day we might anticipate more is the day of our release, when we can go home and sit under the shade of our childhood climbing trees. But for many of us the State has rendered this a moot point. We know we will never leave this place for the crimes we once committed and so, folding laundry or peeling radishes, we recount great rodeo performances of the past—Wylie Farte's 98 point ride or Big Tom Jonovitch's sweep of the centennial Chicken Run. Alone in our cells we cast ourselves in these roles. We dream it's us hoisting the "Best Cowboy" trophy before the throngs of spectators, and we revel in the glory of our triumph, the enduring respect it will garner from our peers and captors. Whereas originally the warden had to designate participants, now a raffle must be held to decide the lucky few who will have the privilege to compete. When the numbers are announced over the tinny PA system, we cease all activity and the prison goes quiet. Murderer, thief, and pederast alike squeeze their eyes shut, mouthing the five digits that adorn our gray uniforms.

Of course, the rodeo is also a welcome respite from our daily routine. It breaks up the tedium of the days and carries us through the long months of tilling our inhospitable land, where we manage to grow all mess of vegetables, grain, and legume despite being walled off on three sides by a river as swift and savage as the Nile.

We are under no delusion that the rodeo is free of danger. Without fail a rider gets trampled by a colt or mashes his face against the metal safety railing. Death by goring is a real possibility, as Cooperson can attest from last year when he lost his spleen. Still, we mark our chalk calendars for that brisk April morning when the light licks quick off the surfaces and good humor hangs in the air. We wait for that moment when the gates swing open and throngs of spectators—children cheering from atop their father's shoulders, women watching through slatted fingers—file into the bleachers and fill their lungs for us, a glint of absolution in their faces.

~

Leading up to the rodeo there is a show of public displeasure. A bespectacled journalist from some sitcom city will appear and cast about on the periphery of our daily activities, striking poses of indignant observation. They will ask the warden, proofing his white linen suit, what purpose the rodeo serves, and he will cross a gator-loafered foot over his knee and expound about the woes of underfunding and the palliative effect of healthy releases of violence in the rehabilitation process.

The journalists will offer the least threatening of us cigarettes and inquire if we have a moment to chat. What do you really gain from this event? they will ask, holding their *n*'s. Have you heard of the gladiator fights of ancient Rome? Do you feel exploited by your role? Do you feel dehumanized? They ask about this year's new event, Inmate Jousting, which up until this point we have regarded with zealous excitement, and then they are determined to convince us it is the worst injustice of all.

One of us, usually a man fresh off the chain, will swallow their line. "Yes, oh God yes," the fish will tell the journalist, "this rodeo business is truly a nightmare," and later, like Muther a few years back, the sieve might be found slouched in a corner with his tongue cut clean out of his skull. But despite this unfortunate barbarity, a change in the population's atmosphere can be detected. Though none of us would ever admit it, we begin to consider these questions once the lights are put out and we are left to converse among ourselves.

About this time the letters will start arriving, missives from outraged citizens and national humanitarian organizations beating their chests, and an inmate, invariably one whose claim to public opinion per the prison hierarchy is borderline, will stand in the yard like a sidewalk holy man frothing about our basic human dignity. Those in earshot will grumble at first, then begin to linger, and soon a small crowd will have gathered waving library books and quoting passages from Gandhi or the Greeks of antiquity until a hum has built among the lot of us at mealtime.

More letters will arrive, this time garrulous texts beautifully handwritten by our suddenly doting wives, or else perfume spritzed by mistresses we'd long ago lost hope of ever hearing from again; notes from our children on construction paper, sticker-strewn and scrawled with four different crayons, only the backwards D's blue for the color of daddy's.

The leader of this spontaneous movement, the rabble-rouser, will stand atop a table, a pair of glasses perched on the end of his nose, and start a chant that will spark a succession of protests and escape attempts, each more reckless than the last. The participants of the rodeo will grow anxious, reconsidering their complicity in this spectacle. They will pray in the night asking guidance of we priests beyond the bars of their cement confessionals and receive no answer.

These men will hold their wives a little tighter when they visit and kiss their children more tenderly, recognizing the miracle they represent. They make plans to take classes or start small businesses on the outside and talk about the future as if it were a real unit of time. They become aware of the fragility of their lives in a way they never realized before, and begin to guard themselves from us with a paranoid fervor bordering on the insane.

But inevitably we tire, lose our momentum. Our voices spent and our wills exhausted, we lay our backs against the cool walls of our cells and exhale. We eat and go to sleep when we are told, perform our duties at the laundry or kitchen, and it is as if our grand commotion had been just another block in the prison schedule. Those who shouted the loudest, men whose names seem to fade quickly from the prison consciousness, get their comeuppance. They are found choked in the kitchen walk-in or piked through the neck with the sharpened arm of a pince-nez, no witnesses among us, and the poor soul who abdicated his place in the rodeo—terrible imaginations roam the halls of our house.

We return to farming, tilling the earth, and let our blood recirculate. For long stretches we achieve an equilibrium of malaise in which we inflict no harm on our fellow man, placid like the cows of India joined by our common star. Then from the calm someone will mention the rodeo, offhand, like a funny thing we all witnessed together once upon a time. Inspiration will spark the artisans among us, and the man who was sent here for negotiating bank vaults will build a ship within a bottle whose scale and intricacy would rival the Antikythera mechanism.

We come to realize we were duped, our natural suspicions strummed, made to believe that our lofty expectations were unfounded, that we were undeserving of any enjoyment in this lifetime. The rodeo is a good and noble endeavor.

We tear up the letters we taped to our walls and burn the photos pressed between the pages of our holy scriptures. We harden our hearts against the false promises they came to symbolize, and once again see how dangerous the world outside our walls can be.

~

The morning of the rodeo is ebullient and skillet hot. We are herded into our designated area, square in the meanest glare of the sun, and watch as the spectators amble into the shaded bleachers. The Grand Entry kicks off and the best of our riders perform a choreographed routine on par with any ceremony in the country. Our pride swells in our throats and we go mental as our brethren parade into the arena led by last year's Best Cowboy runner-up, who presents the flag to the Warden. A beauty queen from the nearest town sings the National Anthem and it is all we can do not to shed a tear as her voice soars through the quiet grounds.

The noon heat beats down on our bare heads, and we watch the events unfold as if in a fever dream. The air, fat with the smell of popcorn and barbeque and skunked beer makes us nostalgic for nights long past wetting our sleeves on salty bar tops. Roman breaks his arm falling from his horse during the Calf Rope. Salamanca is hoofed in the spine steer wrestling. Four others are sent to the infirmary following the Joust. The crowd erupts with each misstep, cheering louder the more gruesome the injury. They begin to chant in anticipation of the final event, the Chicken Run, and we join them. The winning barrel racer finishes his last run and the chants grow louder, echoing throughout the arena. Soon the corral can be heard rattling from the bull's approach.

The first of us walks out, taking his position on the red X marked in the dirt. He's a young man, new to the rodeo, and we razz him for his good fortune. His number is announced over the speaker—"Now competing, Prisoner 22593"—and he tips his hat to the crowd. "Grand theft auto," one of us says, "No, vehicular manslaughter," another refutes, and as we argue over who is right, the bell clangs, jolting us back, and the bull tears into the open like a thing from a long ago time, its black hide taut and lathered, showing every tensed muscle.

"OK, folks, here's what you came to see," says the announcer, and as if predetermined, the crowd shifts its chants to *Toro* without breaking stride.

The bull raises its head. *Toro*. The young man crouches at the ready. *Toro*. He stands headlong for an instant as the bull charges toward him then turns tail and bails over the railing.

"So much for bravery," says the announcer. "I guess crime don't make a cowboy."

We are thrilled and sickened to witness the man's cowardice. *Toro*, we find ourselves yelling. We know no matter how the bull performs, he will not make it out of this place alive. The hired rodeo men will come for him at the end of the day for the guards' annual barbeque, and so we cheer his name, like a sort of incantation, for what we have done to his forefathers and will do to his sons.

When the second of us enters the arena, we shake the rails as he trots to his mark. A snap of pride spurs us as we recognize the man from years at the cafeteria or folding linens in the laundry line. A little piece of us is out there dusting his heels. We begin to stomp and holler, nervous for the man, secretly praying for his safe return. We strain our voices as the clowns swing open the steel gate and the bull surges forth. We empty our lungs of the year's anticipation.

The man holds his spot. He holds as the bull acknowledges his presence and holds as the bull paws at the dirt. He holds as the crowd swells and holds as the bull starts his charge. We see the animal before us. The pluming ground. The nostrils matte with dust. And we feel our own worth in play on the man's actions. Our own lives.

He holds as the bull raises its horns, holding even as the crowd turns away in horror—children wailing atop their father's shoulders—holding as the announcer falls silent, holding as the guards drag his body away.

When the rodeo is finished, and the awards presented, we watch as the spectators empty the bleachers, carrying their prison art crafts and souvenirs—Mary's masterful glass ship among them. We hear the men dispatching the bull in the prison's makeshift slaughterhouse, and watch the red pickup ferry its remains off to the kitchen. The afternoon sun bakes the dirt and sweat onto our faces, and we groan with the understanding that now we must clean the grounds and clear away all evidence of the morning's activities. It will be dark by the time we finish and, hungry and exhausted, the glory of the rodeo far behind us, we will dream of hot showers and soft beds. The guards will open the gates of our corral and we will look to them for a hint of mercy. We will ask them for a short respite and a cool drink of water, and they will refuse. We will carry out our duties, before the butchers come for us, imagining the day when we can cross the river, and rest under the shade of the trees for a while.

Definitions

Amy Collini

Karyotin: the substance of chromosomes, stainable with basic dyes

I am fourteen when I go to the national spelling bee in Washington, D.C. Sponsoring newspapers pay the expenses of each speller and their official escort; I am one of only two, out of 222, who choose their father instead of their mother as escort.

This is how I remember my downfall at the national bee: I am sitting in the Comfort Room, having just been escorted off stage after misspelling "karyotin" in the third round. I am slumped into a navy blue armchair, my face wet with tears, my enormous glasses sliding down my nose. The Comfort Room is a transitional space located just off the stage, and the reporters that follow each speller are denied entrance; only family is allowed contact with fallen spellers. A galvanized tub full of sugary carbonated drinks on ice stands in the corner; my little brother helps himself to a can and slurps quickly while no one is paying attention. After two previous bees, this is my first loss, and I feel incapable of even the slightest movement. My brother makes an attempt at hugging me before I collapse in the chair, but after that, my family surrounds me in a semi-circle and just stares at me while I cry.

My mother, standing several feet away, says coolly, "You know, Ames,"—this is her nickname for me when she is being either patronizing or condescending—"sometimes you just need to quit feeling sorry for yourself."

~

Inimical: having the disposition of an enemy

My mother missed the previous two qualifying bees. For the first, the city bee, she decided she didn't want to skip the weekly class where she was learning how to paint flowers on the sides of hand-woven baskets. She is tired of being just a mother; later, when I am in high school, she will go into nursing school, but for now she is still searching for her own identity, and it doesn't include her children. Possibly it never has.

I had never attended a spelling bee before, and I was surprised to see the wooden stands in the middle-school gym filled with anxious parents and siblings. My father sat somewhere to the right in my line of sight, accompanied by my little sister and brother, but I couldn't see them as the spellers were whittled down to a few, and then just two of us. The other speller and I both misspelled *statistician*—I believed the root of the word was "status," and was too nervous to remember I could ask for a definition—but then I was given the word *inimical*, a word I'd never heard. I spelled it correctly, and I won. This victory secured my entry into the regional bee.

That night I brought home the trophy like an offering.

~

Renown: a state of being widely acclaimed and highly honored: fame
The night of the regional bee, the second, my parents get into a vicious fight; this is a routine family procedure. The topic, long since forgotten, doesn't matter; my mother wants to punish my father for some infraction, and no matter how much he begs her to come to the spelling bee for my sake, she refuses to budge. My grandmother, who accompanies us, also pleads with her before we leave, but my mother is resolute, scowling and silent in her burgundy armchair. When we arrive at the university hall where the bee will be held, my father walks again and again to the payphone in the corner of the lobby; he and my grandmother take turns calling her, begging her to come, while I stand amidst the crowd and watch them until we are called to our seats.

Just as before, spellers fall in great clumps until finally it is just a pale-faced blond boy and me alone on the stage. The pronouncer switches to a list of commonly-misspelled words for the final elimination round. When the blond boy misspells the word "renown," substituting a "u" for the "w," I know I have clinched it. I clutch the sides of my blue flowered skirt and spell it correctly, and just like that, I am going to the national spelling bee. I momentarily cover my face to hide from the thunderous applause, unsure of how to react; my father makes his way to the stage, where he bear hugs me and tells me how proud he is. This shot is caught by the newspaper photographer and printed the next day, the clip of which will be tucked into a box and towed with me everywhere through adulthood.

Once again, I cart home a gigantic trophy, but this time in the car my father and I plan to surprise my mother. We will tell her that I lost, and I will act hurt and dejected, and then thrust the trophy at her, a prize mouse brought home by the family cat, dropped on the doorstep with intent to impress and delight. She is shocked and excited when I finally tell her; the house erupts with noisy chatter and planning for the week-long trip to the capital. My mother quizzes me from the little study booklet for spellers, but eventually she loses interest and retreats to her own world again, and tells me to go read the dictionary at the library. I do it once or twice—the *OED* is the edition the bee recommends, and I can barely pick it up—before I quit, overwhelmed by the sheer number of words. I feel both hopeless and complacent: why won't my mother help me? And why should I bother anyway, when I've won the first two bees with my natural talent?

On an afternoon in late May, just before we leave for Washington, D.C., I arrive home from school to find my mother standing in the living room, waiting for me. My heart palpitates and my breath catches; whenever I come home to find her waiting, it usually precedes a grounding or, sometimes, a rage-filled lecture that derails into a beating. But on this day, she bestows me with a gift, some awkward combination of good luck, apology and congratulations. The gray velvet box she hands me contains an oval aquamarine pendant the color of tears; the stone is topped by a single tiny diamond and dangles from a filament of gold chain.

Many years later, when I am a sophomore at Ohio State, I will take the necklace off one night while studying, spooling it into a pile on a textbook on the floor. When I go to look for it later, it will have disappeared. I will look over the carpet a few times but I will never see it again. I don't look very hard.

Relating to Time

Rachel Jamison Webster

Shortly after I turned thirty, I took a trip to Costa Rica that forced me to reconsider my sense of time. Escape from a daily schedule, immersion in nature, and appearance of my first gray hairs all conspired to create one of those drops into groundlessness that most people I know experience—a kind of newness, or cluelessness, we feel first in the terror of puberty then encounter again and again as we revise our lives.

In my twenties, I had become more comfortable with my own strength, and like many of us, had learned to embrace contradictions. I was a yogi in high heels, a feminist in pressed powder, an organic vegetarian shopping at Target, a seeker pursuing a singular journey even as I deepened my commitments to others. And the reading material I brought on our trip reflected these opposing energies. I had a novel, *The Time Traveler's Wife*, a book of feminist theory by Mary Daley called *Pure Lust*, and the new issue of *Vogue*.

I opened the magazine first, and quickly consumed glossy spreads of gowns and handbags before circling back to read the articles. Some that I would have skipped over only months ago, I read now with an absorption that my snobbier self chuckled over. One—about a 40 year-old woman who had shaved years off her face (literally) with a series of abrasions and injections totaling just over $10,000—held my interest down to the sidebars.

"Maybe when we get home, I'll get a chemical peel," I said to my partner.

"Wow," he replied, laughing. "They got to you like clockwork."

The next day, I left the Vogue in the hotel, rented a long board and falteringly taught myself to surf. I was not terribly agile or physically daring, but I managed to stand up on the board, steady myself, and catch a few small waves. And between rounds of exertion and downtime in which I watched picnicking families and clattering palms, I completely lost track of time. Time had flown off its "track," because I was inhabiting it fully, multi-dimensionally, in a day so good it seemed eternal.

I woke up the next morning tenderized by board bruises and a blistering sunburn, wondering how many years I had added to my complexion. That day we hiked in a nature preserve that had been created thirty years earlier when a cattle rancher and his wife decided to let their land return to its naturally complex habitat. Several different birdsongs fretted the air. Trees thirty feet high were curtained with vines and alive with white-faced monkeys—climbing, foraging and chattering to one another. Ferns pressed through the nooks of trees, lizards scattered among dry leaves, and the path before us coursed with reddish rivulets—leaf-cutting ants, hatted with bright green flakes and purple blossoms, and fully committed to their task. Every creature we saw was busy, alive, making something of time.

That night, I encountered a quote by the writer Starhawk in Mary Daley's book. While watching a snake shed its skin, she commented, "I came to see time not as a thing, but as a relationship." Of course! I thought. Time as interaction. Time as give and take. I thought, what if all the people I know—especially the women—could take everything they'd learned about relationships and apply it to their understanding of time? Wouldn't that give us a deeper, more full-bodied experience with time? Wouldn't thinking this way help us to gauge when the exchange had become too one-sided? Or when we were being bullied by a schedule, for instance, in a way we wouldn't allow ourselves to be bullied by another person? When we were giving and receiving in equal measure, delighting and learning as we do in all healthy relationships?

I thought of the healthy relationships I had created and maintained in my life—with my partner, with my friends. They were challenging. They brought me joy. They made me better, ultimately, more in touch with the inside self than the visible self, thus revising the visible self to be wiser, more generous. Was time doing the same thing with me? And, perhaps the better question, was I doing this with my time?

In its public sense, time keeps us in line, it helps us to make it to meetings on time, and to function in sync. The timekeeping of clocks, wristwatches, and iPhones is related to industrialization, and only became widely used during the nineteenth century, when trains had to run on schedule. In its private sense, however, time is almost a spiritual presence, related to the endless coming to fruition and falling away of natural cycles. The Greeks made this distinction, calling sequential, incremental time *chronos*, and recurrent, sacred time *kairos*, which is an immeasurable, culminating moment in which everything co-exists, everything happens. In its earliest form, *kairos* meant weather, connecting it with natural cycles, and Aristotle used it to describe almost the soul of time, suggesting that each rhetorical mode has its kairos, its most soulful moment of connection.

In our culture, however, we tend to note time less often as a presence—as I did on the beach that day—than as an absence. We know it—like a rogue lover—by its departures, by the marks it leaves on the body when it goes. And this, of course, has to do the way we see time working not only on us as individuals, but on the earth. I think of what thirty years has done to the eroding banks of Lake Erie where I grew up, to the prairie around Chicago where I now live. I think of the steel breakwalls, the almost uninterrupted strip malls, the Walmart going up right now smack in the middle of what used to be Green's Farm. Is there any wonder that we fret about the ravages of time? And do we recognize our role when we expend huge amounts of money using pesticides on our backyards and shoring up our cheekbones and eyelids with chemical creams and Botox?

There are connections here. And time—when we slip through the veneer—is a connective place, where we can commune with mothers, grandmothers, ancestors and other species further back, even where we can know the *kairos*, the right moment in which to act and speak. We don't always remember this, but we can inhabit time in a daily way that reconnects us with time in a recurrent and eternal way.

Thinking about this has allowed me to become more astute, and more in tune with my own rhythms and sense of time. I can see now when someone is trying to control my time inappropriately and that has helped me to make smarter decisions in terms of relationships and career. I have only a few years here, but I do have the opportunity to inhabit those years as fully as possible, to experience the eternal—through nature, art, and love—in the everyday.

I've seen now what can unfold in a tract of land in which wildness has been respected, which is to say *relationship* has been respected. Thirty years ago, that wildlife preserve was a clear-cut ranch owned by

McDonald's and now, because of stewards who respect the process of growth and time, it is alive. The ants break up the leaves, they free the pollen that feeds the trees to grow, and every inch of the rainforest is teeming with the interdependence that is the foundation of evolution and the *kairos* in which everything acts from its being.

CONTRIBUTORS

Colleen Abel is the author of *Housewifery*, a chapbook (dancing girl press, 2013). A former Diane Middlebrook Poetry Fellow, her work has appeared in numerous venues including *The Southern Review, Colorado Review, Mid-American Review, West Branch, Pleiades, Cincinnati Review* and elsewhere. She lives in Wisconsin.

M. M. Adjarian is a writer and professor. She has published creative work in *The Provo Canyon Review, The Milo Review, From the Depths,* and *Empty Sink Publishing.* Her articles and reviews have also appeared in *Arts+Culture Texas, Bitch Magazine, Kirkus,* and the *Dallas Voice,* as well as in several academic journals and compendiums. Currently, she is working on a family memoir titled *The Beautiful Dreamers.* She lives in Austin.

Damon Barta once lived in a place where he could see for miles in every direction. He now lives safely among trees. His work has appeared in several print and online journals. Selected fiction can be found at http://damonbarta.site88.net/.

Evan Beaty lives in San Antonio, Texas.

William Black's fiction and critical essays have appeared in *Crazyhorse, Threepenny Review, Southern Review, The Sun, World Literature Today, Boulevard,* and elsewhere.

Michelle Bracken is a fiction candidate in the MFA program at California State University, San Bernardino. Her work has appeared in *Litro Magazine.*

Tally Brennan is a recovered computer programmer, happy to have emerged from the cubicle as a writer of fiction. Her stories have appeared in journals including *Rosebud, PMS/Poem, Memoir, Story, Room of One's Own, Kaleidoscope, Minetta Review, Meridian, Epiphany,* and on line at *JMWW, Hobo Pancake,* and *Lady Jane Miscellany.* A story of hers was selected for inclusion in *Writing Aloud,* InterAct Theatre's series of readings by professional actors. She is grateful to the Leeway and Astraea foundations for their support and encouragement.

Matt Broaddus is currently a first year PhD student in English at the University of North Carolina at Chapel Hill. He received his MFA in creative writing from New York University. His poetry has recently appeared in *Whiskey Island, Barnstorm, Switchback,* and elsewhere. He is originally from Virginia.

Justin Brouckaert's work has appeared in *The Rumpus* and *Passages North,* among other publications. He is a James Dickey Fellow in Fiction at the University of South Carolina, where he serves as fiction editor of *Yemassee.*

Caroline Bruckner is a writer and screenwriter based in Vienna, Austria. Her short film *The Confession* won the Student Academy Award and was nominated for an Academy Award (Best Live Action Short) in 2011. The children's book *Moritz* was published through H&M for the UNICEF All For Children initiative. Caroline's short fiction has been featured in *Crack the Spine, Diverse Voices Quarterly, Forge, The Minetta Review, Westview, Willow Review,* and others.

Jennifer Bryan grew up in Spokane, Washington. She received an MFA from Bowling Green State University and a PhD in English from the University of Nebraska-Lincoln. She was the 2011 Kimmel Foundation Award writing recipient. Her stories have appeared in *The Missouri Review, LIT, Isthmus, Fifth Wednesday, /nor,* and other literary journals. She recently completed a novel titled, *You'll Be Here Soon*. She lives in Illinois with her husband and daughter and teaches composition at Bradley University.

Craig Buchner's short stories have appeared in *Tin House, Hobart, SmokeLong Quarterly,* and other literary journals. Craig teaches writing and lives in Portland, OR. You can find more of his work at www.craigbuchner.com.

Kate Lister Campbell lives with her husband in Brooklyn, NY, but is originally from Kansas City, MO. When not writing, she helps to design job training and placement programs for people with barriers to employment. Her work has recently appeared in *Bluestem Magazine* and *Foundling Review*. She is a student at The Writers Studio, NYC.

Joanne M. Clarkson's fourth poetry collection, *Believing the Body*, was published in 2014 by Gribble Press. She was awarded a 2014 GAP grant from Artist Trust to complete her next full-length volume. Joanne's poems have appeared recently in *Rhino, Nimrod, Blood and Thunder: Musing on the Art of Medicine* and *Saranac Review*. She serves on the Board of the Olympia Poetry Network and is Poet-in-Residence for the Northwest Playwrights' Alliance. She has a master's degree in English and has taught but currently works as a Registered Nurse. See more at http://JoanneClarkson.com.

Moriah Cohen's poetry has been published or is forthcoming in *Hayden's Ferry Review, Hoot: A Mini Literary Magazine on a Postcard, Stone Highway Review,* and *Narrative* where she was runner-up in this year's "30 Below" contest. She received her MFA from Rutgers University's Newark Campus. Currently, she teaches at Ramapo College.

Douglas Cole has had work in *The Chicago Quarterly Review, Red Rock Review,* and *Midwest Quarterly*. More of his work is available online in *The Adirondack Review, Salt River Review,* and *Avatar Review,* as well as a recorded story in *Bound Off*. He has published a poetry chapbook, *Interstate,* through Night Ballet Press, a novella chapbook called *Ghost* in the Overtime series of *Workers Write Journal,* and has another chapbook, *Western Dream,* forthcoming from Finishing Line Press. He is the winner of several awards, including the Leslie Hunt

Memorial Prize in Poetry, the Best of Poetry Award from *Clapboard House*, First Prize in the "Picture Worth 500 Words" from *Tattoo Highway*, as well as an honorable mention from *Glimmer Train*. He is currently on the faculty at Seattle Central College and is the advisor for their literary journal, *Corridors*.

Amy Collini's essays have appeared or are forthcoming in *Slice, Indiana Review, Soundings Review, Pithead Chapel, Rappahannock Review, Ilanot Review, Literary Mama,* and elsewhere. She lives in Columbus, Ohio, with her husband and two young sons and is currently working on a novel.

Michael Compton is a screenwriter from Memphis, Tennessee. His poetry and prose have appeared in *African American Review, Forge, The New Encyclopedia of Southern Culture, The Tulane Review*, and others.

Paul Crenshaw's stories and essays have appeared or are forthcoming in *Best American Essays,* anthologies by W.W. Norton and Houghton Mifflin, *Glimmer Train, Ecotone, North American Review,* and *Brevity*, among others. He teaches writing and literature at Elon University.

Michelle Donahue is a current MFA candidate in Creative Writing & Environment at Iowa State where she was the managing editor of *Flyway*. Her work has appeared in *Hobart, Whiskey Island, Front Porch Journal*, and others.

Helen Ellis is the author of the novel, *Eating The Cheshire Cat* (Scribner). Her short stories have appeared recently or are forthcoming in *FiveChapters, Blue Mesa Review, Monkeybicycle, The Weekly Rumpus, The Normal School, Faultline Journal*, and *Crab Creek Review*. She is working on a collection.

Vickie Fang is a reformed trial lawyer with a recent MFA degree. She is now writing full time and has completed a literary thriller about two antagonists from the Chinese Cultural Revolution who meet again in contemporary America—kind of an Amy Tan meets *Breaking Bad*. She has won first place awards from the Maryland Writers' Association for both short fiction and the novel, was a finalist for a *Glimmer Train* fiction competition, and has been awarded The Maryland Art Council's largest grant for excellence in fiction. She would love to hear from readers and can be reached on her website: Vickiefang.com.

Jordan Farmer is originally from Logan, West Virginia, and is currently a Ph.D. student studying creative writing at the University of Nebraska-Lincoln. His fiction has been a finalist of both the *Sycamore Review* Wabash Fiction Prize and *Cutbank*'s Montana Prize in Fiction and has appeared or is forth coming in the *Southwest Review, Southern Humanities Review, Appalachian Heritage, Pembroke Magazine, Kestrel*, and others. He is currently finishing a novel set in a juvenile detention center and a collection of stories.

Shirley Fergenson is the literary fiction specialist at The Ivy Bookshop. This piece is part of a collection of linked stories she began during her Masters in Fiction Writing at Johns Hopkins University. When she is not reading, writing, or selling, she rides her bike and gardens. She lives in Baltimore with her husband, whom she met and married in the aisles of The Ivy.

M.K. Foster's poetry won the *2013 Gulf Coast Poetry Prize*, has been recognized with an Academy of American Poets Prize, and has appeared or is forthcoming in *The Account: A Journal of Poetry, Prose, and Thought*; *H.O.W. Journal*; *B O D Y*; *The Journal*; *Ninth Letter*; *Radar Poetry*;and elsewhere. She is currently an MFA candidate at the University of Maryland, College Park, where she teaches academic and creative writing.

Jennifer Givhan was a PEN/Rosenthal Emerging Voices Fellow and a 2015 National Endowment for the Arts poetry fellowship recipient, as well as the 2013 *DASH Literary Journal* Poetry Prize winner, an Andrés Montoya Poetry Prize finalist, and a 2014 Prairie Schooner Book Prize finalist for her collection *Karaoke Night at the Asylum*. She earned her MFA from Warren Wilson College, her Master's in English from Cal State Fullerton, and her work has appeared in over seventy literary journals and anthologies, including *Best New Poets 2013*, *Prairie Schooner, Indiana Review, Rattle, The Collagist, cream city review*, and *The Columbia Review*. She teaches at Western New Mexico University and online at The Rooster Moans Poetry Coop. You can visit Givhan online at jennifergivhan.com.

Lynn Gordon's fiction has appeared in *Epiphany, The Southampton Review, Hobart, Zone 3, South Dakota Review*, and elsewhere. She lives in Northern California.

Mike Gray received his MFA from Florida Atlantic University in 2012 and currently serves as an English Instructor at Hazard Community and Technical College in Kentucky. His fiction has appeared in *Carte Blanche, The Rockford Review, Foliate Oak, Riverwind*, and others.

David Hornibrook is the recipient of a Pushcart Prize and the Michael R. Gutterman award from the University of Michigan. His work has appeared in *Day One, Five Quarterly, The Columbia Review, Flyway* and elsewhere. He holds an M.F.A. from the Helen Zell Writer's Program.

Born in Brown County, Texas, **Landon Houle** currently lives in South Carolina and works as an editor at In Fact Books. She is a winner of *Permafrost's* Midnight Sun fiction contest and *Crab Creek Review's* fiction contest, and her essay "The Plains We Cross" was listed as a notable in *The Best American Essays*. Her work has appeared or is forthcoming in *Beloit Fiction Journal, Confrontation, The Long Story, Natural Bridge, Harpur Palate, River Styx,* and elsewhere.

Ginny Hoyle's work has appeared in *Copper Nickel, MARGIE, Pilgrimage, Wazee* and elsewhere. She collaborates with Colorado artist Judy Anderson to create freeform artist books and installations. Examples of their work are held in numerous fine arts collections, including Stanford, Scripps College, and Baylor. She works in Collections at the Denver Museum of Nature and Science as a sort of volunteer bone librarian and she's a member of Denver's Lighthouse Writers Workshop.

Joshua Idaszak is from Washington, DC. He has lived and worked in Australia, Turkey, and Spain, and will be attending the MFA program at the University of Arkansas this fall.

Meng Jin was born in Shanghai, China, and now lives in New York City where she is an MFA candidate in fiction at Hunter College. Her fiction has appeared in *Bound Off* and *Drunk Monkeys*, and is forthcoming in *The Masters Review.*

Karen Kasaba's stories, essays, and articles have appeared in *Swink, Wilderness House Literary Review, Red Wheelbarrow, Santa Barbara Magazine* (Fiction Competition Winner), *Hawai'i Review, Chariton Review, The Summerset Review, Westways, Byline, American Cinematographer, Los Angeles Times*, and the *Santa Barbara Independent*, among others. She has completed a novel, *Coalblack*. A member of WGAw, her work as a playwright and screenwriter has earned multiple awards including an Emmy nomination.

Sam Katz was born in Korea and now lives in Philadelphia. His fiction has appeared in *The Good Men Project, Southern Humanities Review*, and *Tin House Flash Fridays*. You can see Sam waving from a bike at katzsam.wordpress.com.

Sally Rosen Kindred is the author of two poetry books from Mayapple Press, *No Eden* (2011) and *Book of Asters* (2014), and a chapbook, *Darling Hands, Darling Tongue* (Hyacinth Girl Press, 2013). Her poems have received two awards from the Maryland State Arts Council, and have appeared in *Blackbird, Quarterly West*, and *Linebreak.*

Erika Kleinman has work published or forthcoming in *The Rumpus, The Apple Valley Review*, and *Salon*. She is essays editor for *The Nervous Breakdown*. She lives in Austin, Texas with her husband and two young daughters.

Virginia Konchan is the author of *Vox Populi* (Finishing Line Press) and the short story collection *Anatomical Gift* (forthcoming, Noctuary Press). Her poems have appeared in *The New Yorker, Best New Poets, The Believer, The New Republic*, and *Verse,* her criticism in *Boston Review, Colorado Review*, and *Jacket2*, and her fiction in *StoryQuarterly, Joyland*, and *Requited*, among other places. She lives in Montreal.

Elizabeth Langemak lives in Philadelphia, Pennsylvania.

Danielle LaVaque-Manty lives in Ann Arbor, Michigan. Her fiction has appeared in *Glimmer Train, The Alarmist, Punchnel's, Great Lakes Review*, and *Midwestern Gothic*, and is forthcoming in *The Pinch*.

Stephanie Lenox is the author of the poetry collection Congress of Strange People (Airlie Press) and the poetry chapbook *The Heart That Lies Outside the Body* (Slapering Hol Press). Poems from a manuscript inspired by office work are forthcoming or have recently appeared in *Poet Lore* and *Juke*d.

Terrance Manning, Jr., is a graduate from Purdue's MFA program in Creative Writing (2014). Recently, he received 1st place in the *Boulevard* Short Fiction Contest for Emerging Writers, the David Nathan Meyerson Prize for Fiction, and *Crab Orchard Reviews's* John Guyon Literary Nonfiction Prize. His work appears or is forthcoming in *Boulevard, Southwest Review, Hunger Mountain, Crab Orchard Review*, and other magazines, and has been selected as a finalist in such contests as the *Cincinnati Review* Schiff Awards for Prose, *Colorado Review*'s Nelligan Prize, and the *American Short Fiction* Short Story Award. He lives and writes in Pittsburgh, PA.

Jill McDonough's books of poems include *Habeas Corpus* (Salt, 2008), and *Where You Live* (Salt, 2012). The recipient of three Pushcart prizes and fellowships from the Lannan Foundation, NEA, NYPL, FAWC, and Stanford, her work appears in *Slate, The Threepenny Review*, and *Best American Poetry*. She directs the MFA program at UMass-Boston and 24PearlStreet, the Fine Arts Work Center online. Her fourth poetry collection, *REAPER*, is forthcoming from Alice James Books.

Mark J. Mitchell studied writing at UC Santa Cruz under Raymond Carver, George Hitchcock, and Barbara Hull. His work has appeared in various periodicals over the last thirty-five years as well as the anthologies *Good Poems, American Places,* and *Line Drives*. Two full-length collections are in the works: *Lent 1999* is coming soon from Leaf Garden Press, and *This Twilight World* will be published by Popcorn Press. His chapbook *Three Visitors* has recently been published by Negative Capability Press. *Artifacts and Relics*, another chapbook, is forthcoming from Folded Word. His novel *Knight Prisoner* was recently published by Vagabondage Press, and another novel, *A Book of Lost Songs,* is coming soon from Wild Child Publishing. He lives in San Francisco with his wife, the documentarian and filmmaker Joan Juster.

Jeffrey Morgan is the author of *Crying Shame*. His poems have appeared in *Bellevue Literary Review, Pleiades, Rattle, Third Coast*, and *West Branch*.

John A. Nieves has poems forthcoming or recently published in journals such as: *Southern Review, Poetry Northwest,* and *Fugue*. He won the 2011 *Indiana Review* Poetry Contest and his first book, *Curio* (2014), won the Elixir Press Annual Poetry Award Judge's Prize. He is an Assistant Professor of English at

Salisbury University. He received his M.A. from University of South Florida and his Ph.D. from the University of Missouri.

James Norcliffe is a NZ poet, editor and writer of novels for young people (mainly fantasy) including the award-winning *The Loblolly Boy*. He has published eight collections of poetry, most recently *Villon in Millerton* in 2007, *Packing My Bag for Mars* and *Shadow Play* both in 2012. In 2010 he took part in the XX International Poetry Festival in Medellin, Colombia and in 2011 the Trois Rivieres International Poetry Festival in Quebec. This year sees *Essential New Zealand Poems: Facing the Empty Page* a major new anthology of NZ poetry co-edited with Siobhan Harvey and Harry Ricketts.

Born and raised in Gaithersburg, Maryland, **Maggie Nye** is a current MFA candidate at the University of Alabama in Tuscaloosa. Her fiction appears in Paycock Press's anthology *Defying Gravity*. This is her first essay.

Brenda Peynado has work appearing or forthcoming in *The Threepenny Review*, *Black Warrior Review*, *Pleiades*, *Cimarron Review*, and others. She received her MFA from Florida State University where she was a Kingsbury Fellow. She is currently on a Fulbright Grant to the Dominican Republic.

Vincent Poturica lives in Gainesville, FL, but he will soon be moving with his soon-to-be wife to Long Beach, CA. His stories and poems have appeared or are forthcoming in *Birkensnake*, *Bodega*, *FRiGG*, *Heavy Feather Review*, and *SmokeLong Quarterly*. He has never been to Baltimore, but, someday, he would like to visit. He tweets @vpoturica.

Sean Prentiss is the author of the memoir, *Finding Abbey: a Search for Edward Abbey and His Hidden Desert Grave*. Prentiss is also the co-editor of *The Far Edges of the Fourth Genre: Explorations in Creative Nonfiction*, a creative nonfiction craft anthology. He lives on a small lake in northern Vermont with his wife Sarah and serves as an assistant professor at Norwich University. Seanprentiss.com.

Mark Pritchard is the author of two books of short stories, *How I Adore You* and *Too Beautiful and Other Stories*. His short fiction has been published by *Crony, New Lit Salon, Fiction Attic,* and *Vending Machine*. He has interviewed authors and blogged on *The Rumpus* and *SF Metblogs*. He is the former co-editor and publisher of *Frighten the Horses*, and began writing as a film reviewer for the *Daily Texan* and the *Austin Sun*.

Sharon Rawlette lives in Virginia's Northern Neck, 20 miles from the hospital where she was born. She holds a PhD in philosophy from New York University, and her essays have appeared or are forthcoming in *Salon*, *Orion*, and *Brevity's Nonfiction Blog*. You can find her online at sharonrawlette.wordpress.com.

Lately (2012 or forthcoming), you can read **Dani Sandal** in the *Raleigh Review*, *Adirondack Review, New Orleans Review, Puerto del Sol, Monkeybicycle, Camroc Press, Mad Hatter's Review, PANK, Doctor T.J. Eckleburg Review, THRUSH Poetry Journal, Deep South Magazine*, and *Stirring: Sundress Publications*. She is also included in *Wigleaf's* Top 50 shorts for 2013. Dani holds an MFA from George Mason University, and has the continuous pleasure of raising the coolest kid ever, Holden.

Claire Seymour is a student living in Brooklyn, New York. Her writing has appeared in *Thistle Magazine*, and is forthcoming in the *Chautauqua Literary Journal*. She has won several awards, being named most recently as one of the four finalists for the Norman Mailer Creative Nonfiction Award.

Suzanne Simmons is a poet and essayist who lives in the lakes region of New Hampshire. She holds an MFA in Poetry from New England College. Her work has appeared or is forthcoming in *Calyx, The New York Times, Talisman, Fifth Wednesday, Smartish Pace*, and other journals. Her work received the Editor's Prize for Poetry from *Fifth Wednesday* (2008) and has been nominated for the Pushcart Prize. She teaches English at Manchester Community College.

Karen Skolfield's book *Frost in the Low Areas* won the 2014 PEN New England Award in poetry and the First Book Award from Zone 3 Press. She received the 2015 Robert H. Winner Memorial Award from the Poetry Society of America and the 2015 Arts & Humanities Award from New England Public Radio, and has received additional fellowships and awards in 2014/2015 from the Massachusetts Cultural Council, Ucross Foundation, Split This Rock, Hedgebrook, Vermont Studio Center, and the Sustainable Arts Foundation. New poems appear in the Academy of American Poets Poem-A-Day, *Baltimore Review, Hobart, Indiana Review, MIRAMAR, Pleiades, Southword Journal*, and others; she teaches writing to engineers at the University of Massachusetts Amherst, where she earned her Master of Fine Arts. www.karenskolfield.com

Douglas Smith was born in San Juan, Puerto Rico. His first book is *Judgments*. His work can be read in *Quarterly West, Cimarron Review, Hayden's Ferry Review, Washington Square, Mid-American Review*, and many other magazines. Two of his poems have just appeared in *The Southern Poetry Anthology, Volume VII: North Carolina*, published by Texas Review Press. A contributing editor at *Lake Effect*, he lives in North Carolina and teaches at Guilford College.

Bill Snyder has published in *Atlanta Review, Poet Lore, Folio, Cottonwood*, and *Southern Humanities Review* among others. He was the co-winner of the 2001 Grolier Poetry Prize, and the winner of the 2002 Kinloch Rivers Chapbook competition and the *Consequence* Prize in Poetry, 2013. He teaches writing and literature at Concordia College, Moorhead, MN.

Tamie Parker Song lives and writes in Sitka, Alaska. Other essays of hers can be found in *Connotations, Cirque Journal*, and terrain.org.

Diana Spechler is the author of the novels *Who by Fire* and *Skinny*. She has written for *The New York Times, The Wall Street Journal, Glimmer Train Stories, The Southern Review, The Paris Review Daily, Esquire, GQ, Brevity*, and elsewhere. She teaches writing in New York City and for Stanford University's Online Writers' Studio. Learn more at www.dianaspechler.com.

Marjorie Stelmach's most recent book of poems is *Without Angels* (Mayapple, 2014). Earlier volumes include *Bent upon Light* and *A History of Disappearance* (University of Tampa Press) and *Night Drawings* (Helicon Nine). Individual poems have recently appeared in *Arts & Letters, The Cincinnati Review, Image, The Iowa Review, Kenyon Review online, New Letters, Prairie Schooner, Tampa Review*, and others, as well as twice on Poetry Daily.

J.R. Tappenden is the founding editor of Architrave Press. She earned an MFA in poetry from the University of Missouri – St. Louis where she also served as the university's first Poet Laureate. Her poems have appeared or are forthcoming in *491, Ithaca Lit, Flyway, Euphony*, and elsewhere.

Paige Towers earned her B.A. from the University of Iowa and her MFA from Emerson College, where she also taught Creative Writing and Composition. She currently lives in New York City, teaches in the Writing Center at Monroe College in the Bronx, and is at work on a memoir about ASMR. Her work has appeared in *McSweeney's, Catch & Release, So to Speak, BioStories, Our Iowa Magazine, Honesty for Breakfast* and *Spry Literary Magazine*.

Jen Town's poetry has appeared or is forthcoming in *Mid-American Review, Cimarron Review, Epoch, Third Coast, Lake Effect, Crab Orchard Review, Waccamaw Journal, Unsplendid*, and others. She earned her MFA in Poetry from The Ohio State University in 2008. Her manuscript, *The Light of What Comes After*, was a finalist for both the Moon City Poetry Award and the *Cider Press Review* Book Award in 2014.

Michael Trocchia is the author of *The Fatherlands* (MPP 2014) and the forthcoming collection of poems *Unfounded* (FutureCycle 2015). His poems and prose have appeared in journals such as *Asheville Poetry Review, The Boiler, Camera Obscura*, and *Mid-American Review*. Work is forthcoming in *Heavy Feather Review* and *The Worcester Review*.

Mitchell Untch has been published in *The Los Angeles Review, New Millennium Writers Contest, The Monadnock Anthology, Nimrod Intl., The Wisconsin Review, Out of Ours, Aurorean, The Unrorean (Broadsheet), Jabberwock Review, Blood Orange, The Coachella Review, The Beloit Poetry Journal, The Hawai'i Review, Confrontation, Kestrel, Quiddity Magazine, Booth, The Fourth River, Sierra Nevada Review, South Dakota Review, South Dakota Review, Solo Novo, upstreet, Lucille Clifton Commemorative (Squaw Valley), Natural Bridge, Prism, U.S. Worksheets 1 40th Anniv. Issue, Southern Humanities, Georgetown Review, ABZ Poems, Off the Coast, Poet Lore, North American Review, Assaracus, Knockout, Bicycle Review,*

Glassworks, Lake Effect, Owen Wister, Literary Anthology for Pacific West Writers, and *Grey Sparrow.*

David Wagoner has published 20 books of poems, most recently, *After the Point of No Return* (Copper Canyon Press, 2012). He has also published ten novels, one of which, *The Escape Artist*, was made into a movie by Francis Ford Coppola. He won the Lilly Prize in 1991, six yearly prizes from *Poetry*, two yearly prizes from *Prairie Schooner*, and the Arthur Rense Prize for Poetry from the American Academy of Arts and Letters in 2011. In 2007, his play *First Class* was given 43 performances at A Contemporary Theatre in Seattle. He was a chancellor of the Academy of American Poets for 23 years. He edited *Poetry Northwest* from 1966 to 2002, and he is professor emeritus of English at the U. of Washington. He teaches at the low-residency MFA program of the Whidbey Island Writers Workshop.

Victor Walker is a former university professor and a full-time writer. His short stories have appeared in *New Black Voices, The Wisconsin Review, The Long Story, The MacGuffin, The Red Rock Review* and other literary publications. A Chicagoan, he is presently living in Easton, Pennsylvania.

Jane O. Wayne is the author of four books of poetry, the latest of which is *The Other Place You Live* (Mayapple Press, 2010). A poem of hers along with an interview appeared in Catherine Rankovic's *Meet Me: Writers in St Louis* (Penultimate Press, 2010). She has recent poems in *Boulevard, Southern Poetry Review, New Mexico Poetry Review, Sou'wester,* and *Journal of American Medical Association.*

Mark Lee Webb is a native of Kentucky, but as a teenager lived in California. He knows where a skeg is on a surfboard and how to get from Malibu to Westwood via Mulholland. But he also knows how to find Paris without leaving Kentucky. He's Editor and Publisher of *A NARROW FELLOW,* Journal of Poetry. Mark presented his newest book, *WHATEVERITS,* at the 2014 University of Louisville Conference on Literature and Culture. Finishing Line Press published it in 2014. He was recently awarded a writing residency at the Noepe Center on Martha's Vineyard.

Jacob Weber learned to speak Korean and to love literature during six otherwise wasted years in the Marine Corps. Afterwards, he published a few poems and earned a B.A. and an M.A. in English, the latter in University of Illinois-Chicago's writing program. After his M.A., he wrote nothing for ten years, had kids, and became a translator. Korean was a saturated market, so he learned Tigrinya. It has been his immense privilege to help a few families from Ethiopia and Eritrea to adjust to life in America. "American as Berbere" is his first published work of fiction. He has been blogging lately about getting back to writing and his doubts along the way at workshoperetic.blogspot.com.

Rachel Jamison Webster is a Professor of Poetry at Northwestern University and author of the full-length collections of poetry, *September* (Northwestern University Press 2013) and *The Endless Unbegun* (forthcoming 2015) as well as two chapbooks, *The Blue Grotto* (2009) and *Leaving Phoebe* (forthcoming 2015), both from Dancing Girl Press. Her poems and essays have recently appeared in many journals and anthologies, including *Poetry, Tin House, The Southern Review, The Paris Review, Narrative* and *Labor Day: Birth Stories from Today's Best Women Writers* (FSG 2014). You can read more about her at www.racheljamisonwebster.com.

Kate Wheeler grew up in North Carolina among green things. She received her MFA from Sarah Lawrence College, and her work has appeared in Electric Literature's *Recommended Reading* and *The Westchester Review*. She lives just outside of Brooklyn.

Carolyn Williams-Noren is a 2014 winner of a McKnight Artist Fellowship, selected by Nikky Finney. She has recent poems in *Gigantic Sequins* and *Bluestem* and forthcoming in *Sugar House Review* and *Calyx*. She's the founder and caretaker of a Little Poetry Library in the Minneapolis neighborhood where she lives with her family.

Daniel Enjay Wong received his BA from Stanford University and plans to attend medical school. His stories have appeared in *Tin House, PANK, Spork Press, Monkeybicycle, JMWW,* and elsewhere. He lives in Los Angeles. Find out more at www.dwong.net.

Amy Wright is the Nonfiction Editor of Zone 3 Press and *Zone 3* journal and the author of four poetry chapbooks. She received a Peter Taylor fellowship for the Kenyon Review Writers Workshop, an Individual Artist's Fellowship from the Tennessee Arts Commission, and was recognized as an Emerging Writer at the Southern Women Writers' Conference. Her work appears in a number of journals, including *Brevity, DIAGRAM, Denver Quarterly, Drunken Boat, The Kenyon Review, McSweeney's Internet Tendency, Passages North, Quarterly West,* and *Tupelo Quarterly*.